ISLAM AND RELIGIOUS EXPRESSION IN MALAYSIA

The ISEAS – Yusof Ishak Institute (formerly Institute of Southeast Asian Studies) is an autonomous organization established in 1968. It is a regional centre dedicated to the study of socio-political, security, and economic trends and developments in Southeast Asia and its wider geostrategic and economic environment. The Institute's research programmes are grouped under Regional Economic Studies (RES), Regional Strategic and Political Studies (RSPS), and Regional Social and Cultural Studies (RSCS). The Institute is also home to the ASEAN Studies Centre (ASC), the Temasek History Research Centre (THRC), and the Singapore APEC Study Centre.

ISEAS Publishing, an established academic press, has issued more than 2,000 books and journals. It is the largest scholarly publisher of research about Southeast Asia from within the region. ISEAS Publishing works with many other academic and trade publishers and distributors to disseminate important research and analyses from and about Southeast Asia to the rest of the world.

ISLAM AND RELIGIOUS EXPRESSION IN MALAYSIA

MOHD AZIZUDDIN MOHD SANI

YUSOF ISHAK INSTITUTE

First published in Singapore in 2020 by
ISEAS Publishing
30 Heng Mui Keng Terrace
Singapore 119614

E-mail: publish@iseas.edu.sg
Website: <http://bookshop.iseas.edu.sg>

All rights reserved. No part of this publication may be reproduced, stored in a retrieval system, or transmitted in any form or by any means, electronic, mechanical, photocopying, recording or otherwise, without the prior permission of the ISEAS – Yusof Ishak Institute.

© 2020 ISEAS – Yusof Ishak Institute, Singapore

The responsibility for facts and opinions in this publication rests exclusively with the author and his interpretations do not necessarily reflect the views or the policy of the publisher or its supporters.

ISEAS Library Cataloguing-in-Publication Data

Name(s): Mohd. Azizuddin Mohd. Sani.
Title: Islam and religious expression in Malaysia / by Mohd. Azizuddin Mohd. Sani.
Description: Singapore : ISEAS – Yusof Ishak Institute, 2020. | Includes bibliographical references and index.
Identifiers: ISBN 978-981-4881-35-7 (paperback) | ISBN 978-981-4881-36-4 (PDF)
Subjects: LCSH: Freedom of speech—Religious aspects—Malaysia. | Islam and civil society—Malaysia. | Islam and state—Malaysia. | Radicalism—Religious aspects—Malaysia.
Classification: LCC BL65 F74A99

Typeset by Stallion Press (S) Pte Ltd

CONTENTS

Foreword	viii
Preface	xi
Acknowledgements	xvi
List of Acronyms and Abbreviations	xviii

1.	**Freedom of Expression**	**1**
	Introduction	1
	Freedom of Expression in Malaysia	2
	Freedom of Expression and the Critiques	11
	Human Dignity	16
	Conclusion	22
2.	**Islamization Policy and Islamic Bureaucracy**	**25**
	Introduction	25
	Historical and Contemporary Background	
	of Islamization Policy: An Overview	26
	Multiple Facets of Islamization Process	28
	Institutionalization of Islamic Bureaucracy	28
	1. Public Service	29
	2. Judiciary	30
	3. Security	31
	4. Economy	32
	Education and Human Capital Development for	
	Islamization	34

	Islamization through the Media	47
	Moral Policing	54
	Syariah Index	57
	Malaysia's Constitutional Framework and Islamization Policy	58
	Conclusion	63
3.	**Inter-Religious Expression**	**65**
	Introduction	65
	Inter-Religious Expression in Malaysia	67
	Blasphemy	69
	Hate Speech	70
	Obscenity	72
	Religious Expression in the Press	74
	Interfaith Commission: A Way Towards National Unity?	76
	Conclusion	78
4.	**Intra-Religious Expression**	**81**
	Introduction	81
	Religious Expression Model	83
	Secular or Islamic State in Malaysia?	85
	Freedom of Religion and Intra-Religious Doctrine	90
	Public Speech	94
	Publication and Broadcasting	97
	Blasphemy	99
	Dress Code	102
	Private Speech	104
	Conclusion	110
5.	**Extreme Expression and Radicalization**	**113**
	Introduction	113
	Theory of Radicalization and Counter-Radicalization	117
	ISIL Media Propaganda	120
	Concerns over Malaysians' Involvement in ISIL	123
	The Strategy of Recruiting	123
	Funding	126
	Efforts in Combating ISIL Threats in Malaysia	128
	Conclusion	133

6.	**New Malaysia under Pakatan Harapan**	**135**
	Introduction	135
	Hate Speech	141
	Inculcation of Islamic Values Continued	145
	Islam and Education	152
	Religious Publications	155
	Recent Developments under the PH	158
	Conclusion	161
7.	**Conclusion: Seeking for a Genuine Freedom of Religious Expression**	**163**
	Introduction	163
	Future Challenges for Political Islam	167
	Future Challenges for Religious Expression	171
	Future Challenges for Freedom of Expression in Malaysia	175

Bibliography	181
Index	209
About the Author	225

FOREWORD

Islamic religious expression takes various forms globally from peaceful piety-oriented ones to the most brutal and violent ones.

The September 11 attack in New York has come to be viewed as the most violent public Islamic religious expression that led to the development of intense Islamophobia globally. It was subsequently made more intense by continuous Islamic jihadist attacks conducted in various parts of the world, from the United Kingdom to Chechnya, from Bali to Colombo. When videos of the beheadings of innocent individuals by the Islamic State and the Levant (ISIL) of the Middle East were shown on the Internet, the whole world was shocked and bewildered as to how much more violent Islam could become. Not surprisingly, thereafter, hatred towards Islam came to be generalized and embedded in the negative perceptions and narratives of billions throughout the world.

The majority of Muslims themselves could not provide any explanation or rationale to these abhorrence violent religious expressions. They could not give any credible reason and even if they could, most of them sounded weak and defensive, even evasive.

When President Barrack Obama delivered his speech in Cairo on 4 June 2009 on "the new beginning between the United States and Muslims around the world, one based on mutual interest and mutual respect ... by expanding partnerships in areas like education, economic development, science and technology, and health ...", the world paused for a moment, with some segments of the Muslim and non-Muslim populace offering euphoric responses.

When Obama addressed the issue of economic development and opportunity, he emphasized how human progress cannot be denied, in spite of the crisis faced by the world, including among Muslim communities across the globe. He then specifically referred to "the astonishing progress within Muslim-majority countries from Kuala Lumpur to Dubai" based on innovation and modernization whilst enjoying peace, prosperity, progress, and political stability.

It could be argued that the gist of Obama's speech is that Islamic religious expression throughout history has been intellectually positive. He stressed on the peaceful manner of the expression that benefitted human civilization. Peaceful Islamic religious expression has continuously dominated the history of Islam that, in turn, has enabled it to contribute to world civilizations in the longue durée term.

The astonishing progress within Muslim majority countries, in which Kuala Lumpur (read: Malaysia) was singled out by Obama clearly demonstrated his appreciation of the peaceful nature of Islamic religious expression in Malaysia.

Based on a lengthy research and observation, Professor Azizuddin's *Islam and Religious Expression in Malaysia* elaborates with impressive empirical evidence on democracy and social accommodation among the different religious groups in the country that has generally brought about peace, stability, progress and prosperity to Malaysia and Malaysians irrespective of religious and ethnic orientation.

Against the grain of Islamophobia and intensely negative global narratives and viewpoints about anything Islam or Islamic, Professor Azizuddin painstakingly narrated and analysed the various dimensions of Islamic religious expression in peaceful and stable Malaysia. His contribution is a small oasis and a hopeful narrative within the cacophony of a chaotic discourse on contemporary Islam and society globally.

He successfully unpacked the complexity of the nature of Islamic religious expression in Malaysia based on rich ontological evidence of the Islamization policy and Islamic bureaucracy in Malaysia to the interaction between what could be viewed as the practices of traditional Islam within a Weberian-informed modern bureaucracy.

What is impressive of this study are its coverage, breath and depth. Professor Azizuddin's investigation has not only been on inter-religious expression between Muslims and non-Muslims but also intra-religious expression among Malaysian Muslims, consisting of Malay Muslims, Indian Muslims, Chinese Muslims and the converts group. To the best of my knowledge, this is the first scholarly attempt to dissect the community of Muslims in Malaysia beyond the demographically larger constitutional Muslim Malays.

He also did not fail to address the controversial issue of Islamic terrorism, radicalism and extremism in Malaysia. However, he did this by emphasizing on the "deradicalization" efforts by Malaysian authorities to keep terrorism under control. The added bonus of this book is that Professor Azizuddin gives an informed assessment of the new Pakatan Harapan government and how it deals with Islamic matters.

This is an impressive work by a young, energetic and highly productive Malaysian academic whose observations are serious and valid. This book is a must read for specialists on Malaysia. For those who are beginning to get interested in Malaysia, hopefully this book shall excite them to know more about this complicated yet arguably model of a peaceful Islamic majority country.

Shamsul A.B. FASc
Distinguished Professor and
UNESCO Chair (Communication & Social Cohesion) @ UKM,
Founding Director, Institute of Ethnic Studies (KITA),
The National University of Malaysia

PREFACE

Religious Expression in Perspective

Freedom of expression is a fundamental liberty enshrined predominantly in the constitution of modern Western secular states, with every individual, regardless of his or her ethnicity, socio-economic standing, and religious belief, guaranteed the right to exercise such freedom. Setting this preconceived notion aside, practical implementation of freedom of expression is not totally absolute even to the staunch defenders of human rights. There is an ongoing debate and controversy surrounding the types and substances of the said expressions that warrant constitutional protection. Moreover, the extents and impacts of freedom of expression remain a contentious and divisive issue in many liberal societies. It is not an exaggeration to claim that considerable numbers of advocators of free expression who are willing to support certain controversial practices, including pornography and hate speech, stopped short of recognizing other practices, most notably religious expression. There is no doubt that the possibility of reaching unanimous consensus on this issue amongst civil society groups and activists is remote, albeit one should take note that religious freedom continues to be a dominant subject in public discourse over the last century. In relation to this, the issue concerned may also be examined from the perspective of whether religious expression would somehow inflict or affect political instability or dynamism in bringing political transformation in a country. Therefore, this book will analyse these debates from the context of religious expression in Malaysia.

It is argued that the ultimate goal of safeguarding racial and religious sensibilities continues to be the main barrier to exercising unhindered practice of religious expression in Malaysia. In fact, there is a tendency (and as often the case) for the state authority to exert strict and sometimes excessive legal and political control over the media, prohibiting any forms of provocative or offensive expressions that may harm religious sensitivity of groups or communities from being cited or disseminated in the country. Notwithstanding Islam's official status under the Federal Constitution (*hereafter* "Constitution"), publications or circulation of articles, including editorial pieces and public opinions, that may deemed offensive to Islam and other religious believers either, intentionally or otherwise, are strictly prohibited. No local media in the country, including those operated by the opposition parties, are exempted from complying with this policy directive.

In the Malay community, many of them are of the view that Malaysia's restrictive policies over freedom of expression, either to safeguard national security or for societal benefits—even at the expense of other ethnicities—are justifiable and allegedly with strong constitutional backing. The Constitution stipulates that Malays are inherently Muslims in terms of their religious affiliation (Article 160) and Islam is the official religion of the Federation. Hence, upholding and defending the interest and sanctity of Islam and Muslim Malays are paramount in the agenda of the ruling government policy either previously under Barisan Nasional (BN) government, Pakatan Harapan (PH) government or currently under Perikatan Nasional (PN) government.

At the same time, the Constitution, by virtue of Article 11, acknowledges the rights of other ethnicities in the country (e.g. Chinese, Indian, Sikh, Iban, and others) to freely profess and practise their religions and beliefs. Insofar as protecting these aforementioned rights, the actions of the Malaysian government seemed to give the impression that it intends to strike a balance in preserving the rights of all ethnicities in practising their respective religion and customs. The government assumes an instrumental role in exerting control over the local media, prohibiting the latter from openly displaying or disseminating any forms of articles or news that questioned or ridiculed the faith of its citizens.

There is no doubt that the Malaysian government has for so long constantly and actively monitored and scrutinized religious expression activities in the country. This policy orientation is made with the ultimate goal of securing and retaining a peaceful and harmonious multiethnic and multireligious society. Rendering such protection seems to be justifiable as the government claimed that this is ingrained in the constitutional framework. This overriding goal is largely achievable by strict government controls over a myriad of social and political spheres of the society, ranging from religious expression in the press to blasphemy, religious authority, interfaith commission, and dress code. This state of affairs coexists with the state-driven Islamization policy which, to a considerable extent, affects the practices of religious expression in the country.

This book explains how the government and society alike address and manage the sensitive issues of religious expression in Malaysia. Can religious expression directly and indirectly affect society within the setting of Islamization process in the country? What types of practices and activities of religious expression are allowed and what are disallowed by the State? These questions will be analysed and used to explain the policy and practice of religious expression in Malaysia.

This book is significant for two major reasons. First, it provides a considerable contribution to the growing body of literature on the theoretical and philosophical framework of religious expression. Nonetheless, what is conspicuously absent is the comprehensive analysis and ground breaking research or publication on the theoretical and philosophical framework of religious expression within the context of Malaysia against the background of state-driven Islamization policy. The gaps in this area of study have rendered this book necessary. This book is one of the first attempted studies to comprehensively identify and analyse the varying facets of interventionist actions engaged by state apparatuses and associated actors over matters and activities pertinent to religious expression in the country. The outcome of this book offers some observations on the practice and policy of religious expression in Malaysia based on the theoretical perspective of freedom of expression. Included in this book is a comprehensive description and analysis of the issues and challenges associated with religious expression in Malaysia, including the issues of radicalization and terrorism.

Lastly, the findings of this book make significant contributions to the cumulative knowledge on the influential interventionist role played by the Malaysian government, state and religious authorities in dictating and governing the acceptable practices and concept of Islam. Underpinning empirical analyses are the varying policy and legislative frameworks and responses adopted at the federal and state levels, some of which may have direct and indirect negative repercussions not only on the behaviours and expressions in the public and civil society alike, but also in the well-established Islamic traditions and domestic rituals in the country. More importantly, the outcome of this book reveals a close correlation between the impact of social, political and legal Islamization on the ways in which religious expression are practised in the country. This reflects a reality: the ruling government, associated actors and institutions have purportedly imposed various forms of legislative and policy restrictions on activities and behaviours related to religious expression.

Scholarly analyses on the Islamization policy in Malaysia since the 1980s continue to abound. The process of Islamization which figured prominently during then Prime Minister Mahathir Mohamed's two administration periods (1981–2003 and 2018–20) and his predecessors involved greater integration of Islamic ideas, values, laws and systems into nearly every aspect of the public sphere, from governance, ceremonial setting, education, finance to economy. Throughout the documented history of the country's Islamization process, there are gaps for which this book intends to fill. One of the predominant question of discourse is to what extent this process of the government's commitment to Islam has left its mark on the public domain and society at large, especially among the country's sizable non-Muslim population with regards to the practice of religious expression. Relevantly, this book identifies and observes how members of civil societies react to the perceived eroding of their civil liberties and rights in freely exercising religious expression, a development which is widely seen as intrinsically linked to the Islamization process.

Overview

There are seven chapters in this book. This introduction has briefly discussed about the book and the concept of religious expression in

Malaysia. Chapter 1 explores the politico-legal aspect of freedom of expression in Malaysia. It analyses the critiques on the practices of free expression and how restrictions made by the government are justifiable. Chapter 2 traces and examines the multiple facets of state-driven Islamization policy in Malaysia. It also explores the roles and structures of the Federal Constitution, as well as bureaucratic apparatus and legislative framework involved in that process. Chapter 3 continues the discussion by critically analysing inter-religious expression in Malaysia. It presents a general analysis of the issues and challenges associated with inter-religious expression relayed through various avenues and tools. Chapter 4 elaborates on Islam and intra-religious expression in Malaysia. Particular attention is given to the identification and examination of the major elements constituting religious expression models. Chapter 5 focuses on the issues of extreme expression and radicalization. The Islamic State and the Levant (ISIL)'s recruitment strategies of utilizing the social media, in particular, have attracted Malaysians to join the group. It observes the background of ISIL as an emerging threat to the global and regional arena and the efforts taken by the Malaysian government to counter the ISIL threats. Chapter 6 explores the PH government's perspective of Islam and religious expression since it took over power from BN in 2018. This book attempts to see whether there are differences in policy and practices particularly in governing Islam and religious expression. Chapter 7 and also the final chapter provides the conclusion of the book and states the future challenges of religious expression in Malaysia.

ACKNOWLEDGEMENTS

This book is based on two research projects: (1) "Bureaucratic Islam and Islamization in Malaysia" (2014), a Visiting Research Fellowship Scheme sponsored by the ISEAS – Yusof Ishak Institute, Singapore; and (2) "Discovering the Theory and Practice of Religious Expression in Malaysia" (2012–14), an Exploratory Research Grant Scheme (ERGS) sponsored by the Ministry of Higher Education Malaysia. It is a new initiative to explore a new theory or concept namely "religious expression" within the context of Malaysia. In spite of this, the ongoing debates of religious expression typically attempt to separate the rights from dignity in the cases of obscenity and hate speech. Therefore, in exploring the concept of religious expression in Malaysia, we managed to trace the foundation of the concept to Islamic teachings which are in one way or another embedded in the social values and legislations of the country, especially through the Islamic Penal Code and other *Syariah* laws. This book is truly an attempt to explore deeper into the concept of religious expression and gives a clear perspective in the Malaysian context.

I am indebted to all sponsors who have provided me with funds to successfully complete this book. I want to express my gratitude to my colleagues, Associate Professor Dr Mohammad Zaki Ahmad and Associate Professor Dr Ratnaria Wahid, who are also my co-researchers for the ERGS research. My gratitude goes also towards Dr Ummu Atiyah Ahmad Zakuan, Dr Dian Diana Abdul Hamed Shah, Associate Professor Dr Norhafezah Yusof, and Azahar Kasim who assisted and inspired me throughout my journey to make this book a reality. I also want to thank the Research and Innovation Management Centre (RIMC), Universiti Utara Malaysia (UUM) for rendering me assistance in getting and completing the research. Very special thanks also go to the ISEAS – Yusof Ishak Institute for its unwavering support throughout my career, particularly in 2014 when I was a Visiting Fellow, and for publishing this book, one of my major contributions in the field of political science.

This book would also not have been possible without the generous assistance of my colleagues and administrative staffs at the College of Law, Government and International Studies (COLGIS), UUM. Finally, I would like to thank my loving family, Rafidah, Nusra, Amni, Ariez and Adelia for their unwavering support and inspiration. For their efforts and sacrifices during the preparation of this book, I dedicate this book to them.

Prof. Dr Mohd Azizuddin Mohd Sani
Universiti Utara Malaysia
2020

LIST OF ACRONYMS AND ABBREVIATIONS

ABIM	Angkatan Belia Islam Malaysia
AIS	Academy of Islamic Studies
Art.	Article
DAP	Democratic Action Party
GE	General Election
GEPIMA	Indian Muslim Youth Movement of Malaysia
IIUM	International Islamic University Malaysia
ISA	Internal Security Act
ISIL	The Islamic State and the Levant
ISMA	Ikatan Muslimin Malaysia
JAWI	Jabatan Agama Islam Wilayah Persekutuan
JIM	Jamaah Islah Malaysia
JKSM	Jabatan Kehakiman Syariah Malaysia
JUST	International Movement for the Just World
KAGAT	Kor Agama Angkatan Tentera
KMM	Kumpulan Mujahidin (Militan) Malaysia
MACMA	Malaysian Chinese Muslim Association
MCA	Malaysian Chinese Association
MIC	Malaysian Indian Congress
PEKIDA	Pertubuhan Kebajikan Islamiah dan Dakwah
PERKASA	Pertubuhan Peribumi Perkasa
PH	Pakatan Harapan
PKPIM	Persatuan Kebangsaan Pelajar Islam Malaysia

PKR	Parti Keadilan Rakyat
PMO	Prime Minister's Office
PN	Perikatan Nasional
PUM	Malaysian Ulama Association
RTM	Radio and Television Malaysia
SA	Sedition Act
SAC	Syariah Advisory Council
SC	Malaysian Securities Commission
SUHAKAM	Malaysian Human Rights Commission
UiTM	Universiti Teknologi MARA
UKM	National University of Malaysia
UM	University of Malaya
UMNO	United Malay National Organisation
UMT	Universiti Malaysia Terengganu
UNIZA	Universiti Sultan Zainal Abidin
USIM	Universiti Sains Islam Malaysia
USM	Universiti Sains Malaysia
UTM	Universiti Teknologi Malaysia
UUM	Universiti Utara Malaysia
YADIM	Yayasan Dakwah Islam Malaysia

1

FREEDOM OF EXPRESSION

Introduction

There is an argument that the right to free expression can be potentially used to stir national security. Former Prime Minister of Malaysia, Najib Tun Razak admitted that race and religious issues are sensitive in Malaysia, and stressed that "(We need) political management (which) includes race relations. If we can refrain from uttering words or committing acts which can offend other races, then *temperature-raising incidents* can be avoided" (*The Star* 2010, p. 4). In objection, Anwar Ibrahim, the main opposition leader back then, implied that the Barisan Nasional (BN) government, led by the United Malays National Organisation (UMNO) as the most dominant political party in the coalition, was behind the tensions. He argued that "This is the last hope—to incite racial and religious sentiments to cling to power ... immediately since the disastrous defeat in the March 2008 election, they have been fanning this" (Mydans 2010, p. 4). It seems ironic when Malaysia has Article 10 of the Federal Constitution that protects people's right to free expression and many laws such as the Sedition Act (SA) and Penal Code against religious and racial hatred but hate speech is still being exploited to further the political agenda and interests of certain political groups and parties. This raises a question: can we curb free expression for national security in Malaysia?

One more crucial issue, which needs to be addressed, is on the restrictive laws which are essential for political stability, racial harmony and economic prosperity. Are these laws merely used as tools for the government to cling to power and restrict any political contestation and people's mobilization against it? So far, there have been mixed responses on this issue and the debate is worldwide. The government argues in favour of the restrictive laws in sustaining racial and religious harmony in Malaysia. This chapter will argue about the processes in implementing freedom of expression in Malaysia.

Freedom of Expression in Malaysia

According to Andrew Tan (2004), national security in Malaysia has several objectives, in particular:

1. Preserving the Federal Constitution, including the position of the Malay rulers, Islam as the religion of the Federation, the special rights of the Malays in maintaining Malay political supremacy, and the legitimate rights of the other races.
2. Protecting national unity and racial harmony in realization that any internal ethnic conflict would be detrimental.
3. Sustaining the economic development in a multiracial society in order to strengthen internal resilience and especially the survivability of Malays in the globalized world.
4. Guarding against internal security threats such as the communist insurgency, racial conflict and extremist groups.
5. Safeguarding national sovereignty and territorial integrity of the Federation.
6. Preserving a stable and peaceful environment in the areas of strategic interests domestically, regionally and globally.

These objectives could change due to changes in political, economic and social circumstances.

To the Malaysian government, the country has to be protected from threats such as racial and religious conflicts and economic recession.

Thus, it allows for certain restrictions of freedom of expression in the name of national security. In Malaysia, freedom of expression is assured by Part II of the Federal Constitution under Article 10 (1) entitled "Freedom of Speech, Assembly and Association". Article 10 (1) states that (a) every citizen has the right to freedom of speech and expression; (b) all citizens have the right to assemble peacefully and without arms; and (c) all citizens have the right to form associations. Citizens have the right to freedom of speech, but Section 2 of the Article limits the right where Parliament may allow by law imposed:

> (a) On the rights conferred by paragraph (a) of Clause (1), such restrictions as it deems necessary or expedient in the interest of the security of the Federation or any part thereof, friendly relations with other countries, public order or morality and restrictions designed to protect the privileges of Parliament or of any Legislative Assembly or to provide against contempt of court, defamation, or incitement to any offence

The government has sought to protect institutions i.e. the Parliament, courts, and federal and state governments from scandalous criticism by citizens and foreigners practising freedom of expression. For instance, the Malaysian government welcomed the twelve weeks' imprisonment (reduced to six weeks on appeal) of Murray Hiebert, a *Far Eastern Economic Review* journalist, on 4 September 1997 for his article entitled "See You in Court", which scandalized the court and threatened to undermine the credibility of judicial institutions (Hilley 2001, p. 228). Hiebert was sentenced to imprisonment after he wrote a "defamatory" article about the speedy processing of a lawsuit brought by the wife of a prominent Court of Appeals judge. Addressing the growing level of spurious litigation in the Malaysian courts, Hiebert highlighted the Malaysian Ringgit (RM) 6 million damages being sought by the mother of Govind Sri Ram against the International School of Kuala Lumpur for "unfairly dropping" her son from the school debating team. Noting that the student's father is Court of Appeals judge Gopal Sri Ram, Hiebert commented that "many are surprised at the speed with which the case raced through Malaysia's legal labyrinth". Awaiting appeal, Hiebert had his Canadian passport held for two years (Hilley 2001, p. 228).

Furthermore, Article 10 (4) explains the reasons for restricting freedom of expression:

> In imposing restrictions in the interest of the security of the Federation or any part of thereof or public order under Clause (2) (a), Parliament may pass law prohibiting the questioning of any matter, right, status, position, privilege, sovereignty or prerogative established or protected by the provisions of Part II, Article 152, 153 and 182 otherwise in relation to the implementation thereof as may specified in such law.

The provision of Article 10 (4) was part of the amendment of the Federal Constitution in 1971 and was enforced on 10 March 1971 as a reaction to the racial conflict of 13 May 1969. In this incident, the government blamed the opposition for manipulating freedom of expression to inflict racial sentiments and dissatisfaction among the non-Malays, particularly Chinese and Indians, over the special rights of Malays with respect to particular occupations and higher posts in the public sector (Comber 1983, p. 63). A State of Emergency was declared after the racial clash. Thus, the Federal Constitution had been amended to prohibit citizens and non-citizens, including members of parliament during Parliamentary sessions, from questioning Part III of the Federal Constitution on Citizenship, Article 152 on National Language, Article 153 on Malay special rights and Article 181 on Saving for Rulers' sovereignty (Yatim 1995, p. 168). The Malaysian government justified the 1971 amendment to the Constitution on the following terms:

> It is clear that if no restriction on public discussion about sensitive issues, interracial fright and fear are surely unavoidable. If no action being taken to assure peoples' rights and interest in the constitution, this country could face another racial conflict or even more devastating crisis (Malaysia 1971, p. 2).

The protection of Article 10 of the Constitution is available to citizens only. Based on the *Attorney General versus Wain (No. 1)*

(1991), a non-citizen or a foreign company or news agency cannot lay claim to this right. Article 10 (1)(a) must be read in the light of other articles of the Constitution which curtail this freedom. For instance, Article 126 empowers the courts to punish expressions or actions that amount to contempt of court. Articles 63 (4) and 10 (4) subject Parliamentary proceedings to the law of sedition. Mark Koding, a member of parliament, found this out to his discomfort when he was convicted for a Parliamentary speech demanding the closure of Chinese and Tamil schools. Under Article 25 (1)(a), an order to deprive a person of his citizenship can be based on his disloyal conduct as manifested in his speeches irrespective of the fact that free expression is his constitutional right (Faruqi 2002).

In addition to the justification for restricting freedom of expression in the Constitution, Part XI under Article 149 lists subversive conducts and activities in detail. According to Article 149 (1) of the Constitution, those conducts and activities are actions taken or threatened by any substantial body of persons, whether inside or outside the Federation:

(a) to cause, or to cause a substantial number of citizens to fear, organized violence against persons or property; or
(b) to excite disaffection against Yang di-Pertuan Agong or any Government in the Federation; or
(c) to promote feelings of ill-will and hostility between different races or other classes of the population likely to cause violence; or
(d) to procure the alteration, otherwise than by lawful means, of anything by law established; or
(e) which is prejudicial to the maintenance or the functioning of any supply or service to the public or any class of the public in the Federation or any part thereof; or
(f) which is prejudicial to public order in, or the security of, the Federation or any part thereof.

Article 149 gives Parliament the power to create law as a response to subversive actions with or without a state of emergency being declared. Mohamed Suffian Hashim (1987, p. 316) argues that in the event of serious subversion or organized violence, Parliament may pass laws that are repugnant to the fundamental rights safeguarded elsewhere in the Constitution. Laws, which intent to stop and prevent subversive acts, are legal even though they are against certain provisions in the Constitution under Article 5 (personal freedom), Article 9 (prohibition of citizens from explusion and freedom of movement), Article 10 (freedom of speech, assemble, and establishing an association), or Article 13 (the right to own property) and those outside of Parliament's legislative power. Article 149 (formerly Article 137) was criticized by one of the drafters of the Constitution. A member of Reid Commission, Judge Abdul Hamid condemned the Article:

> If there exists any real emergency, and that should only be emergencies of the type described in Article 138 (now Article 150), then and only then should such extraordinary powers be exercised. It is in my opinion unsafe to leave in the hands of Parliament power to suspend constitutional guarantees only by making a recital in the Preamble that conditions in the country are beyond reach of the ordinary law. Ordinary legislation and executive measures are enough to cope with a situation of the type described in Article 137 (now Article 149) (SUARAM 1998, pp. 217–18).

What concerned Judge Abdul Hamid most was that Article 149 gave power to Parliament to abrogate any laws pertaining to human rights as well as freedom of expression. That concern became a reality when the controversial law of the Internal Security Act (ISA) that allows detention without trial was created under Article 149 (Hashim 1987, p. 317). In addition to ISA, there are also several laws either created or amended under Article 149 purposely to restrict freedom of expression such as the Official Secret Act (OSA), the Sedition Act (SA), and the Printing Presses and Publications Act (PPPA).

Since the 11 September 2001 terrorist attack in New York, the government has sought to emphasize the seriousness of terrorist threats and Malaysia's potential vulnerability to terrorism to justify taking special measures for national security. In his Budget Speech on 20 September 2002, Mahathir said:

Today, there are Muslims who have become fanatical to the extent of using violence, including bombing and resorting to murder as well as plotting to overthrow the Government. If they had been successful in executing their plans, the nation will plunge into instability and utter chaos, resulting in the deterioration of the economy. We have spared the nation from this turmoil with the rule of law practised by the Government. The ISA has indeed saved the Nation (Fritz and Flaherty 2003, p. 2).

Clearly, the government tries to justify the existence of the ISA on grounds of national security.

From a national security's point of view, the government argued that they managed to curb subversive elements in the country that intentionally seek to disturb national security. As reinforced by Mahathir on 28 October 1996: "The threat is from inside … So we have to be armed, so to speak. Not with guns, but with the necessary laws to make sure the country remains stable" (Mendes 1994).

There are two political arguments that strongly support the restriction of free expression in Malaysia. First, Malaysia is obsessed with social stability. Due to the large gap in economic well-being within society, communal politics are potentially explosive. Cultural sensitivities, especially concerning race and religion, are the main obstacles to the implementation of political freedom in Malaysia. Great care is taken not to impinge on the religious sensitivities of various groups. Given the fact that Islam is the religion of the Federation, care is taken not to publish articles that cast a slur, intended or otherwise, on Islam or its adherents. The media, including those operated by the opposition, follow this policy. Malays, by constitutional definition, are Muslims and with the inclusion of some aspects of Chinese, Indian, and tribal culture, no media can publish articles that question or ridicule faith (Moses 2002).

Mahathir criticized Western liberal democracy for tolerating hate speech:

Malaysian democracy is not a liberal democracy and not bound to accept every new interpretation of democracy in the West where democratic fanatics have pushed devotion to a pedantic notion of democracy to include the protection of neo-fascists or the empowering of a vocal minority of political activists over the silent majority of ordinary citizens (Leigh and Lip 2004, p. 320).

The government has taken the initiative to restrict hate speech in order to maintain peace and stability in a communally divided society like Malaysia. This includes expression advocating the overthrow, forcibly or even peacefully, of the ruling government. There are two court cases that are in line with Mahathir's decision to restrict hate speech. Justice Raja Azlan Shah, in *Public Prosecutor versus Ooi Kee Saik & Ors* (1971), adopts a strict interpretation of free expression. He observes that freedom of expression should be given the greatest latitude, but "free and frank political discussion and criticism of government policies cannot be developed within an atmosphere of surveillance and constraint" (Yatim 1995, p. 170). He further argues against the "absolutism" approach by saying that:

> But as far as I am aware, no constitutional state has attempted to translate the 'right' into an absolute right. Restrictions are a necessary part of the right ... The dividing line between lawful criticism of government and sedition is this—if upon reading the impugned speech as a whole the court finds that it was intended to be a criticism of government policy of administration with a view to obtain its change or reform, the speech is safe. But if the court comes to the conclusion that the speech used naturally, clearly and indubitably has the tendency of stirring up hatred, contempt or disaffection against the government, then it is caught within the ban of paragraph (a) of section 3 (1) of the (Sedition) Act (Yatim 1995, p. 170).

The Federal Court sets out the principal guidelines to determine if criticism transgresses the limits of freedom of expression and constitutes sedition within the ambit of the SA. In this case, Justice Wan Sulaiman, in *Public Prosecutor versus Oh Keng Seng* (1977), maintained that a speech stating that "the army is composed of one hundred percent of one ethnic group consequent on the government's policy to favour that ethnic group to ensure political hegemony" is clearly illegal under the SA because the speaker intentionally incites hatred between races or contempt or to excite disaffection against the government. He explains that:

> words having a tendency to bring about hatred or contempt of any ruler or against any government, or promote feelings of ill-will and hostility among the various ethnic groups can be uttered before a handful of persons and yet be seditious under our law (Yatim 1995, p. 171).

Hate speech has had negative impacts in Malaysia. On 30 September 2005, hate speech became a global issue when the daily newspaper *Jyllands-Posten* (The Jutland Post) published an article which consisted of cartoons of the Prophet Muhammad, one of them showing the Prophet wearing turban in the shape of a bomb. They were perceived by many Muslims as an attempt to intentionally depict him as the source of terrorism. These cartoons triggered worldwide protests and a ban on Danish products especially in Muslim countries. In Malaysia, the fifth Prime Minister, Abdullah Ahmad Badawi closed a Borneo-based paper, the *Sarawak Tribune*, indefinitely for reprinting the cartoons. Lester Melanyi, an editor of the newspaper, was forced to resign from his post for allowing the reprinting of the cartoons. Abdullah described their publication as insensitive and irresponsible and had also declared possession of the cartoons illegal. The paper apologized for what it called an editorial oversight. Malaysia's third-largest Chinese-language daily, *Guang Ming*, was also suspended from publication for two weeks for one of the cartoons in its 3 February 2006 edition (BBC 2006; *Media Guardian* 2006).

The setback of press freedom in Malaysia is that all mainstream media were controlled by the government or companies that have close links with the government. For instance, *Utusan Melayu* and *Utusan Malaysia* newspapers were published by Utusan Melayu (M) Berhad, which had a special relationship with UMNO. In October 2006, a business deal between the Malaysian Chinese Association (MCA), one of BN component parties, and media tycoon Tiong Hiew King solidified the monopoly of the Chinese press, with all top four Chinese dailies—*Sin Chew Jit Poh, Guang Ming, China Press* and *Nanyang Siangpau*—concentrated in the hands of a firm political-business alliance. In 2007, Media Prima Berhad, with close links to UMNO, acquired all the private television stations including *TV3, NTV7, 8TV* and *TV9*. It also has a 43 per cent equity interest in The NST Press (Malaysia) Berhad (NSTP), one of Malaysia's largest publishing groups that publishes leading newspaper titles such as the *New Straits Times, Berita Harian* and *Harian Metro*. The group also owns two radio networks, *Fly FM* and *Hot FM* (Azizuddin 2010).

Second, the government utilizes the ISA as a device to quell dissent and bypass the due process of law in protecting public security. Mahathir, in the budget speech in September 2002, hailed the ISA as the main instrument that "saved" the country and further asserted that liberal Western countries have now realized (since 11 September 2001) the importance of such preventive laws in safeguarding the security of the nation (SUARAM 2003). The US-led war on terror has undoubtedly been a major setback for human rights struggle in Malaysia. In the past, the US State Department's annual human rights report criticized Malaysia's use of detention without trial. These days, with the United States itself detaining hundreds of individuals without trial under the PATRIOT Act, the State Department's report on Malaysia appears hypocritical and is viewed by some Malaysian human rights activists with disdain because of its double standards (Netto 2004, p. 94). The UK has also implemented detention without trial under the Anti-terrorism, Crime and Security Act 2001. Although the ISA is designed to counter subversive activities in Malaysia, the law is also disproportionately prejudiced against those who engage in opposition politics, or groups that oppose government policies and as such are deemed "political" by the Attorney General. Section 3 of the ISA also empowers the home minister to prohibit organizations and associations of a political or quasi-military character. Once prohibited, an organization is incapacitated from applying for a licence to hold an assembly or procession. Section 7 forbids training or drilling for the use of arms. Section 8 permits prohibition, in the national interest, of flags, banners, badges, emblems and uniforms. Under Section 47, the Yang di-Pertuan Agong (King) may proclaim any area in Malaysia as a "security area". Restrictions may then be imposed on entering or remaining in this area (Sections 48–50). The Officer in Charge of a Police District may exclude any person from this area (Section 51) and may put the area under curfew (Section 52) (Faruqi 2002, p. 22).

There is generally less scope for spontaneous protest because of legal prohibition and the requirement for police permits for any public gathering. The Police Act 1967 effectively circumvents the rights to free expression and free assembly, and confers wide discretionary powers on the police to regulate assemblies, meetings and processions in both public and private places. Under the Act all public assemblies of three or more persons require a police permit. The Act gives the police the power to stop and use force against participants in thwarting these events, whether in public or private places. The Act, in addition, provides the police with powers to regulate the playing of music in public places and to prohibit the display of flags, banners, emblems or placards and the use of loud speakers, amplifiers and other devices. The police can also confiscate the offending items. Violators, including those participating in illegal assemblies, can be fined between RM2,000 and RM10,000 and can be imprisoned for up to one year (SUARAM 2003, p. 93). The Penal Code also places restrictions on the right to peaceful assembly. The Code defines "unlawful" gatherings and riots, police powers of dispersal and penalties upon conviction. Under Section 141 of the Code, an assembly of five or more persons is designated an "unlawful assembly".

Freedom of Expression and the Critiques

Many question the intentions of the Malaysian government in restricting free expression. Vitit Muntarbhorn (1994, p. 4) argues that many ASEAN governments, particularly the Malaysian government, restrict political and civil rights not to promote prosperity, but "to perpetuate the longevity of the regime in power". A critic of the West's human rights campaign, Chandra Muzaffar (1993, pp. 30–31) laments that:

> southern elites deprive their people of their basic human rights ... The arbitrary exercise of unlimited power which is not checked by strict adherence to the principles of accountability must lead inevitably to the suppression of the masses.

Such criticisms suggest that unlimited state power to restrict civil liberties can be detrimental to the very quality of life such control is supposed to protect. Anwar Ibrahim (1996a, p. 28) said: "it is altogether shameful, if ingenious, to cite (national security) as an excuse for autocratic practices and denial of basic rights and civil liberties". At the same time, this debate cannot be seen in crude terms merely as a tool manipulated by a political or capitalist regime, or an artificial screen behind which to hide a wilfully illiberal government. The debate of the last two decades is an episode in the long-term post-colonial politico-cultural project.

In many Commonwealth constitutions, such as in India, Jamaica and Malta, Parliament is empowered to enact "reasonable regulations" on free expression. The significance of the word "reasonable" is that courts are invested with the power to review the validity of legislation on the grounds of reasonableness, harshness or undemocratic nature of the restrictions. However, the drafters of Malaysia's basic charter deliberately excluded the word "reasonable" from the law. Article 10 (2) states that "Parliament may by law impose ... such restrictions as it deems necessary or expedient" on a number of prescribed grounds (Faruqi 2002). Article 4 (2)(b) makes Parliament the final judge of the necessity or expediency of a law and bars judicial review on the ground of lack of necessity or expediency. Therefore, Parliament is authorized to restrict free expression on fourteen broad grounds under Articles 10 (2), 10 (4), 149 and 150. It is so wide and the government has no difficulty in fully defending laws like the SA, OSA, ISA and PPPA in accord with the basic charter. For example, Sections 3 (3), 6 (1), 12 (2) and 13A of the PPPA confer on the minister "absolute discretion" to grant, refuse or revoke a licence or permit and makes the minister's decision final and unquestionable in a court of law (Faruqi 2002).

Parliament, however, is not supreme. The Constitution supplies the ultimate yardstick against which every law can be measured. In *Dewan Undangan Negeri versus Nordin Salleh* (1992), it was held that Parliament may restrict free expression only on the grounds specified in the Constitution. Similarly, *Madhavan Nair versus Public Prosecutor* (1975) ruled that any condition limiting freedom of expression not falling within the provisions of Article 10, clauses (2), (3) and (4) cannot be valid. Thus, the general grounds of "state necessity", "public policy", "public interest", "good government", "efficiency" and "common sense" are not constitutionally permitted grounds for depriving a citizen of his right. Restrictions on free expression must be confined to those articulated in the Constitution (Faruqi 2002).

There is a new development with regard to the "reasonable regulation" in the Constitution. In the University Kebangsaan Malaysia 4 (UKM 4) case on 1 November 2011, the Court of Appeal ruled that Section 15 (5) of the Universities and University Colleges Act (UUCA), which prohibits students from involving in politics, is unconstitutional and violates freedom of expression. Judge Mohd Hishamuddin Mohd Yunus, in his twenty-one pages written judgement, argues that:

> ... the restriction on freedom of speech is permitted by Clause (2)(a) of Article 10 ... in the interest of 'public order or morality'. ... In addition, the restriction must also be reasonable. Any restriction imposed on freedom of speech by Parliament must be a reasonable restriction, and the Court if called upon to rule ... has the power to examine whether the restriction so imposed is reasonable or otherwise. ... I fail to see in what manner that section 15 (5)(a) of the UUCA relates to public order or public morality. I also do not find the restriction to be reasonable. ... Clearly the provision is not only counter-productive but repressive in nature (Court of Appeal of Malaysia 2011).

With this preceding case, the government has to amend the UUCA and accept the principle of "reasonable regulation" as part of Article 10 for future legislation and legal proceedings.

There were pressures from the opposition, civil society movements, the Malaysian Human Rights Commission (SUHAKAM), and some dissenting leaders in the ruling BN to reform the mainstream media. For example, Khairy Jamaluddin, UMNO Youth deputy chief, advocated for the repeal of the PPPA (*The Star* 2008) and Koh Tsu Koon, acting president of Gerakan (one of the BN component parties) and former chief minister of Penang, suggested abolishing the ISA (*The Star* 2008, p. 27). Besides aiming towards a new mandate for his leadership and ruling party in the 13th General Election in 2013, Prime Minister Najib Tun Razak has taken drastic measures to reform the Malaysian legislation. He surprisingly made his argument based on the equilibrium between national security and liberty. Najib argued that a balance between national security and individual freedom is needed in a modern democracy. The government should take this responsibility, argued Najib, to ensure the welfare and well-being of the people. Interestingly Najib further stressed:

> For instance, the freedom of speech guaranteed by the Federal Constitution does not mean that anyone is free to spread slander and incite the flames of hatred. To illustrate a simple example, the government is responsible for preventing false alarms about a bomb in a packed stadium. This is because such freedom only causes panic that might lead to injury and loss of lives (Najib 2011, p. 64).

This argument is similar to the judgement of Judge Oliver Wendell Holmes in *Schenck versus United States* (1919) regarding the First Amendment of free speech:

> The most stringent protection of free speech would not protect a man in falsely shouting fire in a theater and causing a panic. ... The question in every case is whether the words used are used in such circumstances and are of such a nature as to create a clear and present danger that they will bring about the substantive evils that Congress has a right to prevent (Hargreaves 2002, p. 259).

The only difference from Najib's statement is that Holmes' judgement was based on the suspension of free expression during war, and not during peacetime like currently in Malaysia.

However, the argument above has given Najib, as announced in his Malaysian Day address on 16 September 2011, a justification to pledge for transformation under the National Transformation Policy (NTP) (2011–20) by setting up a parliamentary select committee on electoral reforms, announcing the repeal of the ISA, abolishing the annual renewal policy for the press under the PPPA, tabling a new bill to replace and amend the UUCA as well as doing away with Section 27 of the Police Act that requires all public gatherings to have a police permit (*New Straits Times* 2012, p. 2; *The Star* 2011). Najib also promised to repeal the SA, but later decided to retain and strengthen the law. These changes in policy are relatively new to Malaysia. However, there is no clear indication that these changes will bring more freedom of expression to the people.

However, in the 13th General Election on 5 May 2013, the BN won with a reduced majority of 133 parliamentary seats from 140 seats in the previous 12th General Election in 2008. Meanwhile the Pakatan Rakyat (PR), a pact of three parties namely the Malaysian Islamic Party (PAS), People's Justice Party (PKR) and DAP, managed to get 89 seats compared to 82 seats in the 2008 general election. Unexpectedly soon after the 2013 general election, the police arrested six PR leaders and NGO activists—Tian Chua, Thamrin Ghafar, Haris Ibrahim, Muhammad Safwan Anang, Hishammuddin Rais and Adam Adli Abd Halim—under the SA for allegedly calling for street demonstrations to topple the government. Moreover, home ministry officers on 23 May 2013 seized 1,408 copies of PKR's *Suara Keadilan*, 1,602 copies of PAS' *Harakah*, and 70 copies of DAP's *The Rocket* for violating their publishing permit by selling to the public, instead of parties members only (*The Star* 2013, pp. 1–3).

The Home Ministry also announced that from 2008 until June 2015, 409 cases have been investigated under the Sedition Act 1948. In terms of charging rate, it stands at only 6 per cent of the total cases investigated. There were 138 investigations later classified as no further action (NFA). Meanwhile, there were 99 cases under investigation, while 116 cases were returned by the Attorney-General's Chambers requesting for further probe. Only 30 cases had been referred to the Deputy Public Prosecutor (Anand 2015). In the Parliamentary sitting in April 2015, the provision of detention without trial, used to be enforced under the ISA, was reintroduced through the Prevention of Terrorism Act 2015 (POTA), and used to retain and strengthen the SA. Recently, Human Rights Watch (2015, p. 2) produced a report entitled "Creating a Culture of Fear: The Criminalization of Peaceful Expression in Malaysia", which states that

> a spiraling corruption scandal involving the government-owned 1 Malaysia Development Berhad (1MDB), whose board of advisors is chaired by Prime Minister Najib, led the government to block websites

and suspend newspapers reporting on the scandal and to announce plans to strengthen its power to crack down on speech on the Internet.

These actions taken by the government especially after the 2013 General Election have raised doubts on the transformation agenda promoted by Najib. This later led to the defeat of Najib's government by the opposition Pakatan Harapan (PH) in the 2018 General Election, the first defeat for BN since Malaysia's independence.

Human Dignity

There are constant debates between the concepts of human rights or human liberties with human dignity. However, "human rights" as a concept is dubious or rather confusing. As we observe a debate between liberal universalists and relativists, there are disagreements especially on the issues involving culture and religion. Basically, there are two theories of human rights i.e. universalism and relativism. The idea of universalism is "Human Rights, because they rest on nothing more than being human, are universal, equal, and inalienable. They are held by all human beings, universally … Human rights, being held by every person against the state and society, provide a framework for political organisation and a standard of political legitimacy" (Donnelly 2001). Meanwhile relativism focuses on the cultural perspective. Relativists argue that:

> Relativism (or cultural relativism) is the assertion that human values, far from being universal, vary a great deal according to different cultural perspectives. Some would apply this relativism to the promotion, protection, interpretation and application of human rights which could be interpreted differently within different cultural, ethnic and religious traditions. In other words, according to this view, human rights are culturally relative rather than universal (Ayton-Shenker 1995).

Shad Saleem Faruqi (2004a) explains that there is a sort of "human rights epidemic" that is sweeping many lands, meaning that:

> The human rights argument is so much in vogue that a lot of causes, though highly contentious in nature and not central to the dignity of human beings, are brought under the umbrella of a human rights claim.

> Homosexuality, pornography, blasphemy, abortion on demand and same sex marriages are all being treated as human rights issues. Homosexual couples are seeking to adopt children in the like manner of their heterosexual counterparts. Children are seeking a right to divorce their parents. A publication from the Law School in Exeter lists the right to outdoor recreation, the rights of the unborn and freedom from unwanted publicity as fundamental liberties. Clearly there is an over-zealousness in some human rights claims and a failure to distinguish ordinary civil claims from fundamental human rights (Faruqi 2004a, p. 14).

When arguing about freedom of expression, it is always in conflict with some other rights such as the right to privacy, for example the right to sing loudly at home can disturb the right to privacy of a neighbour. Sometimes, the amorality of the human rights concept makes others uncomfortable, particularly regarding the issues of hate speech and pornography. That is why in searching for a better concept to protect the people and common good, human dignity is a choice that can resolve the confusion in the concept of human rights. That is also the reason why European and African states, particularly Germany and South Africa, embedded the concept of human dignity in their constitutions.

Historically and contemporarily, the term "human dignity" has theological origins that may affect its interpretation and understanding. The concept of human dignity has deep roots in many religions, as well as in moral and political philosophy (Clifford and Huff 2000, p. 334). Human dignity played a historical part in the development of religious and philosophical approaches to human rights (Kretzmer and Klein 2002). Human dignity is foundational for the tradition's understanding of distributive justice, the common good, and the right to life. Other perspectives, both religious and secular, may conceive of human dignity in similar terms with a similar sense of its inherent worth or value and other implications, but may posit different sources for that dignity (Kamali 2002, p. 67). Human dignity is one of the most emphasized themes in the Holy Qur'an (Aramesh 2007). For example:

> "We have honoured the sons of Adam; provided them with transport on land and sea; given them for sustenance things, good and pure; and conferred on them special favours, above a great part of Our creation" (17:70). And: "Proclaim! (Or read!) In the name of Thy Lord and

Cherisher, who created- Created man, out of a (mere) clot of congealed Blood- Proclaim! And Thy Lord is Most Bountiful- He who taught (the use of) the pen- Taught man that which He knew not." (96:1–5). According to teachings of the Holy Qur'an, God (Allah) gave human beings the best shape and form: "O Iblis! What prevents thee from prostrating thyself to one whom I have created with my hands? Art thou haughty? Or art thou one of the high (and mighty) ones?" (95:4) Not only that He created human being by His hands and gave humans the best form, but He called the spirit of human being His spirit to give honour and dignity to human beings: "I breathed into him my spirit." (15:29; 38:72) He taught him all the names. And He taught Adam the names of all things; then He placed them before the angels, and said: "Tell Me the names of these if ye are right." (2:31) And behold, we said to the angels: "Bow down to Adam:" and they bowed down: not so Iblis: he refused and was haughty: he was of those who reject Faith. (2:34) He gave human being intellect and freedom of the will. (16:78; 23:78; 32; 9; 46:26; 67:23) And He made human being His Khalifah (Representative) in the earth. (2:30; 33:72) (Aramesh 2007).

Malaysia has always had the intention to protect Islam. Therefore, when arguing about human dignity, the concept is always interpreted from an Islamic perspective, particularly for the Malay community.

Within the community and in traditions, the Malays have strongly applied human dignity where Malay customs (*adat*) co-exist comfortably with Islam. Malay culture has been described by Western observers as valuing "refined restraint", cordiality, and sensitivity while Malays themselves are described as courteous and charming (and less positively, as fatalistic and easy to take offence). In comparison with other cultures and peoples such as the Chinese and Europeans, the Malay's proper conduct of speech generally tend to be regarded by themselves as *halus* (soft) and others as *kasar* (rough) (Wilson 1967, p. 132). This is to stress that *halus* behaviour applies also to non-verbal behaviours such as removing the shoes before entering a home, consuming some of whatever refreshment is offered, adopting a specific posture when passing between people who are seated, using only the right hand when eating or in passing things, avoiding physical contact with the opposite sex, and beckoning in a certain way (Goddard 1997). Malay culture is richly verbal, with a large stock of sayings (*peribahasa*), short evocative verses (*pantun*), and narrative poems (*syair*). The importance of speech (*percakapan*) to proper conduct is because it has a secondary meaning of "courtesy, manners". For instance, the collocation *tahu bahasa* (know speech) is explained by Hussain Abdullah (1990, p. 26f.) as *sopan santun* "well mannered". Other similar expressions are *melanggar bahasa* (attack speech) "breach etiquette" and *kurang bahasa* (less/under-speech) "ill-mannered" (Goddard 1996). Malays believe that proper speech will affect manners, and manners will definitely affect the dignity of a person.

One important concept in Malays' psyche and interaction is the social emotion of *malu* "shame, propriety". It is usually glossed in bilingual dictionaries as "ashamed", "shy", or "embarrassed". However, these translations do not convey the fact that Malays regard a sense of *malu* as a social good, somewhat akin to a "sense of propriety" (Goddard 1996). Michael G. Swift (1965, p. 110) equals *malu* with "hypersensitiveness to what other people are thinking about one". As identified by some anthropologists that the need to avoid *malu* has been the primary force for social cohesion—not to say conformism—in the Malay village. *Malu* is largely a negative reaction to the idea that other people could think something (anything) bad about one, a prospect which is powerfully unpleasant to Malay sensibilities (Goddard 1996).

What is interesting to the Malays is that *malu* is also related to the social concept of a person's dignity or *maruah*. Other meanings of *maruah* are "self-respect", "pride", and the like. *Maruah* involves both what others think about one and what one thinks about oneself. It is a notion resonant with moral implications in which a person with *maruah* would not lower himself or herself to knowingly do something wrong. This portrays *maruah* as a kind of wholesome confidence in one's moral standing in the eyes of others. Other closely related concepts are *harga diri* "self esteem" (*harga* "value", *diri* "self") and *nama baik* "(one's) good name". This cluster of concepts is of primary concern to Malay social ideology. As Nen Vreeland et al. (1977, p. 113) remarks: "an individual's *amour propre* [is] in many respects his most treasured and jealously defended possession". *Maruah* and a concern for one's *harga diri* bear a clear relationship to the emotion of *malu*. Feeling *malu* "shame" implies a threat to one's *maruah* "dignity", because *malu* is induced by the prospect that other people are thinking bad things about one; conversely, maintaining one's *maruah* will largely pre-empt any unpleasant sense of *malu*. The relationship is similar to that remarked by Mario Jacoby (1991, p. 24) in a discussion of the psychology of shame, "shame-anxiety", and dignity in the European context: "... one could regard shame as a 'guardian' of dignity. Shame-anxiety puts us on guard against 'undignified' behaviour, sensitising us to whether or not a given event will be experienced as 'degrading'."

What do such concepts have to do with characteristic Malay speech patterns? These concepts of shame and dignity are clearly explained in the Malays tradition as among the most essential values embedded in the Malay psyche. For instance, the relations between the ruler and the ruled are based on the idea of a social contract that emerged from the concepts of "sovereign" (*daulat*) and "disloyal" (*derhaka*) (Zainal 1970, p. 20). The social contract was believed to have existed from a myth or dialogue between Sang Sapurba representing the ruler and Demang Lebar Daun representing the ruled in a classical literature called *Sejarah Melayu* (The Malay Annal) written by Tun Sri Lanang. In the dialogue as discussed by C.C. Brown (1970), the concepts of shame and dignity are so crucial in guiding the relation between the ruler and the ruled. The Malay political system can collapse if both sides disobey the rule as shown in the dialogue below:

> Sri Tri Buana said; "What is it that you wish me?" And Demang Lebar Daun replied: "All my descendants shall be your highness subjects and they must be properly treated by your highness' descendants. If they do wrong, however greatly, let them not be disgraced or insulted with evil words: if their offence is grave, let them be put to death, if that is in accordance with Muhammadan (Islamic) law." And the King replied, "I will give an undertaking as you wish but in return I desire an undertaking from you ... that to the end of time your descendants shall never be disloyal to my descendants, even if my descendants are unjust to them and behave evilly". And Demang Lebar Daun replied, "So be it, your highness". And that is why it has been granted by Almighty God to all Malay rulers that they shall never put their subjects to shame: however

greatly they offend, they shall never be bound or hanged or insulted with the evil word. If any ruler puts his subjects to shame, it is a sign that his kingdom will be destroyed by Almighty God. Similarly it has been granted by Almighty God to Malay subjects that they shall never be disloyal or treacherous to their rulers, even if their rulers should behave evilly or inflict injustice (Brown 1970, p. 16).

As observed by Vreeland et al. (1977, p. 117), this is to suggest that "The social value system is predicated on the dignity of the individual and ideally all social behaviour is regulated in such a way as to preserve one's own *amour propre* and to avoid disturbing the same feelings of dignity and self-esteem in others." That is to say, in ordinary conversations, Malays cooperate to assist the safeguarding of each other's *maruah* "dignity" and to steer away from the possibility of incurring or inducing *malu* "shame" (Goddard 1997). Therefore, the concept of human dignity is not something new in the Malay tradition. It, however, needs to be further strengthened and developed in order to make it relevant to Malaysia's current context and practice for the common good.

It has been argued that although the Malays face rapid development and modernization, they still embrace and prioritize certain values closely linked with human dignity. The Malay values of patience, respect and togetherness are applied through tactful actions in everyday social interactions, but more importantly, they are also achieved through linguistic indirectness, hedges and other "positive politeness strategies". According to Lim Beng Soon, by avoiding disagreements, criticisms, complaints and any other face-threatening acts (FTAs) that might reduce the desirability of the addressee and using hedges or even white lies to avoid conflicts, one shows forbearance, achieves harmony and demonstrates togetherness, thus meeting the essential requirements of Malay etiquette (Yuan 2003, p. 1). For example, Malays are warned to guard against speaking in a direct manner as it may lead to serious consequences: "*berapa tajam pisau parang, tajam lagi lidah manusia*" [knives and machetes are not as sharp as human tongues]. Malay culture has significant implications for negotiation processes and outcomes. In negotiations, the Malays' compromising and obliging conflict-handling styles are probably manifestations of their collective nature, which prioritizes group over personal interests. In compromising and obliging styles, negotiators are more concerned with maintaining relationships and safeguarding their partner's feelings, hence the seemingly perceived "weak-styles" in goal-oriented negotiations. To the Malays, even though achieving their goals in a negotiation is important, their values in preserving harmony and respect for elders take precedence in the negotiation process (Lailawati 2005, p. 8). This, for the Malays, will preserve their integrity and dignity in human relations.

It is clear that Asian countries, particularly Malaysia, should have a strong argument on human dignity and place it in the national constitution and legislation. This is not limited to the Malays only, but should involve other multireligious communities as well. This is because the protection of human dignity will make the people better off for the common good. I agree with Guy E. Carmi (2008) that, despite several possible understandings of human dignity, this understanding is most common among legal systems that utilize human dignity as a central constitutional tool, and serves as the basis for the Malaysian model. Under this understanding, the regulation of speech to promote social norms is warranted. In particular, the regulation of speech that is perceived as infringing upon dignity is advanced. Thus, the ban on hate speech is perceived as advancing the human dignity and equality of minorities, and the regulation of pornography is often perceived as promoting the same values for women. But this conception of dignity also comes into expression in maintaining the dignity and honour of individuals via defamation laws and, in some cases, via criminal insult laws. These characteristics of human dignity explain the ideology and motivation of virtually all Western democracies, with the exception of the United States, to regulate hate speech and libel, and, in some cases, to restrict pornography and promote civility (Carmi 2008).

Conclusion

As the "slippery slope" argument would suggest that any restrictions on political expression, once permitted, have a sinister and nearly inevitable tendency to expand. Allowing the practice of one kind of restriction means that many other acts of censorship are allowed as well. The risk of censorship is serious and omnipresent because it can be perceived as acts of repression. Malaysia imposes some additional restrictions on civil liberties. Under the banner of "national security", the Malaysian government limits free expression by arguing from the context of safeguarding race relations and national stability. While democracy as a political ideal is sought, restrictions may be imposed on political processes as necessary to protect other fundamental values. The perceived need of a strong government that is able to deal with competing demands of an ethnically diverse society may be seen as undemocratic and denying people their legitimate rights (Ahmad 1989, p. 17). In Malaysia, unlike in the West, it is not the restriction of free expression that is being questioned but rather government domination of the channels of political expression to weaken opposition and eliminate criticism.

The problem with freedom of expression in Malaysia is that the ruling government exploits the fragile political situation to its benefit. Through policies and the exercise of power, it is able to suppress dissent and criticism from political oppositions, NGOs and the public. Although opposition parties, trade unions, professional associations and other cause-oriented groups are allowed to operate, systematic actions have been taken to curb their activities and their rights to free expression. Permits are denied for public gatherings organized by the opposition parties. Laws such as the ISA, OSA, PPPA, SA, and the Penal Code are invoked to limit political expressions and hinder opposition parties, NGOs, and the public from freely communicating their views and mobilizing their constituencies. These actions gravely impede the opposition's effectiveness in contesting equally in the political arena. Respecting the right to free expression and tolerating dissent and criticism are crucial, as long as hatred and intolerance toward different races, religions, and cultures and deliberate attempts to undermine national security and social stability are avoided. In Malaysia, the right to free expression has been limited by the government, not just on these grounds but to insulate it from criticism and to preserve its power. This is clearly in contrary to democratic values as the limitation on free expression aims not only at the common good but also to neutralize political contestation and opposition. Therefore in the next chapters, the discussion will focus on the issue of religious expression in Malaysia. Before that, the policy of Islamization and the roles of Islamic bureaucracy will be explored in order to understand the practices of religious expression in Malaysia.

2

ISLAMIZATION POLICY AND ISLAMIC BUREAUCRACY

Introduction

Considerable restrictions over certain types of religious expression practices in Malaysia imply the State's subtler and consistent intention not only to maintain racial and religious harmony within the country's multiethnic society, but also ultimately to protect the sanctity of Islam. Safeguarding the primacy of Islam as the official religion of the Federation serves as *raison d'etre* for the Malaysian government and state-religious authorities to carry out Islamization policies and programmes in which Islamic values, principles, laws and systems are integrated into every aspect of national life.

Within the broader context of domestic political landscape, the impetus for Islamization coincided with the deliberate tactical political measures employed by the UMNO-led ruling government to continue to remain in power amidst the background of burgeoning socio-political climate oriented towards Islamic primacy and conservatism which emerged since the 1970s. Hence, this chapter explores and examines the characteristics of state-driven Islamization policy in Malaysia and its historical narrative development. Greater attention will also be paid to the driving factors of and socio-politico ramifications arising from this policy. An understanding of the government's intents, rising Islamic revivalism and the existing national constitutional and legislative framework offer some insights into why the State acted in such ways.

Historical and Contemporary Background of Islamization Policy: An Overview

The origin of Islamization policy in Malaysia can be traced back to the early 1960s. Nevertheless, historical accounts of the early period following the post-independence Malaya reveal that the signs of Islamization process were already visible. The country's first Prime Minister Tunku Abdul Rahman paved the way by establishing the Muslim Welfare Organisation of Malaysia (PERKIM: Persatuan Kebajikan Islam Malaysia). Since its establishment in 1960, PERKIM has been a "non-partisan" *da'wah* organization entrusted to care for recent converts to Islam and to educate the Muslims about Islam. Even so, it was during the period between the 1970s and the 1980s that the policy had gained impetus with the steadily revival of political Islamist movement in the country. During this period, social, legal and political Islamization process in Malaysia coincided and, to a significant extent, was influenced by a landmark of geopolitical events unfolded outside the country—the Iranian Revolution of 1979–82 and revivalism of conservative Islamism in sub-Indian continent.

By the late 1980s, the push to Islamize the country began to figure prominently in government agenda under the prime ministership of Mahathir Mohamed (1981–2013). UMNO in its formative years not only assumed the mantle of defender of Malay rights, but also of propagator of Islamic values and teaching, setting up a number of good-will *da'wah* organizations to support Muslims at the community level (Hassan 2003). As surmised by prominent social-political commentators, this policy-orientation formed part of the Party's political strategy to counter and neutralize the growing political support to the Malaysian Islamic Party (PAS) from considerable sections of the Malay-Muslim populace (Ali 2012, p. 76; Ahmad Fauzi 1998, p. 268).

The critical role played by *da'wah* and youth organizations in expediting Islamic revivalism in Malaysia through education and missionary activities cannot be understated. Among the mainstream Islamist groups that actively promoted religious conviction among Muslim population in Malaysia were Persatuan Kebangsaan Pelajar Islam Malaysia (PKPIM: National Association of Islamic Students Malaysia), Angkatan Belia Islam Malaysia (the Muslim Youth Movement of Malaysia) or popularly known as ABIM, and Jamaah Islah Malaysia (JIM: the Congregation for Islamic Reform).

Sharing the same commonality as a non-political affiliated organization, their organizational memberships and leaders were predominantly made up of Muslim educated youths, both local and foreign educated. It is no exaggeration to say that the dramatic progression of Islamization and religious revivalism in Malaysia was made possible by these organizations. They played a pivotal role in pressuring the government to entrench Islamic values and laws into the nation's system and embraced "a holistic Islamic perspective of social, economic, and spiritual development" in the country (Ali 2008, p. 76). Advocating the impetus to develop and modernize the country through an Islamic model and social system, both ABIM and PKPIM in particular were critical to the then ruling government for dismissing Islamist identity and value in the government's social and economic policy. Aside from successfully getting a large segment of the Muslim population to turn to Islam as a way of life through propagation of positive and practical messages about Islam, these Muslim youth organizations consequently received tremendous support and recognition from the Muslim *ummah* at large—the worldwide community comprising all adherents of the Muslim faith.

Spearheaded by ABIM under the leadership of a popular and charismatic student activist—Anwar Ibrahim, numerous *da'wah* organizations and groups assumed decisive and active roles in planning, organizing and implementing an array of activities and programmes designed to revitalize and push for the Islamization of Malaysian society and institutions. The rapid political ascendancy of Anwar Ibrahim was nothing short of remarkable. Anwar Ibrahim was appointed as the Secretary General of ABIM in 1972, and two years later, became its president. He was a popularizing force behind ABIM, successfully propelled the organization into a powerful civil society and Islamic lobby among Malaysian youths until he became an UMNO member and subsequently entered federal level politics under Prime Minister Mahathir Mohamad's administration (ABIM 2010).

Multiple Facets of Islamization Process

State-driven Islamization policy has arguably left a comprehensible mark in nearly every sphere of society and national life in Malaysia. Nowhere of this policy is more profound than the establishment of Islamic bureaucratic machineries and institutions. The succeeding section discusses this development in detail.

Institutionalization of Islamic Bureaucracy

By the 1990s, Islamic identity had become well entrenched in social, political and legal systems in the country. One development which prominently associated with the aforementioned trend is what Abbott and Gregorios-Pippas (2010, p. 143) referred to as "institutionalization of Islamization within the bureaucracy". Administrative bureaucracy and institutions with Islamic identity and governance ethic flourished, revealing the seriousness of both the federal and state governments to heighten Islamic profile and image of the country through formalized administrative, bureaucratic or socio-economic institutions.

While a significant number of Islamization measures have increasingly been integrated into the life of the country's mainstream society, including institutional transformation based on Islamic model, none of these practices is more conspicuous than during the administration of Prime Minister Mahathir Mohamed. In 1984, he publically announced his intention to "Islamise government machinery", describing "the inculcation of Islamic values in government ... the laws of the nation although not Islamic based, can be used so long as they do not come into conflict with Islamic principles" (Islam 2005, p. 126). Henceforth, the operational framework of government machinery would adhere to Islamist principles and values but stopped short of discriminating other ethnic groups. This state-driven transformation of government bureaucratic institution into Islamic-based institution can be observed through four main sectors in the government, specifically the public service, judiciary, security and economy.

1. *Public Service*

Evidence of "institutionalisation of Islamization within the bureaucracy" in Malaysia can be seen in the public service sector. This is evident with the incremental government support for the establishment of a fully-fledged government department with strong Islamic identity and system. One notable example of such bureaucratic institution is Jabatan Kemajuan Agama Islam Malaysia (Department of Islamic Development Malaysia) or widely known by its acronym: JAKIM (Abbott and Gregorios-Pippas 2010). Originally, it was set up as a subsidiary division of a government department known as the Bahagian Ugama (Division of Religious Affairs), which later became known as the Bahagian Hal Ehwal Islam (Division of Islamic Affairs) in 1984 (Ryan 2010). To further advance the development of Islamic institutions and the administration of Islamic law, the Division was eventually transformed into JAKIM in 1997.

The government's efforts to infuse Islamic values into the federal administrative machinery of the country are executed through JAKIM. While at the state level, one particular institution with similar function is Majlis Agama Islam dan Adat Istiadat Melayu (Council for Islamic Religious Affairs and Malay Customs). JAKIM in particular is responsible for spearheading the standardization of Islamic legislation. During the administration of Prime Minister Mahathir Mohamed, the Islamic Development Foundation was created in alignment with his statement of strengthening the integration of Islamic value and identity in national life and government bureaucracy (Funston 2006).

Meanwhile, Jabatan Kehakiman Syariah Malaysia (JKSM: the Department of Syariah Judiciary Malaysia) was established in 1998 to restructure and coordinate the administration of justice in *Syariah* courts. It also aimed to improve the infrastructure, procedure, and quality of service. Financial assistance was provided to states to upgrade the infrastructure or to increase the remuneration of judges and legal officers of *Syariah* courts. The states which accepted assistance subscribed to a "joint service scheme", where judges and legal officers in the *Syariah* courts may be promoted and transferred between different states and the federal government. JKSM is headed by the Director-General who is also a Chief Syariah Judge. The Director-General is in-charge of the

Department of Syariah Judiciary for the Federal Territories. JKSM also has a group of *Syariah* appeals court judges who have the jurisdiction to hear cases from the Federal Territories' *Syariah* courts as well as cases from states that have entered into the joint service scheme (Shuaib 2012).

2. Judiciary

Federal Constitution stipulates that the administration of Islamic law is to be placed under the jurisdiction of the states. Hence, all matters pertaining to Islamic law are within the purview of the state's legislative power, statutes and *Syariah* courts. There are thirteen states and a unit known as the Federal Territories (i.e. Kuala Lumpur, Labuan, Putrajaya) that make up Malaysia. The structure of Islamic courts is outlined in the Administration of Islamic Law Enactments of the respective states and the Administration of Islamic Law Act (Federal Territories) 1993 for courts located in the Federal Territories. These legislative instruments provide three principal authorities with three separate functions: the Majlis Agama Islam (Islamic Council), the Mufti, and the *Syariah* courts. Each authority is accountable to the ruler of the respective state (Zin 2012).

The current structure of the Islamic judiciary in Malaysia is the result of a nationwide judiciary restructuring exercise which occurred between the 1980s and the 1990s. During that period, each state and the Federal Territories had enacted legislation governing the power of Islamic judiciary. These acts established a three-tiered *Syariah* court structure that resembles the structure of Malaysia's civil courts. The lowest court in the hierarchy is the *Syariah* subordinate court. This is the court of first instance for most matters and consists of a single judge called a *Syariah* subordinate court judge. On the other hand, the *Syariah* high court has supervisory and revisionary jurisdiction over all *Syariah* subordinate courts, either through its own motion or upon the application by an interested party (Zin 2012). Like the subordinate court, the high court consists of a single judge with the title "*Syariah* Judge".

The Syariah Court of Appeal comprises of a panel of three judges consisting of the Chief Syariah Judge and two judges selected from standing panels. The Court of Appeal has the jurisdiction to hear appeals from both lower courts in criminal and civil cases. Decisions by the Syariah Court of Appeal are final. In each of the states, the *Syariah* judiciary is headed by the Chief Syariah Judge of the respective state. The Chief Syariah Judge is directly responsible to either the Sultan of the respective state or to the Yang di-Pertuan Agong (in the case of states which are not governed by Sultans).

Supervisory authority at the federal level for the above mentioned courts is assigned to the Department of Syariah Judiciary. The Department also seeks to promote coordination and uniformity in the administration of Islamic law throughout the country. It does not, however, as underlined by Zin (2012), possess any binding power over individual states, which retain ultimate authority over their own systems.

3. *Security*

The Islamization policy has not only transformed the public service and judiciary with stronger Islamic identity, but it has also extended to other realms. The country's security services, particularly the military and the police, are no exception from this transformation. One notable instance of "institutionalisation of Islamization of bureaucracy" is the establishment of Kor Agama Angkatan Tentera (KAGAT: Religious Corp of Malaysian Army).

Officially formed on 19 April 1985, KAGAT is the 16th corps of the Malaysian Army. The initial move to establish KAGAT began in 1979. The formation of the corps received endorsement from the Armed Forces Council on 24 January 1980 during its 197th meeting. Nearly six years later, the Armed Forces Council approved the terms of transfer of the Islamic Religious Affairs officers from the Public Service Department (JPA) to KAGAT in March 1986. The underlying reason behind the government's move to inculcate Islamic values in the military was due to the fact that the majority of Malaysian military personnel are Malays and Muslims (Burhanuddin 2014, p. 20).

The uniqueness of KAGAT lies with the fact that it serves all three branches of the Malaysian Armed Forces, and not restricted only to the Malaysian Army. KAGAT is assigned with the following roles:

i. Plan, coordinate and implement *da'wah* programmes for all members of the Armed Forces.
ii. Teach and propagate Islamic knowledge with emphasis on high morals, positive attitudes, *esprit de corps* and give a better

understanding of the role of the Armed Forces from an Islamic perspective.
iii. Implement and enforce laws and rules pertaining to Islamic Administration as ruled by the various state authorities.
iv. Assist in boosting morale among soldiers of the Armed Forces (Burhanuddin 2014, pp. 29–30).

There is no specific and formal field formation for KAGAT. Instead, members of the corps are distributed throughout all three services of the Malaysian Armed Forces. The most senior officer is the Director who holds the rank of a Brigadier General.

Unlike KAGAT, the police only experience the Islamization process quite recently. Bahagian Agama dan Kaunseling Polis Diraja Malaysia (BAKA PDRM: Division of Religion and Counselling, Royal Police of Malaysia) was established on 3 April 2007 (Haron 2007). BAKA PDRM is put under the command of the Inspector General of Police. It is divided into three units: Religious Unit, Counselling Unit and Administration Unit. It is operationalized in all levels including Bukit Aman headquarter, contingents, and districts. Other levels where BAKA PDRM operates include the General Operations Force, Federal Reserve Unit, Training Institute, Marine Unit, and Air Unit.

Historically, the importance of religion was noticed by PDRM since the 1980s. Back then, religious knowledge, especially about Islam, was embedded into the course syllabus for training police personnel. There was a Religious Unit within the organizational structure but on a smaller scale. The bigger scale of Religious Unit only came into existence on 13 May 2005 after the Commission on the Improvement of Operation and Management of PDRM tabled a report suggesting that the said Unit should be strengthened in order to boost the morale and spiritual development of the police officers (Haron 2007). Henceforth, BAKA PDRM came into being following the establishment of Religious Unit and Counselling Unit to reinforce police integrity through Islamic values (Teh and Jamsari 2013).

4. Economy

Perhaps the most visible aspect of the Islamization process in Malaysia is the setting up of Islamic institutions of various kinds in the economic sector. For instance, the Islamic Banking Act 1983 provides for the licensing and regulation of Islamic banking businesses. The Takaful Act 1984 authorizes and provides regulation for insurance businesses.

The Banking and Financial Institution Act 1989 (*hereafter* BAFIA) in particular provides laws for the licensing and regulation of institutions involved in banking, finance, merchant banking, discount house and money-broking businesses. Under Section 124 of BAFIA, there is no law prohibiting or restricting any licensed institution from conducting Islamic banking business or Islamic financial business. In addition, the Syariah Advisory Council is tasked with the responsibility to regulate and oversee *Syariah*-compliance in *Syariah* banks. The laws establishing *Syariah* banking, *takaful* (*Syariah*-compliant insurance) and capital markets provide the foundations for the *Syariah* economy and its institutions in the country (Ryan 2010).

The *Syariah* capital market in Malaysia operates under the Securities Commission Act 1993. The market concerned is overseen by the Malaysian Securities Commission (SC), which reports to the Minister of Finance. Section 18 of the Securities Commission Act 1993 establishes the SC's Syariah Advisory Council to regulate and oversee *Syariah*-compliance in the *Syariah* capital market. The *Syariah* capital market includes the *Syariah* equity market, debt market, derivatives and futures market, and interbank money market (Hassan 2009). Other non-banking and *Syariah* financial markets include development institutions, microfinance initiatives, venture capital, and private equity (Hassan 2009).

In the *Syariah* economy, the product and transaction—primary or secondary—must be *Syariah*-compliant. The difference between the *Syariah* economy and the conventional economy is that in the former, *riba* (usury) and *gharar* (risk) are *batil* (invalid) and *haram* (forbidden). Despite its explanation in the Qur'an and hadith, *riba* as a term continues to be debated among the *ulama* (religious scholars). Although it is commonly assumed that *riba* is usury or interest, there are three practices constituting the basic forms of *riba*: *Riba al-fadl* (money exchanged in unequal amounts), *Riba al-nasiah* (changing the total amount due on a loan based on overdue or prepaid loans—penalty or incentive) and the most *haram*, *Riba aljahiliyyah* (charging a penalty for an overdue payment) which has two subsets—*Amhilni azidka* (a penalty fee) or *Da wa taajjal* (financial incentive for early payment) (El-Gamal 2000; Ryan 2010).

The Islamization programme and policy initiated by the Malaysian government managed to bring Islam into the mainstream national economy while spreading awareness about Islamic economy to the Muslims and non-Muslims alike. These government initiatives have established Malaysia as an economically successful and politically stable multicultural Islamic nation that should be emulated by the rest of the Islamic world (Shamsul 1997, pp. 216–22). Furthermore, the endorsement by the United States that Malaysia is a successful moderate Islamic country is no small feat in view of the fact that most of the Islamic countries were lumped together as potentially terrorist-producing countries by the Western media and some of the Western governments (Azmi and Shamsul 2004).

Education and Human Capital Development for Islamization

Islamic education in Malaysia predominantly can be categorized into two types, namely traditional and modern Islamic education. The former may be found in the *pondok* and some *madrasah* religious school system (Buang et al. 2008), while the latter is found in public schools, higher institutes and universities of Islamic studies (Buang et al. 2008; Kayadibi and Buang 2011). Understandably the foremost challenge when implementing the Islamization policy rests on the difficulty confronting the Federal government to cater to the diversity of needs and markets for higher education. It is for this reason that it is imperative for the government to set up institutions of higher learning of varied types. As one would expect, strengthening the Islamization policy and enabling it to be practised successfully would require the allocation of substantial amount of financial investment for human capital development (i.e. scholarship provision, infrastructure building, enhancement of human resources capacity) aimed at producing Islamic scholars, administrators, judges, and educators. In fact, it is required by law to produce these human capitals. For instance, there must be certain types of education requirements in place before somebody can be appointed a *Syariah* judge. Interesting, none of the provision in the Administration of Islamic Law (Federal Territories) Act 1993 governing the appointment of *Syariah* court judges in the Federal Territories imposes any specific minimum religious-based academic qualification for judges.

In practice, however, appointment to the *Syariah* courts and in all states in Malaysia is open only to those who have obtained at least a bachelor's degree. This is because judges are appointed from the ranks of the civil service, and the basic educational qualification required for appointment as a *Syariah* officer within the civil service is a bachelor degree. This degree may be obtained from any recognized institution of higher education either in Malaysia or abroad. In addition to the required bachelor degree, candidates applying for a position in the *Syariah* court must possess a professional qualification in the form of either a postgraduate professional diploma from the International Islamic University Malaysia (IIUM) or other recognized institutions, or a double degree in both law and *Syariah* (LL.B. in *Syariah*) (Zin 2012).

In the Federal Territories, the appointment of *Syariah* judges in the *Syariah* high courts must only be designated to Malaysian citizens and that the person must have at least ten years of experience either as a judge of a *Syariah* subordinate court, a kathi (*qadi*), a registrar, or a *Syariah* prosecutor, and be "learned in Islamic law". These requirements are stipulated in the Administration of Islamic Law (Federal Territories) Act 1993. With respect to the judges of the *Syariah* subordinate court, the Act simply states that the appointee should be from among "members of the general public service of the Federation". Similarly, in the State of Selangor, appointees to the *Syariah* court must have at least ten years of experience as a *Syariah* lawyer (*peguam syarie*), a prosecutor, a registrar, or a member of the *Syariah* courts, and also learned in Islamic legislation. Meanwhile, *Syariah* subordinate court judges are appointed from the general public service or the Syariah Judicial Legal Service (Zin 2012).

Therefore, the Federal government assumed the responsibility of producing human capital in the field of Islamic studies or *Syariah* laws. Understandably, one of its strategies to attain this goal of human capital development was to establish institutions of higher learning. The first higher institution on Islamic Studies in Malaysia, Kelang Islamic College (Kolej Islam Kelang), was established in 1949. The early group of academic staffs employed in the college originated from Egypt. In fact, Al-Azhar University gave accreditation to the graduates of Kelang Islamic College in 1961 as equivalent to the bachelor and master degrees conferred at the same university. Nilam Puri Foundation of Higher Learning (Yayasan Pengajian Tinggi Nilam Puri) was another well-known Islamic institution which was established on 18 September 1965 in Kelantan. The setting up of Nilam Puri Foundation paved the way for the establishment of other Islamic centres of higher education in Malaysia. For example, the Academy of Islamic Studies (AIS) was established at the University of Malaya (UM) while the Faculty of Islamic Studies (FIS) was set up in 1970 in the National University of Malaysia (UKM), IIUM in 1983, and more recently, the University of Islamic Science Malaysia (USIM) in 2000, as well as the establishment of many more Islamic education institutions, both public and private (Kefeli et al. 2007). For example, AIS in UM currently consists of eleven individual departments, namely the department of *Fiqh* and *Usul*; the department of *Syariah* and Management; the department of *Syariah* and Economics; the department of *Syariah* and Law; the department of Aqidah and Islamic Thought; the department of Al-Quran and Al-Hadith; the department of *Da'wah* and Human Development; the department of Islamic History and Civilisation; the department of *Siasah Shariyyah*; the department of Islamic Education programme; and the department of Applied Sciences with Islamic Studies (Kayadibi and Buang 2011).

There are a diversity of courses offered by both the department of law and *Syariah*. Some of these courses encompass the traditional Islamic law (*fiqh*); the administration of Islamic law in Malaysia, which deals with subjects such as jurisdiction, Islamic family law, Islamic law of succession, Islamic procedure, Islamic criminal law, Administration of *fatwa*, *wakaf*, *zakat*, *bayt al-mal*, Islamic judiciary system, and Islamic banking law. Other non-Islamic related law courses taught in these departments include Malaysian legal system, constitutional law, contract law, criminal law, tort law, property law, and evidence (Abdullah 2001).

Such diversity of course subjects offered by these departments is due to the academic background of their faculty members. For example, AIS of UM notes that its lecturers come from different academic backgrounds. Those who teach Islamic Law courses are mainly trained in the universities in the Middle East while the local lawyers are mainly involved in teaching courses relating to Malaysian Law (Abdullah 2001). Furthermore, this assortment of courses offered intertwines with the institution's efforts to enhance its international reputation. Numerous lecturers and scholars from different parts of the world were invited to teach Islamic studies in English and Arabic languages. They have a close relationship with other scholarly communities from the Middle Eastern countries especially Egypt, Saudi Arabia, Syria, Iraq, Turkey and Gulf States as well as western countries particularly the United Kingdom, the United States, and Canada (Kayadibi and Buang 2011).

In addition to UM, UKM, IIUM and USIM, a range of courses related to Islamic studies are taught in the faculties of non-Islamic studies of other universities in the country. Notable examples are the Universiti Sains Malaysia (USM), Universiti Malaysia Terengganu (UMT), Universiti Sultan Zainal Abidin (UNIZA), Universiti Utara Malaysia (UUM), Universiti Teknologi Malaysia (UTM), and Universiti Teknologi MARA (UiTM) (Bakar and Mohamad 2012).

In an effort to increase understanding and knowledge of Islam, values and its historical civilization amongst the university students and youths alike, the curriculum content at public universities in Malaysia has undergone transformation. This development was particularly evident during the tenureship of Prime Minister Mahathir. One example of which was the introduction of Islamic Civilization as a compulsory subject in all Malaysian public universities. He believed that Islam should be understood by every Malaysian. Mahathir reiterated that this subject was not intended to teach the tenets of Islam in order to convert people to the religion, but it focused more on the learning of Islamic civilization. According to Mahathir, the method was similar to the teaching of "History of the British Empire" during the British colonial era. With this move, he hoped to erase fear and doubt of certain quarters of the non-Muslims towards Islam and Muslims. This effort is also seen as trying to strengthen the inter-ethnic relationship in Malaysia (Ahmad 2010).

As previously mentioned, these Islamic-trained graduates are expected to enter the job market and subsequently helped to strengthen the Islamization policy in the country. According to Ibrahim Abu Bakar and Mohd Nasran Mohamad (2012), many graduates from FIS of UKM, for instance, have joined the Malaysian Public Service as Islamic religious teachers in primary and secondary national schools, as college and university lecturers in Islamic education, Islamic studies, Islamic history, Arabic and Islamic Civilization, Islamic law, Islamic banking, and Islamic finance. In addition, graduates from FIS of UKM have also joined various Islamic-based institutions in Malaysia, such as Islamic banks, Islamic religious departments, department of state for Islamic affairs and Malay customs, Islamic councils, including JAKIM. They also elaborate that the graduates from FIS of UKM and other universities offering Islamic studies programmes in Malaysia and abroad are able to become Islamic religious teachers, *imams*, lawyers and judges in the *Syariah* courts, Islamic religious departments and other related establishments. This is because they argue that both federal constitution as well as state constitution have placed the responsibilities of the respective governments to spread Islam among the Muslims and Muslim children and youths through the national education system and curriculum as well as through Islamic religious education system and curriculum for Malaysian Muslims and their children. These two kinds of educational systems, the national and Islamic religious education, employ those graduated from Islamic studies programmes as Islamic religious teachers for subjects related to Islam such as Islamic theology, law, tradition, worship, history, mysticism at the primary and secondary levels. The federal and state governments support and finance Islamic education in the national school system and the Islamic religious school system, the buildings of the mosques and their maintenance because Islam is the religion of the Federation in the Federal Constitution of Malaysia (Bakar and Mohamad 2012).

In a survey conducted in 2011, most Islamic studies graduates chose education as a career, instead of other fields which also offered numerous opportunities. In 2010, 71,565 people graduated in arts and social science of whom 1,804 were Islamic studies graduates. The Director of Academic Development Management Division in the Higher Learning Department, Zarida Hambali, informed that out of a total of 1,804 graduates, 62.8 per cent have sought to work in the education sector as teachers, *J-Qaf* (basic Islamic teachings) teachers and teachers in religious schools (*Bernama* 2011). According to Zarida, there are ample opportunities available for them since many new schools and colleges are opened. Meanwhile, the Director of AIS, UM, Ruzman Md Noor said that Islamic studies graduates would have little problem securing jobs because opportunities are in abundance for them especially in the education sector. He added that Islamic studies graduates have a bright future in terms of employment (*Bernama* 2011).

Zeti Akhtar Aziz, Governor of the Central Bank of Malaysia, mentioned in December 2006 about the contributions of the International Centre for Education in Islamic Finance (INCEIF) to human capital for the future growth of Islamic finance. She said: "Malaysia has placed strong focus on human capital development through training and education" (Zeti 2006, p. 1). Based on this remark, human capital is developed through education and training. If INCEIF develops human capital through its education and training in Islamic finance, AIS of UM and FIS of UKM develop human capital through education and training in Islamic studies (Bakar and Mohamad 2012).

The Malaysian government intensified its Islamization efforts in the early 1970s by sanctioning a number of cabinet level offices and national Islamization policies. In 1971, the government formed the National Cultural Congress (NCC) to include Islamic morals in all sectors of Malaysian governance (JAKIM 2006; Funston 2006). The government also funded the Institut Da'wah dan Latihan Islam (INDAH, Islamic Propagation and Training Institute) and Pusat Penyelidikan Islam (PPI, Islamic Research Centre) (Islam 2005).

The government assigned a deputy minister to the Malaysian National Council for Islamic Affairs who was responsible for Islamization commitments in 1973. The Council managed to get a full-ministry in 1997 which showed that the administration of Islam had become a federal priority (Funston 2006; Ryan 2010). Other evidence of this institutionalization of Islamic bureaucracy is when the Majlis Raja-Raja (Council of Rulers) established the Majlis Kebangsaan Bagi Hal Ehwal Ugama Islam Malaysia (Malaysian National Council for Islamic Affairs). The Council was put under the Prime Minister's Office (PMO) in 1968.

From the constitutional perspective, the Federal Constitution of 1957 designated the states with a list of functions and jurisdiction in administering and enforcing Muslim law, as did the state level statutes regulating matters of relevance to personal and family law. The ensuing years after the adoption of the 1957 Constitution saw a series of amendments to the constitutional provisions, wherein the Islamization process was further strengthened and Islamic identity visibly entrenched in the country. Tamir Moustafa (2014, p. 161), for example, argues that this development was evident in the 1976 amendment of the Constitution relating to semantic changes in Islamic legislation and jurisprudence. Several notable examples include the substitution of the terminology "Muslim law" with "Islamic law", whilst the new term "Muslim courts" is replaced by "*Syariah* courts". He went on to illustrate the same trend of semantic shift which soon appeared in numerous state and federal statutory laws: the "Muslim Family Law Act" of 1984 (Federal Territories) became the "Islamic Family Law Act"; the "Administration of Muslim Law Act" of 1984 was converted to the "Administration of Islamic Law Act"; the "Muslim Criminal Law Offenses Act" became the "Syariah Criminal Offenses Act"; and lastly, the "Muslim Criminal Procedure Act" became the "Syariah Criminal Procedure Act". Why are these semantic changes of terminology so critical to the government's Islamization efforts? Moustafa further explained that in all of these amendments, the shifting of terminology was intended to exchange the object of the law (Muslims) for the purported essence of the law (as "Islamic"). Such shift came during a period when revivalism of *da'wah* movement was picking up considerable steam in Malaysian political life.

A series of global and domestic events unfolded in the twentieth century also served as catalysts in fuelling the steady progression of Islamization in Malaysia. One such event that had left profound effects on the domestic scene was the religious revivalism movement among Muslims worldwide that emerged in the 1970s (Ali 2008, p. 72). Citing examples of such movements that occurred in the Indian subcontinent countries (e.g. Pakistan, India and Bangladesh), this phenomenon to a considerable extent affected and raised the level of religious consciousness among sizeable numbers of Muslim population in the country. Muslim youths, in particular, emerged as the most influential and dynamic players in pushing for the dissemination of Islam and strengthening religious convictions among Muslims. Such movements also received broad based support from a network of religious groups like the Indian-originated Muslim organization, Jamaah Tabligh, and the Malay-based Darul Arqam. In addition, Malay-Muslim students who studied at local universities actively and enthusiastically participated in a myriad of Islamic activism and education programmes, most of which were organized by ABIM. Religious revivalism among the Muslim youth was not only confined to the local university students. Many Malay students who studied or graduated from foreign tertiary institutions, such as in Egypt and the United Kingdom, instigated the push for political emergence of Islamization in Malaysia upon their return from abroad.

The Iranian Revolution of 1979 ushered in a period of Islamic revivalism in many countries with predominately Muslim populations, and Malaysia is no exception. Regarded as a momentous geopolitical event during the Cold War era, the Revolution not only disposed American-sponsored Shah regime and was replaced by Shi'ite cleric-back Muslim Republic, but it also ignited a wave of socio-political struggle among disgruntled Malay society "against of what they perceived as corrupt influences of Western lifestyle" (Thaib 2013, p. 53).

The Revolution in many ways inspires a large segment of the Malay-Muslim population to spread revolutionary and conservative types of Islamic teachings in Malaysia. This new generation of Muslims managed to collectively identify themselves with their Muslim counterparts in Palestine, Libya, Pakistan, Algeria, and the Southern Philippines as an *ummah*. A nationalistic dynamic eventually prevailed as the perpetuating ideology in a solely Malaysian context.

Activism also flourished at UM, UKM and the International Islamic University (IIU), which hosted a new generation of significant Islamic constituents (Garza 2012). Scholar Mohamad Abu Bakar (1991, p. 220) attributes an internal re-education about the holistic nature of Islam as the primary cause of Malaysian revivalism. This new consciousness in religious teaching created a greater awareness and understanding of Islam among many Malay-Muslim populace and a heightened feeling that as *ad-din*, or a way of life, Islam needed a greater role in the public sphere (Miller 2004).

Even as early as the 1970s, criticism was levelled against the ruling government coalition led by UMNO for its perceived failure to rigorously and aggressively promote and uphold Islam in government policy agenda and administration. PAS President Asri Muda and associates claimed that the government was not doing enough to advance Islam and to defend Malay's interests economically, politically, and culturally. Whereas Islamic identity, system and value were well entrenched in the government policy since the mid-1970s, the policy was only officially acknowledged under the administration of Prime Minister Mahathir Mohammad.

In harnessing the legitimizing power of Islamic symbolism and discourse in the country, Mahathir sought to co-opt the steadily ascendancy of *da'wah* movement. Mahathir took office in 1981 to begin what became a twenty-two-year reign over Malaysian politics. Although he pursued a variety of policies, he was credited for modernizing Malaysia's economy to become one of the Asian Tigers. With regard to political Islam, his focus was to defeat PAS' challenges. PAS was trying hard to gain support among Muslims especially those from the rural areas of Malay heartland and this was a source of great concern to UMNO. To counter the political influence of PAS and secure his party's political survival, Mahathir readily pursued various range of Islamic policies by embracing Islamic themes and projects, and became more accommodating to Islam (Miller 2004).

Mahathir (then Acting Prime Minister) announced in March 1981 that the government would be setting up an Islamic Consultative Body (ICB) to ensure that national development programmes were in conformity with Islamic values. This committee signifies the beginning of Islamization policy becoming the official policy of the state. It was made up of Islamic experts in politics, law, administration, sociology, economics, engineering, medicine, agriculture, and Islamic philosophy. It had the responsibility of analysing and evaluating policies and technology with the intention of modifying them to be in line with Islamic values. According to Mohamed Aslam Haneef (2009), the ICB was assigned the task of discussing and deliberating on various issues concerning Islam and its development and to put forward these proposals to the government for consideration. The government seemed to indicate that the New Economic Policy (NEP), which began in 1974, was being Islamized or at least being injected with Islamic values. This would also imply that meeting the "Islamic standard" was going to be the requirement of all policies, thus elevating Islam to a central role in policy formulation and decision making (Haneef 2009).

Soon after that, the government announced the Inculcation of Islamic Values Policy later in 1981, which was meant to cover government administration. The government over the years crystallized this policy to instil some forms of universal Islamic values such as Trustworthiness, Responsibility, Sincerity, Dedication, Moderation, Diligence, Cleanliness, Discipline, Cooperation, Integrity and Thankfulness that would enable the country to have an effective, strong, just and progressive administration (Prime Minister's Office 1986; Ministry of Information 1986). Haneef (2009) argues that this was to create a dynamic work ethic which would increase productivity. The policy's main intention was an attempt at improving individuals in their thinking, behaviour and value orientation, rather than imposing Islamic law or some other external aspects of Islam (Haneef 2009). To make the policy successful, Mahathir was even more prepared to accommodate the dissenting Islamists. A big boost came when he managed to persuade the ABIM leader Anwar Ibrahim to join UMNO just prior to the 1982 elections and later helped him strengthen the Islamization policy.

This Islamization policy initiated many programmes. Among others were the use of Islamic terminologies and salutations, the building of Islamic complexes and research institutes, the organization of international conferences, broadcasting of Islamic programmes on radio and television, and conducting Islamic courses for the public. The more substantive programmes were added. Most notable of these programmes involved the establishment of an international Islamic university, the introduction of Islamic securities, banking and insurance systems. Other initiatives undertaken by the State were the amendments to the Constitution to increase the power of Islamic legal authorities, reforms of Islamic administration, laws and courts, and serious efforts to promote uniformity and coordination between states (Horowitz 1994a, p. 22; Thaib 2013, p. 48).

By the 1980s, the Islamization policy showed numerous signs which were pervasive in people's daily life. Muslim women started to wear *hijab* in mass. There were also segregation of sexes and tremendous proliferation of Islamic literature and cassette tapes. The public also appeared to renew their interests in the pure Islamic way according to the *Qur'an* and the *Hadith* (*Sunnah*). Besides, the presence of religious organizations was mushrooming. These were definitely many clear and palpable signals in Malaysia about the reach of the Islamic resurgence (Kumar 2012). Implementation of Islamization policy at the government level reached its crescendo and this was prominently demonstrated when Prime Minister Mahathir Mohamed declared Malaysia as an Islamic state on 29 September 2001.

During his twenty-two years of rule, the religious bureaucracy expanded at an unprecedented rate, and aspects of Islamic law were institutionalized to an extent that would have been unimaginable in the pre-colonial era. Besides the proliferation of state institutions, primary and secondary education curricula were revised to include more materials on Islamic civilization, and radio and television contents followed suit. But it was in the field of law and legal institutions that the most consequential innovations were made (Moustafa 2014).

Abdullah Ahmad Badawi (2006, p. 3), who succeeded Mahathir in 2013, propagated a new national policy of Islamization called "*Islam Hadhari*". He explained that *Islam Hadhari* is not a new religion, a new teaching or a new *mazhab* (denomination). It is an effort to bring the *ummah* back to the basic tenets of Islam, back to the fundamentals as prescribed in the Qur'an and the hadith which formed the foundations of Islamic civilization. Therefore, *Islam Hadhari* aimes to achieve ten main principles:

 i. Faith and piety in Allah;
 ii. A just and trustworthy government;
 iii. A free and independent people;
 iv. A vigorous pursuit and mastery of knowledge;
 v. A balanced and comprehensive economic development;
 vi. A good quality of life for the people;
 vii. The protection of the rights of minority groups and women;
 viii. Cultural and moral integrity;
 ix. The safeguarding of natural resources and the environment; and
 x. Strong defence capabilities.

In a Parliamentary session on 27 August 2007, he reiterated that Malaysia is a Muslim country and governed according to Islamic principles. He said that Malaysia firmly believes in the principles of Parliamentary democracy guided by the country's highest law, the Federal Constitution (*Bernama* 2007a). Badawi argued that the *Islam Hadhari* approach does not mean that Malaysia is a theocratic country. He explained that:

> The government that I lead is a government based on the principles of Parliamentary democracy and is answerable to Parliament. At the same

time, the Cabinet comprises ministers who profess Islam, Buddhism, Hinduism, Christianity and others respectively, who reach consensus based on discussions and come out with the national development policies. ... I also dismiss the argument that it contravenes the social contract negotiated by our past leaders. We must remember that the Federal Constitution was successfully drafted on the basis of compromise and cooperation demonstrated by the three major races in the country when fighting for independence (*Bernama* 2007, p. 1).

He argued that this administrative approach had been practised by the Malaysian government for over fifty years, and the unique formula had been tested and its effectiveness had been proven. The adoption of Islamic principles in the country's administration did not in any way change the social contract or the Constitution (*Bernama* 2007).

Islam Hadhari was also looked upon as a general framework for the development of Muslim *ummah*, shielding them from engaging in the violent trend of *jihad*, extremism, and militaristic Islamic groups, such as al-Qaeda and Jumaah Islamiah. Malaysia had the experience of dealing with the violent attempts by militant Islamic movements, most notably the al-Maunah and Kumpulan Mujahidin (Militan) Malaysia (KMM) in 2002 and 2003 respectively. Abdullah openly criticized and disavowed the violent streak in the Islamic jihadist movement (Kling 2006, p. 180). The introduction of *Islam Hadhari* was designed to erase Islamophobia among the non-Muslims especially in Malaysia. On the policy front, one of the means adopted by Abdullah was to encourage dialogues between Muslims and non-Muslims in order to wipe out the stereotype of alleged violence nature of the Muslim community.

Pertaining to democracy, Badawi (2006, p. 114) believed that *Islam Hadhari* is entirely consistent with the democratic principles on the basis that the concept is all about living peacefully and respecting each other in a society. *Islam Hadhari* encourages consensus building (*musyawarah*) as an effective approach to resolving problems, and acknowledges the consultative process (*shura*) as the best means of dealing with various societal issues. Abdullah also urged that people of goodwill, civil societies, and institutions of higher learning can all play their part in promoting critical dialogues between the non-Muslim and Muslim worlds. While it is necessary on their part to find a common ground with people of other faiths, Muslims must also open up the discourse within their own faith—a more open and diverse Islamic discourse. The observance of the canon of accountability in Islam is often matched by respecting the people's views. Morally upright Caliphs even accommodated opinions that are different from theirs. In fact, there is a hadith that even eulogizes differences of opinion within the *ummah* as a sign of divine blessing. It explained why at different points in Muslim history, there were healthy discussions and debates about religious and political matters among scholars and certain segments of the populace (Badawi 2006, p. 39).

Upon taking over as the Malaysian prime minister in 2009, Najib Tun Razak introduced the concept of 1Malaysia. In order to promote the Islamization policy, Najib decided not to continue to practise Abdullah's concept of *Islam Hadhari*. Instead, Najib projected a concept of *Wasatiyyah* beginning in 2010, which was embedded together with the 1Malaysia policy. The concept of *Wasatiyyah*, an Arabic term that translates into "moderation", derived from the word "*wasat*", is found in chapter 2 verse 143 of the Qur'an. An advantage of this method is that it provides a more neutral position on *Wasatiyyah*, averting the possible bias of the politician's pragmatism and expediency (Wan Mansor, Mujani, and Rozali 2013).

Najib introduced the concept of *Wasatiyyah* amidst a convention attended by local Islamic scholars and leaders. Najib clearly intended *Wasatiyyah* to primarily serve as a supporting ideology to his bigger scale multiethnic unity campaign "1Malaysia". Therefore, Jabatan Kemajuan Islam Malaysia (JAKIM, Department of Islamic Development) uses its new motto, "1Malaysia 1Ummah" (Wan Mohamad 2011, pp. 53–55). In many accounts, the premier underlined the role of *Wasatiyyah* in fending off religious extremism (especially in Islam) and promoting a more united Malaysia based on tolerance and mutual cooperation.

The moderation solution in Malaysia is based on three criteria. First, the conviction and commitment of *Wasatiyyah* towards moderation and its underlying philosophy of "public reasonableness" are urgently needed in Malaysian society. The harms of past colonialism that restrict interactions between Malays, Chinese and Indians by means of "divide and control" must be abated and alleviated. This willingness to engage in a political discourse must be guided by the impetus of *Wasatiyyah's* concept of "so that you know each other". Second, *Wasatiyyah's* philosophy is based on the universal values of Islam but grounded on contextual realities. A strong understanding of history and the colonial effects on Malaysia, as well as reliable social sciences on the Malaysian society must be considered in order to make the best and just decisions. Although realizing the need to correct past societal harms, corrective measures must be done moderately; drastic measures must be avoided. Third, divisive political culture of using race as a basis of rights and obligations should be re-examine from time to time in order to avoid unjustified exploitation of power under the pretext of Islam and Malay. Inter ethno-religious relationships must always be cognizant to the fact that differences are created so that humanity can grow, not the opposite (Wan Mansor, Mujani, and Rozali 2013). Hence, Najib announced the establishment of the Institute of Wasatiyyah Malaysia on 17 January 2012 in order to promote the concept of *Wasatiyyah* to the public. This institute is now operationalized under the Prime Minister's Office.

There is nothing new about this policy. In fact, it is a continuation of previous policies by Najib's predecessors. To implement this Islamization policy throughout several decades since the 1980s, the government obviously needs a functioned Islamic bureaucracy to govern it.

Islamization through the Media

To understand the roles of Malaysian media in reporting religious matters, it is pertinent to trace the policy of Islamization in Malaysia. Zulkiple Abdul Ghani (1996) argued that the progression of Islamization of media in the country had already transpired since the 1970s. In his observation, both the radio and television had played an instrumental role in amplifying Islamic discourses for the past three decades. It was evident from the early 1970s onwards that television, in particular, might be a potent force for Islamization and the government was fully aware of this notion. In 1973, the government-owned Radio and Television Malaysia (RTM) began televising no more than thirty minutes a week of Islamic content, and existing entertainment programmes were frequently criticized by *da'wah* groups for purveying decadent and non-Islamic, Western material. Later on, a Religious and *Da'wah* Unit was set up within RTM that year, and three years later it was producing and broadcasting twenty-two programmes a week. To date, Islamic programmes make up over 10 per cent of the total output of broadcasting hours. The impact of Islamization again witnessed another Islamic media development when in July 2001 the first twenty-four-hour broadcast of Islamic radio was launched. The establishment of radio IKIM.fm was seen as another mechanism in promoting and educating Muslims about development and social change from the Islamic perspective. The establishment of the Religious and *Da'wah* Unit in RTM, and IKIM.fm later on, can be assumed that there were high demands for Islamic media (Ahmad and Harrison 2007, p. 14).

Cursory analysis on the Malay-language press represented, for example, by *Utusan Malaysia* and *Berita Harian*, including *Sinar Harian*, shows a noticeable absence of any discourse on religions other than Islam, stopping short of announcing themselves as "Islamic" newspapers (Merican 2005). Ahmad Murad Merican (2005) argues that Malay idea about Islam as portrayed in the Malay dailies are largely confined to Malay society, in that Islam is viewed as monolithic, and the only legitimate faith in Malaysia and for the Malays. In the first instance, both dailies have mainstreamed Islam to be of the Sunni doctrine and Shafi'i school. Other sects such as Shi'ism, and other theological schools such as Hanafi, Hambali and Maliki are excluded from news coverage or commentaries. With Islam being the religion of the Malays, and that constitutionally defined, being Malay is also being a Muslim, Merican (2005) explains that one finds a number of constructs on Islam in the Malay dailies. First, the Islam portrayed is of the Sunni and Shafi'i school; second, Islam is exclusivist, and not equalled to other religions; third, Islam is Malay and intertwined with Malay culture and customs; fourth, Islam is compatible to modernization; fifth, Islam is a religion of peace; sixth, religion (read: *agama* and not Islam) is separated from politics; seventh, Islam is a total way of life (*syumul*) in that it encompasses all aspects of life; and eighth, there are constant reminders of the *akhirat* (the hereafter), especially in commentaries and essays (Merican 2005).

Merican (2005) further argues that in the 1980s, the concern with being Islam and the reassertion of Islamic identity was linked to the problem of Malays having to confront the issue of cultural, economic, educational and political survival, and the conflict between two competing interpretations of Islam as projected by UMNO and PAS, two main Malay-based political parties. UMNO had been induced to make some concessions, for instance the propagation of *Penerapan Nilai-nilai Islam* (Inculcation of Islamic values) during Mahathir Mohamad's premiership and his successor Abdullah Ahmad Badawi with *Islam Hadhari* (Civilisational Islam), which serves to further enhance the importance of Islam in Malaysia. In addition, there is continuous problem of the search for Malay identity *vis-à-vis* the Islamic identity (Azizuddin 2013a). Since being Malay is defined as one who practises Malay customs and is a Muslim (in accordance to Article 160 of the Malaysian Constitution), it is inconceivable to be Malay but not Muslim at the same time. Therefore, Malay identity should be embedded in Islam. Hence according to Merican (2005), the Malay newspapers are daily discourse on Islam and Malay society with regards to their concerns for ritual practices, items on *ulama*, the history of Islam in Malaysia and the Malay world, Quranic interpretations and the hadith (sayings of the prophet), as well as the understanding and use of science and technology in accordance to Islamic norms and values.

Since the last five decades, there have been authoritative/bureaucratic agencies defining about Islam. One such authoritative/bureaucratic agency that saw its expanded role was JAKIM. It was seen as strengthening the role of Islam in Malaysia. On the other hand, the popularly defined Islam can be seen through Islamic movement of *da'wah* groups, which have started to demand a greater role for Islam in public life, including a greater jurisdiction based on Islamic law. Consequently, elevating religious awareness among the Malay population necessitates a more visible implementation of Islam in the context of redressing the economic imbalances among the three ethnic groups, and in countering the rise of materialism and permissiveness among the Malays (Merican 2005).

From the broadcasting's point of view, the Ministry of Information (now Ministry of Communications and Multimedia) stated that all Malaysians should understand that Islam is the official religion and non-Muslims should accept its importance and dominance over other religions (Mutalib 1993). Therefore, in 1988, the ministry, through RTM, announced that Islam will be given airtime over radio and television. There were no specific policies regarding Islamic programmes in Malaysia but JAKIM has come out with a general guideline for entertainment in

Islam. This guideline will assist anyone in Malaysia who is involved in entertainment industries such as singing, music, and dancing. It is, therefore, a general rule in entertainment programmes and has been used by most television stations and production especially when producing Islamic programmes (Buyong and Ismail 2011).

TV al-Hijrah is a state-owned free-to-air television network in Malaysia operated under the al-Hijrah Media Corporation, a Malaysia government-owned company under JAKIM (http://www.tvalhijrah.com/Home.aspx). TV al-Hijrah was established and started its operation on 16 September 2009 as the first Islamic television station. As a new television station, TV al-Hijrah expands its coverage to the whole country through eight transmitters that can freely follow and cover 75 per cent of households. In addition, broadcasting programmes of TV al-Hijrah have also been posted on the Internet for viewing by foreign countries. As stated on its website (http://www.tvalhijrah.com/Home.aspx), the main objective of the establishment of TV al-Hijrah is to become the medium that educate, entertain, and unite the plural society of Malaysia. Moreover, the vision of TV al-Hijrah is to provide various creative and good quality broadcasting contents targeted mainly at youth or those in the group ages of forty and below. The mission of TV al-Hijrah is also to provide suitable contents and programmes that are parallel with *Syariah* principles. In order to achieve that objective, TV al-Hijrah states that its main commitment is to provide contents in the forms of magazine, documentary, drama, news, current affairs, entertainment and sports based on Islamic principles and universal values. Meanwhile, in terms of the contents, the station adopts the concept of Islam as a way of life. TV al-Hijrah produces its own programmes in various genres including talk shows, documentary, drama, children programmes, spiritual zone, entertainment and magazine. The station has also broadcast imported films for the targeted audiences including Muslims as well as non-Muslims. With regard to the *Syariah* compliance and *fiqh* broadcasting, TV al-Hijrah establishes several guidelines for programme productions. The establishment of the guidelines is to ensure that all programmes broadcast by the station must not deviate from the Islamic principles. Furthermore, the broadcasting guidelines also take into consideration the Communications and Multimedia Act 1998 and the Film Censorship and Content Code Act 2002 (Zulkiple 2014).

A study about television programmes conducted in 2011 reveals that in terms of Islamic programme, there were only 13.5 per cent of Islamic programmes in five free-to-air television channels—namely TV1, TV2, TV3, TV9 and TV al-Hijrah—and zero per cent on two other channels NTV7 and 8TV. The total amount of transmission hours allocated for Islamic programmes from 25 September 2011 to 1 October 2011 were 128 hours 30 minutes. TV al-Hijrah had the most Islamic programmes with 67 per cent of its total broadcasting hours followed by TV9 with 23 per cent (Buyong and Ismail 2011).

Both federal and religious state authorities appear to have monopolized the interpretation or understanding of Islamic faith, laws, values and principles and subsequently, strictly imposed them on Muslims within Malaysia. Once a *fatwa* or a decree from state-appointed religious officials is recorded in the official Gazette, public expressions of alternate views and even personal beliefs other than those sanctioned by the authorities are prohibited. The Administration of Islamic Law Act (Federal Territories) Act 1993 and parallel state-level enactments confer a state monopoly on religious interpretation. The Islamic Religious Council, the office of the Mufti, and the Islamic Legal Consultative Committee wield absolute authority in this regard. For instance, the Syariah Criminal Offences Act 1997 further consolidates the monopoly on religious interpretation established in Article 9 of the Administration of Islamic Law Act (Federal Territories) 1993 which criminalizes defiance of religious authorities:

> Any person who acts in contempt of religious authority or defies, disobeys or disputes the orders or directions of the Yang di-Pertuan Agong as the Head of the religion of Islam, the Majlis or the Mufti, expressed or given by way of fatwa, shall be guilty of an offence and shall on conviction be liable to a fine not exceeding three thousand ringgit or to imprisonment for a term not exceeding two years or to both.

Article 12 further criminalizes the communication of an opinion or view contrary to a *fatwa* when it states as follows:

> Any person who gives, propagates or disseminates any opinion concerning Islamic teachings, Islamic Law or any issue, contrary to any fatwa for the time being in force in the Federal Territories shall be guilty of an offence and shall on conviction be liable to a fine not exceeding three

thousand ringgit or to imprisonment for a term not exceeding two years or to both.

In addition, Article 13 criminalizes the distribution or possession of a view contrary to Islamic laws issued by religious authorities stating that:

> Any person who (a) prints, publishes, produces, records, distributes or in any other manner disseminates any book, pamphlet, document or any form of recording containing anything which is contrary to Islamic Law; or (b) has in his possession any such book, pamphlet, document or recording, shall be guilty of an offence and shall on conviction be liable to a fine not exceeding three thousand ringgit or to imprisonment for a term not exceeding two years or to both.

In sum, the government commands a complete monopoly over the interpretation of Islamic law (Moustafa 2014, p. 164).

A 1996 *fatwa* by the Fatwa Committee of the National Council of Islamic Religious Affairs stated that Muslims in Malaysia must only follow the teachings of Islam based on the Sunni doctrine on creed, religious laws and ethics. Other teachings of Islam such as Shi'ism are considered as deviant from Islam (Razak 2013). The Home Ministry was urged to immediately ban printed materials such as books and novels written by Shia followers on the deviant religious doctrine. Senator Noriah Mahat, when debating on the Supplementary Supply Bill (2012) 2013 in the Dewan Negara (lower house in the parliament) on 31 July 2013, said that the ministry should also take stern actions against any such individual so that their writings would not erode the faith of Muslims in the true teachings of Islam. She further said: "If it is not controlled, I fear for young Muslims because they could be easily influenced by Shia teachings as they are a curious lot" (*The Malaysian Insider* 2013, p. 1).

One issue that raised considerable concerns over the exercise of religious freedom and expression in multiracial Malaysia is the controversy on the use of the word "Allah". On 23 June 2014, in a 4–3 majority decision, the Federal Court conferred with the Appeal Court's decision siding with the government and rejected the Catholic Church's bid to get leave to challenge the Home Ministry's ban on the use of the word "Allah" for "The Herald" (*The Star Online* 2014a). In January 2008, the Malaysian cabinet banned a Catholic newspaper, *The Herald*, from using the word "Allah" in their publications. The Malaysian government justified the restrictions on the basis that the word "Allah" refers to God according to the Muslim faith, and as such its use by non-Muslims may touch on sensitivities and create confusion among Muslims in the country (*The Sun* 2008, p. 1). The issues of Shi'ism and "Allah" have affected the practices of religious freedom in Malaysia. The US Commission on International Religious Freedom (USCIRF) 2014 Annual Report placed Malaysia on Tier 2, one level down from Tier 1 (countries of particular concern) which lists countries like Myanmar, China, Iran, Iraq, Pakistan and Sudan, among others. USCIRF found that the intertwining of religion, ethnicity, and politics in Malaysia complicates religious freedom protections for religious minorities and non-Sunni Muslims (Zachariah 2014).

Although the state controlled by UMNO has always been in the role of enforcing Islam on Muslims in Malaysia, since the post-2008 general election, many Malay rights groups such as Pertubuhan Peribumi Perkasa (PERKASA), Pertubuhan Kebajikan Islamiah dan Dakwah (PEKIDA), and Ikatan Muslimin Malaysia (ISMA) have emerged vocally championing the issues of Islam and Malays. They received great support from the Malay press, particularly *Utusan Malaysia* owned by UMNO, because of their common struggle for similar issues, e.g. the publication of an article headlined "Kristian agama rasmi?" [Christianity the official religion?] on the front page of *Utusan Malaysia*.

Malay groups such as PERKASA, UMNO and *Utusan Malaysia* have always shown solidarity in their struggle towards championing the issues of Malay and Islam. For example, about one hundred UMNO Youth and PERKASA members gathered in front of Utusan Melayu (M) Berhad office in Kuala Lumpur on 20 May 2011 to express support for *Utusan Malaysia* which has been accused of publishing lies over issues involving opposition parties. The gathering was filled with cries of "Hidup Melayu", "Hidup PERKASA" and "Selamatkan Utusan", with some participants also holding posters with the words, "Utusan Perkasa Melayu", written on them. Seven UMNO Youth representatives led by its assistant secretary Megat Firdaus Megat Junid and seven PERKASA representatives led by its secretary general Syed Hassan Syed Ali handed a memorandum to the newspaper's deputy editor-in-chief II, Ahmad Abdul

Hamid, expressing their support for *Utusan Malaysia*. Syed Hassan told reporters that one of the four main points contained in the memorandum stated that since its establishment, *Utusan Malaysia* has always fought for the agenda of national development and sovereignty and championed Malay and Islamic interests as stipulated under Article 152 (2) and 153 of the Federal Constitution (*The Borneo Post* 2011, p. 1). Besides, on 25 April 2011, about one hundred PERKASA members and supporters held a protest outside the Malaysian Chinese Association (MCA) headquarters in Kuala Lumpur after the party's call to boycott the Malaysian Malay language daily *Utusan Malaysia*, in response to the daily's "1 Melayu, 1 Bumi" initiative. PERKASA secretary general Syed Hassan Syed Ali defended *Utusan Malaysia*, saying that the newspaper was not being racist as it only defended Malay rights enshrined in the Constitution (Chi 2011, p. 2). Therefore, UMNO and Malay groups like PERKASA seemed to utilize the Malay press especially *Utusan Malaysia* as their mouthpiece for their far right agenda.

Moral Policing

Both federal and religious state authorities seemed to have monopolized the interpretation or understanding of Islamic values and moralities in Malaysia and as often the case, enforcing them through respective state and federal religious apparatus. In January 2005, for example, the Jabatan Agama Islam Wilayah Persekutuan (JAWI: Federal Territories Religious Department) enforcement officers raided Singapore-owned Zouk nightclub in Kuala Lumpur and arrested 100 Muslims who were patrons of the club. The involved religious officers claimed that those arrested were dressed indecently or had consumed alcohol. This event had triggered a protest by a group of anti-moral policing campaigners, who called themselves Malaysians Against Moral Policing. The group had not simply protested to the arrest but also questioned the state's role in defining the morality of its citizens and the use of punitive religious and municipal laws to curb immorality and indecency (Mohamad 2008). Their campaign called for the repeal of provisions in religious and municipal laws that deny citizens their fundamental rights to privacy, freedom of speech and expression, and those that overlapped with the federal penal code. It also called for the appointment of a committee to monitor the process of repealing these laws, including representation from women's groups, human rights groups, civil society organizations, progressive religious scholars and constitutional experts. In addition, the group also called on the need for strengthening of pluralism through community dialogues on the issue of morals in the society. The campaign was endorsed by about fifty non-governmental organizations (NGOs) and more than 200 individuals including prominent government and opposition politicians such as those from the Democratic Action Party (DAP) and Parti Keadilan Nasional (KEADILAN: National Justice Party) (Mohamad 2008). As a result of the various protests, none of those arrested were charged in the *Syariah* court because, according to Abdullah Mat Zin, the minister in the Prime Minister's Office (the *de facto* Islamic Affairs Minister), there was a "lack of evidence which warrants prosecution" (Mohamad 2008).

In response to the Anti-Moral Policing Campaign, a coalition of mainstream Islamic organizations launched a counter-campaign to defend the enforcement of Islamic moral laws. About fifty Islamic organizations including ABIM, JIM, PKPIM, Malaysian Ulama' Association (PUM), Malaysian Chinese Muslim Association (MACMA) and Indian Muslim Youth Movement of Malaysia (GEPIMA) issued a joint statement claiming that the campaign "has caused confusion and ambiguities about the concepts of prevention of sin and the limits of individual freedom in Islam" (Mohamad 2008, p. 160). The organizations maintained that the prevention of sin, especially by the government, is a manifestation of the principles of *hisbah* and *al-amr bi al-ma'ruf wa al-nahy 'an al-munkar* (enjoining good and forbidding evil) which are central to the teachings of Islam. Sharing the same sentiment was the National Fatwa Council, which consists of state muftis and religious scholars who urged the government in its April meeting to uphold the Islamic concept of "enjoining good and forbidding evil" by enforcing those laws more responsibly. The government, responding to the protests from the Muslim majority, shot down the initiative and promised to retain all laws on morality including the *Syariah* laws in order to safeguard the moral of Malaysians (Mohamad 2008, p. 160).

Meanwhile in another related issue, fifty-two unmarried Muslim couples faced charges of sexual misconduct and possible jail terms after being caught alone in hotel rooms by Malaysia's Islamic morality police (*Daily Mail* 2010). Scores of officers fanned out across budget hotels in central Selangor state before dawn on 1 January 2010, knocking on doors and detaining unmarried Muslim couples who were sharing rooms. The detained, mostly students and young factory workers, were expected to be charged with "*khalwat*", or "close proximity". Several unmarried Muslim couples in Malaysia were charged for being in "close proximity". Malaysian *Syariah* law does not allow couples to live together or cohabitate before marriage. Under Malaysia's *Syariah* law, "*khalwat*" is described as couples not married to each other being alone together in a private place. The spokesman of Jabatan Agama Islam Selangor (JAIS: Selangor Religious Department) Hidayat Abdul Rani explained that: "We chose to have this large-scale operation on New Year's Day because many people are known to commit this offense while celebrating such a major holiday" (*Daily Mail* 2010, p. 1). In Selangor, *khalwat* carries a maximum penalty of two years in prison and a fine. The *Syariah* law nevertheless only applies to Malaysia's Muslims, who make up nearly two-thirds of the population, and not to Christian, Buddhist and Hindu minorities. Mohd Asri Zainal Abidin, former mufti of the state of Perlis, conceded that the religious authorities have the right to conduct *khalwat* raids but it must be done in a reasonable and rational manner (*The Star* 2006a). While the actions of *khalwat* among unmarried Muslim couples are sinful, the approaches to prevent such sins from being perpetrated should be modified to educate Muslims on their rights and wrongs. He suggested that state governments have special guidelines for religious departments on the proper way of conducting *khalwat* raids.

In a separate issue in 2009, a Muslim model was sentenced to be caned by authorities after being caught drinking beer at a nightclub. Kartika Sari Dewi Shukarno was sentenced to six lashes by an Islamic court after she was caught with alcohol in a raid on a hotel nightclub in eastern Pahang state. Amnesty International had urged the authorities to "immediately revoke the sentence to cane her and abolish the practice of caning altogether". But Miss Shukarno accepted her punishment and even asked for the caning to be carried out in public to send a clear message to Muslims that they should shun alcohol (*Daily Mail* 2010). The nation's strict *Syariah* laws have been the focus of world attention.

In some cases, such as with *khalwat*, academics and authorities have discussed on imposing the code on non-Muslims in the country as well.

Syariah Index

In an international seminar on the implementation of *Wasatiyyah* through the *Maqasid Syariah* on 8 April 2014, Prime Minister Najib Razak said that Malaysia is aiming towards establishing an international *Syariah* index in evaluating the commitment of countries applying *Syariah* law. The reason for the establishment of such an index is to reject any criticism that Malaysia through its policies is not practising Islam sufficiently. Besides, this will also show Malaysia's commitments in practising the true Islamic teachings according to Sunni doctrine. The concept of *Wasatiyyah* (moderation) will be enforced through the five principles of *Maqasid Syariah* namely religion, life, mind, dignity and property in order to ensure Malaysia's Islamic approach will be followed by other Muslim countries (*Utusan Online* 2014).

The concept of *Syariah* index is not something new. In fact, the *Syariah* index was introduced on 17 April 1999 by Bursa Malaysia (Kuala Lumpur Stock Exchange) containing only Syariah Approved Securities in the Main Board. Bursa Malaysia (2005) elaborated that the objective of *Syariah* index is to meet the demand from investors who want to invest in securities which are consistent with the *Syariah* principles. The *Syariah* index is believed to have improved the development of Islamic financial market by providing information to investors in making a better investment decision. Market participants mainly use the *Syariah* index to help them in investment management, for example as a benchmark to evaluate the Islamic portfolio performance, to create the Islamic portfolio (Index Fund Portfolio), and to evaluate the current and predict the future Syariah Approved Securities performance (Ahmad et al. 2008, p. 114). Thus, almost the same concept will be applied in evaluating public policies and practices of Islam in Malaysia.

In 2015, Malaysia implemented the *Syariah* index. In the inaugural Malaysian Mosque Awards 2014 on 28 August 2015, Najib announced that the *Syariah* index will be introduced to gauge Malaysia's achievements in the implementation of Islamic law. This is definitely a peak of achievement in the Islamization policy. Najib said that the *Syariah* index was developed by JAKIM in collaboration with IIUM and the Islamic Missionary Foundation Malaysia (YADIM). He explained that:

> It is highly polemical; some say our country is Islamic and some say it is not. How are we attempting to fulfill the requirements of Islamic law? There must be some scientific gauge for Islamic law. ... When there is such an index, we will be able to gauge and make comparisons with other countries as to where we have achieved success and where there are shortcomings that we should rectify together (*The Malaymail Online* 2014a, p. 1).

Najib urged the assistance of *ulama* in shaping an administration required by Islam, not only in terms of progress but also fair and equitable distributions of wealth.

Malaysia's Constitutional Framework and Islamization Policy

Conceptualizing the notion of Islamization and religious expression in Malaysia would require some understandings of the Constitution's provisions. Firstly, Article 3 (1) of the Constitution affirms that Islam shall be the religion of the Federation, but other religions may be practised in peace and harmony. Scholars have advanced various interpretations of the aforementioned constitutional article, primarily connecting Islam with its ceremonial, historical and traditional significance (Fernando 2006, p. 249; Harding 2002, p. 21). For instance, Lionel A. Sheridan and Harry E. Groves (1987) argued that Article 3 entails the use of Muslim rites in the religious aspects of the Federal ceremonies (Sheridan and Groves 1987, p. 31; Thomas 2006, p. 29). It is no coincidence that the intention of making Islam as the official religion of the Federation was purportedly assigned primarily for ritualistic and ceremonial purposes. Thomas (2006, p. 31) suggested that Article 3 gives due regard to the elements and traditions that existed in the Malay states long before the colonial period (i.e. the Sultanate, Islamic religion, Malay language, and Malay privilege). On contrary, Shad Saleem Faruqi (2006, p. 1) stressed the ramification of this constitutional article:

> ... the implication of adopting Islam as the religion of the Federation is that Islamic education and way of life can be promoted for Muslims. Islamic institutions can be established. Islamic courts can be set up. Muslims can be subjected to *Syariah* laws in certain areas provided by the Constitution.

Notwithstanding that Article 3 declares Islam as the religion of the Federation, it is only quite recently that some scholars came to the conclusion that this particular provision does not in any sense imply that Malaysia is an Islamic state, but merely acknowledges the religious nature of state ceremonies (Harding 2010, p. 506). That being said, one of the original drafters of the Constitution, Chief Justice Abdul Hamid, the Reid Commission member from Pakistan, opined that the provision on Islam as the religion of the State is innocuous (Thomas 2006, p. 19). Nevertheless, "a secular State" as originally envisioned by the constitutional drafters for the country neither connote to an anti-religious nor anti-Islamic state of governance (Sarwar 2007). Giving effect to this sentiment, it is argued that the Constitution envisages that *Syariah* laws would govern the personal law requirements of Muslims in Malaysia, while at the same time, recognizes that the *Syariah* laws would not be made the supreme law of the country. This dual legal system in the country, civil law and the *Syariah* law, arguably has its erroneous effect to the exercise of the freedom of religion by individual Muslim who seeks to renounce Islam (Abdullah 2007, p. 267).

Despite that Islam holds a special status in Federal Malaysia, certain provisions stipulated in the Constitution imply recognizant of the rights of non-Muslims when dealing with matters concerning their religion and culture. Article 11 of the Constitution, in particular, guarantees freedom of religion, which, based on its literal wording, seems comprehensive enough to safeguard this fundamental right bestowed to Malaysia's plural society. A citizen has the right to profess, practise and—subject to Article 11 (4)—to propagate his or her religion within his or her own community. Religious groups also have the right to manage their own religious affairs or any matters relating to the properties and the establishment of religious institutions. Reading Article 11 at its face value seemingly shows that the provision does not expressly prohibit the conversion of a Muslim, though at the same time, the Constitution does not contain any explicit provision regarding the right to change one's religion. Nevertheless, it is suggested that the same article can be construed broadly to include freedom to relinquish or change one's religious faith (notwithstanding with some limitations imposed on Muslims under specific *Syariah* laws), and even to the extent of becoming an atheist (Thomas 2006, p. 34).

The clause for freedom of religion is reinforced by other constitutional provisions (Thomas 2006). First, to combat subversion, Article 149 of the Constitution permits the enactment of laws which would otherwise be incompatible with certain universally-accepted principles and fundamental elements of human rights, such as freedom of speech and personal liberty. The same article, however, prohibits any enroachment on the rights of people to exercise religious freedom. This, however, does not stop one commentator to question the rising demand for Islam's political and social incursion into public life which he perceived has exceeded its constitutional limits (Lee 2010, p. 8). Second, Article 150 (6A) of the Constitution stipulates that, even in a state of emergency, any emergency law enacted thereafter cannot curtail the freedom of religion. Third, Article 8 prohibits discrimination on the grounds of religious belief against employees of the public sector, covering various areas, in particular, on the acquisition or holding of property, as well as in any trade, business or profession. In fact, freedom of religion is not adversely affected by Article 3 that supports constitutional recognition of Islam as the official religion of the Federation. Of relevance to this argument is that Article 3 (4) seems to imply nothing in Article 3 derogates from any other provision in the Constitution on matters pertaining to freedom of religion.

Even so, it seems that there are still some restrictions imposed against one's rights to fully exercise freedom of religion in Malaysia. Nowhere is this deprivation of rights evident than in Article 11 (5) of the Constitution. It implicitly places restriction to this freedom on the grounds of public order and morality, and thus the right of exercising any religious act that deemed contrary to any general law relating to such grounds is inconceivable. In the case of Muslims, there may be additional restrictions applied to religious freedom by virtue of Schedule 9, List II, Item I of the Constitution. This provision grants power to State Assemblies to enact laws to punish Muslims for offences against the edicts of Islam and human dignity, such as *khalwat* (close proximity), adultery, apostasy, gambling, drinking and deviationist activities (Masum 2009, p. iii). Therein underpins the crux of liberal's view that the aforementioned provision in some ways could deprive individual Muslim in the country to fully exercise the types of human rights universally practised in the Western world, including freedom of expression and religion.

A more controversial provision of the Constitution is subsection 4 pertaining to limitation on the propagation of religion among Muslims. At first glance, it appears that this article contradicts the idea of religious freedom especially for those religions that regard proselytizing as an integral part of worship (Sheridan and Groves 1987, p. 31). Several important arguments against this view have been presented by some commentators. First, laws controlling propagation, as quoted by Masum (2009, pp. iii–iv), are meant "to prevent Muslims from being exposed to heretical religious doctrines, be they of Islamic or non-Islamic origin, and irrespective of whether the propagators are Muslims or non-Muslims". Such restrictions, according to Faruqi (2001), are meant to protect Muslims from organized international missionary activities and to preserve social harmony, rather than prioritizing any particular religion. Second, subsection 4 does not, in and of itself, restrict propagation. Sheridan and Groves (1987, p. 76) argue that this aforementioned provision merely affords such jurisdiction under the state law (or federal law in the case of the Federal Territories) to control or restrict propagation.

Despite the constitutional grounding of religious freedom, there is complication in exercising such right in actual practice. The parameters of religious freedom in the country are not always clear, often obscured by multiple political, social and racial factors. This situation has its consequences in domestic setting. It has not only affected the relationship between Muslims and non-Muslims (sometimes triggering communal friction and conflict), but also raised a myriad of religious issues within the Muslim community itself. This strikes a chord between those who are intent upon carrying out modern liberal interpretation of universal principle of human rights, and those who insist on communally-based, constitutional-contract politics in Malaysia (Mohamad 2008, p. 155).

Perhaps the most problematic aspect of the country's constitutional framework is the apparent side-stepping of constitutional issues and deference to the *Syariah* court on matters which may undermine freedom of religion. This situation reveals a *lacuna* in the national legal system due to overlapping of civil and *Syariah* jurisdictions. On the one hand, constitutional rights and their interpretation fall squarely within the purview of the civil courts (Article 121 (1) of the Constitution). As reiterated by Chew (2007), "it is for the civil to determine whether the limitation of a practice of a religion is constitutional". Harding (1996, p. 138) argues that matters within the purview of Islamic jurisdiction are personal-related rather than constitutional, and that the "constitutional law requires that the jurisdiction of the ordinary courts to rule finally on matters of legality should be preserved". In contrast, conversions out of Islam are perceived as a matter for the *Syariah* court to deal with due to the separation of the civil-*Syariah* jurisdiction in 1988. The problem is that state-enacted Islamic laws for regulating religious conversion have not always been consistent with the liberal's ideas of religious freedom. Moreover, barring a few states, there is no precise legislative enactment on how to deal with apostates or those who seek to convert to another religion (Hasan 2008). Citing an example from *Kamariah bte Ali* (2002), the Court of Appeal deliberated on how applications to the *Syariah* courts were rejected. The Court, however, held that the legislation in question—the state of Kelantan's section 102 of Enactment 4/1994—does not prohibit a Muslim from renouncing his faith. But this cannot be undertaken unilaterally and a declaration of permission must be sought from the *Syariah* court. In *Daud bin Mamat & Others vs. Majlis Agama Islam & Another* (2001), the right of an individual to convert out of his religion is not within the scope of Article 11 of the Constitution and the fact that the plaintiffs are Muslims means that the civil court does not have jurisdiction over that matter.

It is highly unlikely for a Muslim to voluntarily turn to the *Syariah* courts for permission to renounce his faith. This course of action does not necessarily guarantee a rewarding outcome for the applicant. Any attempt to renounce Islam by a Muslim has been made difficult by a series of stringent legislative procedures and as surmised by Abdullah (2007, p. 278), "the generally accepted approach is not to allow renouncement". As demonstrated in many cases brought before the court, the applicant might even be subjected to monetary fine or a lengthy counselling session as stipulated in a number of state religious enactments. For example,

Articles 119 (1) and 119 (8) of the Administration of Islam Enactment (Negeri Sembilan) 2003 impose requirement for a Muslim who seeks to convert to another religion to refer to a *Syariah* court and apply for a declaration that he or she is no longer a Muslim, be subjected to religious counselling for a year, and if the individual is still steadfast with his or her wish, the court may endorse the application (*Refugee Review Tribunal* 2008). Constitutional arguments aside, from an Islamic perspective, apostasy—pronouncing oneself to have or intend to renounce Islam—is considered legitimate regardless of the absent of its official endorsement by any particular religious authority (Abidin 2007).

The progress and traits of *Syariah* laws in Malaysia have been the thematic subjects of scholarly analysis in numerous works. Donald Horowitz (1994b, p. 236) describes the trend regarding the development of such laws in Malaysia as follows:

> Nowhere ... in Asia has the Islamization of law preceded more methodologically than in Malaysia where, in the span of a decade, dozens of new statutes and judicial decisions have clarified, expanded, and reformulated the law applicable to Muslims ... what has been attempted is the creation of two parallel, relatively autonomous systems, one secular and one Islamic.

Miller (2004) acknowledges that these legislative transformations are indeed revolutionary, albeit they are carried out at the state level. Islamic laws continue to be applicable only to the Muslims of Malaysia in accordance with 9th Schedule, List II, Paragraph 1 of the Constitution.

Conclusion

In conclusion, this chapter has provided details of the Islamization policy which started in the 1960s and spread extensively to become a main state policy in the 1970s until today. It is mainly supported and protected by the provisions of the federal and state constitutions. These factors allow national leadership to establish several permanent bodies to promote Islam such as JAKIM at the federal level and *Syariah* courts in all states. Moreover, many institutions such as the IIU, KAGAT and BAKA PDRM were established to promote Islamization policy in the administration. More significantly, Mahathir introduced Islamic banking, securities, and insurance laws and amended the Constitution to increase the powers of Islamic legal authorities.

Several policies were established to support the state's agenda for Islamization such as the Inculcation of Islamic values by Mahathir, *Islam Hadhari* by Badawi and *Wasatiyyah* by Najib. These policies laid out the foundation for implementing Islamic teachings in the public administration and society. This Islamization policy will not be successful if the population is not provided with enough education. Many programmes and courses in Islamic studies and *Syariah* laws were introduced especially at the university level to produce human capital that can assist the government in spreading Islamization policy. In creating awareness about Islam, the media played a significant role. The target of Islamization policy is to ensure that the Islamic way of life will be practised. Therefore, Islam needs to be enforced by the Islamic bureaucracy. There are many clear evidences of the enforcement such as the banning of Shi'ism and the word "Allah" and upholding morality. The establishment of the *Syariah* index is another step of the government's agenda. It is obvious that Islamization has become one of the main agendas of the government in Malaysia's multiethnic society.

3

INTER-RELIGIOUS EXPRESSION

Introduction

Freedom of expression is a fundamental liberty that all modern states should have in their constitutions and implement in the society. But freedom of expression is not absolute even to the defenders of the right. There is a heated debate in identifying the kinds of expressions that warrant constitutional protection. It is rather ironic that some staunch defenders of free expression deny certain other practices including religious expression. Gregory P. Magarian (2010) explains that there are arguments for normative constraints on religious argument and the translation imperative on the ground that religious arguments threaten liberal democracy. They posit two distinctive sorts of danger. First, they contend that religious beliefs cannot provide adequate justifications for coercive governmental actions in conditions of democratic pluralism. Members of a liberal democratic political community should not offer religious arguments in public debate because such arguments by definition urge improper grounds for government action. Any coercion based on religious arguments is unfair to non-believers, because such coercion denies non-believers equal respect and full and fair access to the process of political decision-making (Audi 1989, pp. 259–76; Greene 1993, pp. 1611–33). Second, religious arguments undermine public political debate, and thus threaten liberal democracy, by fostering social and political instability. Religious arguments, on the restrictive theorists' account, carry a distinctive capacity to inspire intolerance of opposing political viewpoints (Audi 1997, p. 5; Rorty 1994, pp. 1–6; Marshall 1993, pp. 843–58; Sullivan 1992, pp. 195–99).

In contrast, some theorists argue that secularism poses a greater threat to liberal democracy than religion. Some compare what they portray as overblown claims of religion's divisiveness to the genuine divisiveness of political advocacy by or for historically disadvantaged racial and ethnic groups (McConnell 1999, pp. 639–48).[1] First, they reject the restrictive concern that leads to religious arguments in public political debate denying non-believers equal respect and regard by underwriting religious justifications for coercive government actions. These theorists maintain that whatever features of insularity or exceptionalism might cause certain religious arguments to alienate non-believers and are equally likely to cause certain secular arguments to alienate believers or others. In any event, they contend that religious arguments in public political debate do not dictate policy outcomes but simply make "one contribution among others in a debate about how political power is to be used" (Alexander 1993, pp. 775–76; Waldron 1993, pp. 817–29). Second, they deny that religious arguments are less accessible than secular arguments to the political community generally. They maintain that non-believers can access the distinctive sources of religious knowledge in the same way anyone can access any source of knowledge—by reading or listening (McConnell 1999, p. 652). The debate can also be examined from the perspective of whether religious expression inflicts or affects political instability or dynamism through political transformation.

Religious sensitivities are seen as one of the main obstacles to the implementation of religious freedom in Malaysia. Richard Neuhaus (1984, p. 82) takes the permissive attack on secular politics to its logical limit, insisting that religion's absence from public life could prefigure a totalitarian state. Great care is taken not to impinge on the religious sensitivity of the various groups. Given the fact that Islam is the religion of the Federation as stated in the Federal Constitution, care is taken not to publish articles that cast a slur, intended or otherwise, on the religion or its adherents. All media, including those operated by the opposition, follow this policy. No media can carry articles that question the faith or ridicule it (Moses 2002, pp. 102–7). Thus, religious expression has always been monitored by the government in order to protect racial harmony in Malaysia. This protection is covered in the Constitution and can clearly be seen in practices relating to certain issues such as religious expression in the press, blasphemy, hate speech, and interfaith commission. Can religious expression harm the society? What is allowed and disallowed? This chapter will examine each of these issues and explain how both the government and society tackle the issue of inter-religious expression.

Inter-Religious Expression in Malaysia

Religion is an integral component of cultural values in Malaysia. Former Prime Minister, Mahathir Mohamad, explains that Malaysian values are based on Malay-Islamic culture and should be protected against the invasion of Western liberal values. He urges the three most basic elements of "Malayness"—feudalism, Islam, and *adat* (traditional customs) as he wrote in 1970 in his book, *The Malay Dilemma*, to be classed as features accepted as realities and perhaps adapted to modern needs (Barr 2002, p. 42). Mahathir accuses the Western liberals of practising unfettered free speech which, he believes, can corrupt Malaysian religious beliefs (Mahathir and Ishihara 1995, pp. 71–86).

Furthermore, Ismail Ibrahim admits that all positive values are Islamic values, e.g. respect for the elderly and good work ethics.[2] He also stresses that all societies have their own measurements of human rights, which are based on local values, religious practices and traditions. Freedom of speech should be used in as appropriate a manner as possible without undermining sensitive issues such as national security, religious beliefs and multiracial harmony. Mahathir has also argued that the aggressive separation of church and state in the West—in effect limiting religion to the private sphere—and the consequent process of secularization have contributed to a moral void in public life and accentuated the negative impulses of individualism (Mahathir and Ishihara 1995, pp. 1–9). In Malaysia, despite the obvious diversity of religions—mainly Islam, Buddhism, Hinduism and Christianity—and a similar process of secularization, it has been argued that religion still plays an important part in everyday life and contributes to group identity and orientation. In fact, most East and Southeast Asians would prefer some constraints in free speech, perhaps in the form of libel laws to protect religions from various forms of defamation and hate speech (Bell 2000, p. 9).

In Malaysia generally, political decision-making is arrived at through processes of consensus rather than confrontation. According to Chandra Muzaffar (1996, p. 4), "None of the major Asian philosophies regards the individual as the ultimate measure of all things." Still another important value is:

> the preference for consultation and consensus ... to take the middle path, the Confucian *Chun Yung* or the Islamic *awsatuha* ... This spirit of consensual *musyawarah* (or *muafakat*) is very much at play as we progress towards a cohesive regional community (Anwar 1996b, p. 4).

However, a strong bureaucracy and an absence of the separation of powers are still characteristics of the Malaysian state. In fact, there has been practically a fusion of the state, the leading political party and the bureaucracy. This appears to conform to the Malaysian emphasis on harmony and consensus, which could obstruct the free exchange of ideas and rigorous political debate (Mahathir and Ishihara 1995, p. 5).

Malaysia also exercises "controlled democracy" which simply means that as much as Malaysia is a democratic nation, the government rigidly stipulates what can be done and said. The media community is not spared from this restriction (Salleh 2004). The government provides guidelines to the media community of what can and cannot be reported. The government utilizes the media as its informational tool to reach out to the population, reporting successes for the country and failures and defamation of the opposition party. All these can be seen as the downside of the Malaysian government. Malaysia views the media as a "double-edged weapon" and thus must be controlled and exploited to the advantage of the government of the day. At the same time, political instability would lead to loss of foreign direct investment and could give rise to internal security problems such as racial clashes or religious confrontations (Salleh 2004).

In Malaysia, we can understand that the fragility and diversity of religious and social structures are potentialities for instability. Efforts must be maintained to ensure that a strong government and racial integration remain intact to facilitate and accommodate further development for the nation. This is clearly evident in several cases of inter-religious expression such as blasphemy, hate speech, obscenity, and issues in the press which will be explored in the next sections.

Blasphemy

Religion is significant in determining the values of Malaysians. Thus, for Malaysians, or Asians generally, their values are influenced by Islamic notions of morality and human dignity. The Mahathir model of Asian values encompasses elements of strong authority, priority of community over the individual, and a strong family-based society, which he argues are based on Islamic values (Azizuddin 2008, p. 4). In the context of the Malaysian state, the fusion of religious and political authority in public life claims to help avoid the moral decadence of the West and irresponsible political speech, and contributes to the tolerance of different religions. Attempts to disrupt religious harmony are severely dealt with in Malaysia. Unlike in England where blasphemy is an offence only against the Church of England, the Malaysian Penal Code in sections 295–298A, relating to Offences Relating to Religion, punishes offences against all religions.[3]

The issue of blasphemy became a worldwide issue especially in the Muslim world when Salman Rushdie published his book, the *Satanic Verses*, in 1988. Malaysia, along with all other Islamic countries, condemned and banned the book because it ridiculed the most sacred symbols of Islam and resorted to profanity and insult to the Prophet Muhammad's family (Faruqi 2004b, p. 20). Chandra Muzaffar (1989, pp. 425–26) talked of the way in which the characters and events in the book were distorted "to suit the author's vile imagination … The right to free speech should not be used—or rather abused—to propagate malicious lies, to pour filth upon the faith of a people". Even though the *Satanic Verses* is a novel and an imaginative work of Rushdie which has nothing to do with religion and politics, the contents of the book are described by many Muslims as an offensive attack on Islam and the Muslim community. The Iranian government even sentenced Rushdie to the death penalty. In Malaysia, although the government did not impose a death sentence on Rushdie, alongside opposition Malaysian Islamic Party (PAS), Islamic non-governmental organizations (NGOs), and many Malay intellectuals, it denounced Rushdie as a blasphemer. The government, in this case, tried to show that it was against any attempts to condemn religion practised by the majority Malaysian people in order to prevent controversy and to protect religious sensitivities.

During the era of Badawi's leadership, blasphemy became more crucial, given its negative impact on Malaysia's multiracial country as discussed in the previous chapter. Blasphemy is applied not only to Islam, but also to other religions as well. In another case, a Tamil-language newspaper, *Makkal Osai*, had its operations shut down for a month in 2007 and its permit suspended for publishing a picture that associated Jesus with cigarettes and beer. However, there was a claim that *Makkal Osai* had been critical of the Malaysian Indian Congress (MIC) in the past, and the MIC which owned a rival paper appealed to the Internal Security Ministry to have the *Makkal Osai* censored for publishing the Jesus picture (North 2007).

Hate Speech

There are serious concerns on the impact of hate speech, which involves religions, on ethnic relations in Malaysia. Hate speech is now expressed openly in the public sphere especially through social media. There is anxiety that this is a time bomb waiting to explode if not managed well.

There are many examples of hate speech in Malaysia, of which three are discussed here. The most highly publicized recent case happened in July 2013 which relates to the photograph posted on the Facebook of Alvin Tan Jye Yee and his partner Vivian Lee May Ling. The photograph showed them eating (apparently) pork rib soup, with the caption "fragrant, delicious and appetising" in the Malay language, during the holy month of *Ramadhan* (the fasting month) which upsets Muslims. Islam does not permit Muslims to eat pork. The photograph also carried the logo indicating that the product was *halal*, or permitted to be consumed by Muslims in Malaysia. The two pleaded not guilty to three charges of violating the Sedition Act, the Film Censorship Act and the Penal Code by "committing acts likely to cause feeling of enmity on grounds of religion". The couple has since apologized for the posting, saying it was meant to be humorous (Azizuddin 2013b).

In another case involving the press, the Malay daily, *Utusan Malaysia*, carried a front-page article on 7 May 2011, headlined "*Kristian agama rasmi?*" [Christianity the official religion?], claiming that the opposition Democratic Action Party (DAP) was conspiring with Christian leaders to take over Putrajaya and abolish Islam as the religion of the Federation. The report, based entirely on unsubstantiated blog postings from "*Bigdog*" and "*Marahku*", was perceived to be written by pro-United Malays National Organisation (UMNO) bloggers, argued that DAP should be charged with sedition for allegedly trying to change the country's laws to project for a future Christian prime minister. In response to the allegation, Ibrahim Ali, the president of PERKASA—a right-wing group—called for a "crusade" against Christians who challenge "Islam's position" in Malaysia. This event was naturally disturbing. Hishammuddin Hussein, then home minister, issued a warning letter to *Utusan Malaysia* over this report (Azizuddin 2013a). Nevertheless, no action was taken against the bloggers who spread the lie.

In an earlier case, the Hindu Rights Action Force (HINDRAF), a coalition of thirty Hindu NGOs committed to the preservation of the Hindu community's rights and heritage, had organized a rally—that later turned unruly—on 25 November 2007 to submit a petition to the British High Commission. The rally has led to agitations against what they see as an "unofficial policy of temple demolition" and concerns about the steady encroachment of *Syariah*-based law. They also accused the UMNO-led government of systematically marginalizing the ethnic Indian community and running a policy of ethnic cleansing. According to Chandra Muzaffar, the statement about ethnic cleansing is dangerous, utterly reckless and a scurrilous allegation as there is no evidence whatsoever of ethnic cleansing in Malaysia (Azizuddin 2010).

The above three cases were acts committed by people from three dominant ethnic groups in Malaysia: the Malays, the Chinese and the Indians. These cases present clear examples of hate speech which have hurt and angered many Malaysians, especially those who advocate for good inter-ethnic and inter-religious relations in Malaysia.

Obscenity

Malaysian law is very strict when it comes to obscenity because all obscene materials, particularly pornography, are outlawed. According to Juriah Abdul Jalil (2015), "Malaysia regards all pornography as illegal and thus does not have any specific law criminalising child pornography." Under the obscenity law, she explained that:

> The laws are scattered and govern all types of pornography under the category of obscene, indecent and offensive materials. The Printing Presses and Publications Act 1998 (PPPA), the Film Censorship Act 2002 (FCA) and Penal Code clearly prohibit obscene and offensive materials in relation to print medium and film, whereas indecent, obscene and offensive online contents are governed by the Communication and Multimedia Act 1998 (CMA) and Content Code (CC) (Juriah 2015, p. 138).

Of all the above laws, Content Code is the only one which is not an Act of Parliament. It is a form of self-regulatory instrument which is mandated by the Communications and Multimedia Act 1998. While adopting it is voluntary, such adoption serves as evidence of the level of compliance of the industry players. Interestingly, the Content Code is the only instrument that comes with a relatively clear definition of obscenity. Thus obscene content has been described in Item 3.0, Part 2 of the Content Code as "content that gives rise to a feeling of disgust because of its lewd portrayal and is essentially offensive to one's prevailing notion of decency and modesty" (Zulhuda 2015, p. 2). The test of obscenity is whether the content has the tendency to deprave and corrupt those whose minds are open to such communications. Among the classes of content that falls within this category are: (i) explicit sex acts/pornography, (ii) child pornography, and (iii) sexual degradation (Zulhuda 2015).

Pornography has been more heavily censored in some Asian countries, for example Singapore, Malaysia, and Indonesia, than in most Western ones. Does the prohibition of pornography unjustifiably violate freedom of expression? Adopting the three-party analysis of interests mentioned above, some may judge what is required in the balance of the interests of the publishers (commercial and ideological interests), the audience/consumers (in erotic excitement) and third-party, or community. Important disagreements may centre on the third-party interests, some may take the view that the community as a whole has an interest in maintaining its moral standards, and that society's morals should, therefore, enter into our judgements. However, this view offends many liberals who uphold a particular mid-level principle, namely, that it is not the business of the state to enforce a society's particular moral ethos. On this view, the maintenance of morals is never a legitimate interest to enter into the balancing calculus. According to Joseph Chan (2000, pp. 70–72), those accepting the legitimacy of, for example, the principle of legal moralism would allow society's morals to be put on the scale; those liberals who are against legal moralism would not. In Malaysia, moralism is parallel with the cultural and religious (Islamic) practices and normally, principles of political morality guide Malaysian society to make this kind of fundamental decision, such as banning pornography. The government has an essential role to represent society's moralism and act on cultural values and religious beliefs.

There is strong consensus amongst Malaysians whether they are Malays (or other indigenous tribes), Chinese, or Indians, to deem materials of a pornographic or sexual nature as immoral and obscene. Pornography is seen as a kind of exploitation as it degrades, endangers, and harms the lives of women. Although many in the business argue that the women's involvement in pornography is voluntary, many Malaysians believe that there is an element of exploitation by the pornographic industry. Mahathir Mohamad argued in this context:

> ... there are limits to freedom, and I believe it is important for every member of a society to know these limits. One good example is pornography. You can have computer animation, which may be ever so creative—and thus should be freely available—but if this 'freedom' is used to produce pornographic films that are purveyed to the impressionable young, then the fruits of the freedom should not be accepted and allowed

by society. In Malaysia, it is not my impression that business ingenuity or creativity has been stifled by our Malaysian value system which sets clear limits to individual freedom and generally emphasises the community over the individual. To the contrary, I believe that our value system has been the foundation for our society's stability and prosperity, at least until the economic crisis struck (Mahathir 1999, pp. 73–74).

On this matter, the government takes the initiative to protect public morality and the traditional way of life from pornography and sexual exploitation.

Harian Metro in 2016 reported that 28,671 teenagers in Malaysia were addicted to pornography (Harisa, Siti and Ahmad 2017, p. 720). Assistant Commissioner Ong Chin Lan of the Royal Malaysia Police's Sexual, Women and Child Investigation Division (D11), in a seminar on "Cyber Protection for Children", revealed that based on data furnished by Dutch police based in Malaysia in 2015, about 17,338 IP addresses involved in child pornography were from Malaysia (*The Star Online* 2018a). Ong said that the sole remit of the newly-launched Malaysia Internet Crime Against Children Investigation Unit (MICAC) was to monitor traffic at pornographic websites, especially those offering child porn (Aliza 2018). It would locate and pinpoint daily in real time Internet users surfing these sites and build a "data library" of these individuals—which portals they frequent, how long they spend on the sites, and the files they upload and download—that will help the authorities in prosecuting them. The Internet Crime Against Children—Child Online Protective Services (ICACCOPS), a programme developed in the United States, would show the porn user's IP address, location, the name of the website where he uploaded or downloaded pornographic materials, the actual time the user surfed the sites and the duration spent. This is the latest effort by the authority to uphold morality against obscenity in Malaysia.

Religious Expression in the Press

One issue that has raised considerable concerns over the exercise of religious freedom and expression in a multiracial society such as Malaysia is the controversy revolving around the use of the word "Allah". A seven-judge panel in the Federal Court on 23 June 2014 conferred with the lower court decisions that the Catholic Church's bid to get leave to challenge the Home Ministry's ban on the use of the word in *The Herald* was rejected in a 4–3 majority decision, thereby siding with the government's decision (*The Star Online* 2014a). The Malaysian cabinet banned *The Herald* from using the word "Allah" in January 2008. It justified the decision by saying that the word "Allah" should not be used by non-Muslims because it is sensitive and can create confusion to the Muslims (*The Sun* 2008, p. 1). The Sikhs also felt threatened because Sikhism's teaching of Guru Granth Sahib has the word "Allah" as well (Singh 2013).

The debate on this issue remains unresolved. Although the High Court held in favour of *The Herald*, the Appeal Court allowed the Malaysian government to ban the newspaper from using the word "Allah" on 14 October 2013. Three members led by Datuk Seri Mohamed Apandi Ali said that there was a 1986 directive by the Home Ministry that prohibited non-Muslim publications from using four words namely "Allah", "Kaabah", "Solat", and "Baitullah". The prohibition was imposed in order to protect the sanctity of Islam and prevent any confusion among Muslims. According to the Appeal Court, if the word was allowed to be used by Christians, it could threaten national security and public order. Moreover, the prohibition was reasonable because the word "Allah" was not an integral part of the Christian faith and practice (Anbalagan 2014).

Proponents of the government suggested that the word "Allah" is exclusive for Muslims only, and by giving Catholics the right to use "Allah", this will only disregard Article 3 of the Constitution because such use will somehow "erode" the position of Islam in the country and cause confusion among Muslims. It is difficult, however, to see the reasoning behind this argument especially since the establishment of Article 3 clearly does not affect the exercise of other rights espoused in the Constitution. Furthermore, in other Muslim countries, even in the Middle East, where both the Muslim and Christian communities use the word "Allah", one hardly hears of any confusion caused.[4]

For those who support *The Herald's* position, the government's censure against *The Herald* arguably violates the freedom of religion under Article 11, freedom of speech and expression under Article 10, as well as equality under Article 8. They claimed that there is a violation of Article 11 pertaining to the right to religious freedom, in that the use of the word "Allah" is part and parcel of the practice of their religion. But the widespread concern among the Muslims is that such use would hit at the prohibition against propagation of other religions to Muslims. It is believed that the Catholic Church would use it as a tool for proselytism among the Muslim majority. However, a non-Muslim would only commit an offence if he uses the word "Allah" to a Muslim but there would be no offence if it is used to a non-Muslim. The High Court opined that the use of the word "Allah" is an essential part of the worship and instruction in the faith of the *Bahasa Malaysia*-speaking community of the Catholic Church in Malaysia, and is integral to the practice and propagation of their faith.

In response to the Federal Court's decision, the Prime Minister's Office said that Malaysian Christians can still use the word "Allah" in church. It said in a statement that the government is committed to the ten-point Cabinet solution which was made in 2011, prior to the Sarawak state election, allowing Christians in Sabah and Sarawak to use the word "Allah" in their Malay-language Bible and aimed at addressing differences in opinion between Muslims and Christians. It called on all parties to respect and abide by the apex court's decision and said it was only applicable to *The Herald*. The government, it said, respects the court's decision and called on all parties to also respect and abide by it (*The Star Online* 2014a).

Interfaith Commission: A Way Towards National Unity?

During Badawi's period as prime minister, the Malaysian Bar Council convened a national conference to discuss a draft bill proposing for the formation of a national interfaith commission in February 2005. Its primary function would be to help the government make clear and establish coherent policies to allow for greater interfaith relationships as well as avoid conflicts arising out of misunderstandings (Yeoh 2005, p. 629). Additionally, it would be empowered to determine whether or not there has been any infringement of freedom of religion, expression, conscience and thought within the context of Universal Declaration of Human Rights and the Federal Constitution. A loose coalition of Muslim NGOs, called the Allied Coordinating Committee of Islamic NGOs

(ACCIN), boycotted the conference, arguing that the interfaith commission, if established, would usurp the functions of existing religious authorities. In particular, it characterized proposals brought by the Malaysian Consultative Council of Buddhism, Christianity, Hinduism and Sikhism (MCCBCHS) which allow Muslims the right to renounce Islam, to facilitate apostasy (*murtad*) through the civil courts and constitutional provisions, and to review religious enactments, as merely "self-serving to non-Muslims" and "anti-Islam". Subsequent to the conference, Prime Minister Badawi announced that deliberations on the proposed formation of the interfaith commission would be shelved because of the heated debates reported in the press. He opined that the statutory body, if willed into being, would be a setback to religious unity in the country. Instead, he suggested that more events promoting inter-religious dialogue be organized and encouraged to strengthen racial harmony through open houses during major festivals celebrated by various races (Yeoh 2005, pp. 629–30).

Ioannis Gatsiounis (2006) argues that if the past is any indication, Badawi will claim tolerance and unity as enduring traits of the Malaysian people. He will swear by *Islam Hadhari*, a political and ideological interpretation of the faith that stresses moderation and technological and economic competitiveness. However, there is a very different reality unfolding on Badawi's watch, one that raises questions about his commitment to *Islam Hadhari* and may have far reaching implications for this "model Islamic democracy". Hardliner Muslims had grown more vocal in 2006, demonstrating at forums held by a coalition of NGOs, known as Article 11, who wanted the government to put its weight behind the Malaysian Constitution, which guarantees equality and freedom of worship, as the supreme law of the land. Article 11 was concerned that *Syariah* (Islamic law) courts have recently taken primacy over civil courts in a number of controversial decisions. The hardliners were also opposed to efforts to establish an Inter-Faith Commission to enhance understanding among Malaysia's various faiths. The latest protest came on 22 July 2006 in the state of Johor Bahru. As Article 11 members gathered in an upper-floor hotel ballroom, some 300 Muslims scowled from behind a police line at the hotel entrance, brandishing signs that read, "Don't touch Muslim sensitivities", "Destroy anti-Muslims", and "We are ready to sacrifice ourselves for Islam". Before that in May

2006, hardliners threatening to storm an Article 11 venue succeeded in bringing the forum to an abrupt end (Gatsiounis 2006).

From a soft approach to encourage dialogues between disputed parties, Badawi has taken a hard stand by saying "Do not force the government to take action" to Article 11 members (Gatsiounis 2006, p. 1). He warned and accused Article 11 members of playing up religious issues and threatening to shatter Malaysia's fragile social balance by highlighting "sensitive" issues which should not be discussed openly. Badawi issued a stern warning to the media to stop reporting on issues related to religious matters. He has also not ruled out using the Internal Security Act,[5] which allows for indefinite detention without trial, against Article 11 members should they continue with their activities. Badawi's stance against Article 11 could be read as in keeping with Mahathir's belief that greater freedom of expression will stoke inter-ethnic tensions. However, according to Gatsiounis (2006), Badawi's position is less encompassing and can be seen as applying a lopsidedly selective application: it allows hostile segments of the Muslim community to use free speech to dictate its limits. In my view, both parties, the hardliners and Article 11 members, should have closed-door discussions to resolve this matter. The government can act as a neutral agent in guiding the forum because if all respective parties do not resolve this sensitive issue, it would have negative implications on the future of race relations in Malaysia.

In a November 2009 event, Muslims paraded a severed cow's head in the streets of Shah Alam, capital of Selangor state, to protest the construction of a new Hindu temple. Thereafter, there are more and more demands to set up an interfaith commission to resolve inter-religious issues which can inflict disharmony in race relations. But the government lacks in initiative to form such a commission due to protest from some hardliners among the ruling UMNO leaders and supporters. This issue remains unsettled.

Conclusion

In sum, this chapter offers observations on inter-religious expression from the Malaysian perspective. Based on the above discussion, Malaysia definitely believes in a more restrictive-stability approach in dealing with inter-religious expression. Cultural sensitivities, especially concerning race and religion, are the main obstacles to the implementation of religious freedom in Malaysia. Great care is taken not to impinge on the religious sensitivities of various groups. This needs to be handled carefully through civilized means.

What is interesting is that Malaysia, an illiberal democracy, seems to be more restrictive in protecting the regime status-quo, political stability and at the same time avoid political change.[6] Religious expression is allowed only if it is approved by the state and religious authorities. This is definitely protected by the Constitution as Islam is a religion of the country, but other religions are allowed to be practised by their followers. There are also many restrictions imposed on religious expression which are included in publications on hate speech, blasphemy and establishing an interfaith commission. What is obvious is that religious freedom and religious expression are very sensitive in the race relations in Malaysia. The government is seen trying to protect political stability and racial harmony in Malaysia, but at the same time it tries to maintain the status-quo as a way of regime security mechanism especially in declaring Malaysia as an "Islamic state". Hence, the issue is complicated but religious issues in a plural society such as Malaysia ideally must be open to civilized, intellectual debates by all sections of the community. While concerns of social stability are understandable, actions must be reasonable and not at the expense of human dignity.

Notes

1. Richard Neuhaus (1984, p. 82) takes the permissive attack on secular politics to its logical limit, insisting that religion's absence from public life could prefigure a totalitarian state.
2. Interview with Ismail Ibrahim, former Chairman of the Malaysian Institute of Islamic Understanding (IKIM), 13 October 2001.
3. Article 298A (1) mentions that:
    Whoever by words, either spoken or written, or by signs, or by visible representations, or by any act, activity or conduct, or by organising, promoting or arranging, or assisting in organizing, promoting or arranging, any activity, or otherwise in any other manner:
    (a) causes, or attempt to cause, or is likely to cause disharmony, disunity, or feelings of enmity, hatred or ill-will; or
    (b) prejudices, or attempts to prejudice, or is likely to prejudice, the maintenance of harmony or unity,

On the grounds of religion, between persons or groups of persons professing the same or different religions, shall be punished with imprisonment for a term of not less than two years and not more than five years.

4. *Titular Roman Catholic Archbishop of Kuala Lumpur* vs. *Menteri Dalam Negeri & Anor*, Current Law Journal 2 (2010): 208 and 214; *High Court Malaya, Kuala Lumpur*, Judicial Review No. R1-25-28-2009, 31 December 2009.
5. The Security Offences (Special Measures) Act 2012 (SOSMA) was gazetted to replace the repealed ISA. It was approved by the *Dewan Rakyat* on 17 April 2012, given the royal assent on 18 June 2012, and gazetted on 22 June 2012. The provision of detention without trial was removed in the new law.
6. There is an exception. There is no mention at all in the Federal Constitution about the non-believers because each Malaysian is assumed to embrace one religion or belief. Malaysia used to encourage Malaysians, especially the non-Muslims, to embrace any religion in order to differentiate themselves from the Communists who were considered as the non-believers. However, there is no indication contemporarily that there is a terminology to differentiate the believers from the non-believers in the Malaysian Constitution.

4

INTRA-RELIGIOUS EXPRESSION

Introduction

Malaysia is a state that embraces communitarianism. Abdullah Ahmad Badawi (2006, p. 47), former prime minister of Malaysia, is critical of the Western values of individualism and once urged the West to learn about the Muslim world because in his view, Muslims see themselves ideally as a collective *ummah*, notwithstanding the occasional disunity among Muslims countries. Malaysia is also a multireligious society prone to inter- and intra-group conflicts if the relations between and within races are not handled and managed well.

From the debate of religious expression, a communitarian approach to speech regulation where the curtailment of a speech and the consequent loss of autonomy are considered less problematic. In a communitarian society like Malaysia, the state is not neutral between conceptions of the good life, but seeks to promote a substantive version of the "common good" and actively strives to create the public and private virtues needed for society to attain that end (Sandel 1982; Taylor 1985; Walzer 1983). Communitarians perceive individuals as having social characters grounded in the communities in which they live (McIntyre 1981). The good of an individual is not conceivable unless understood within some broader views of the good of the community. For communitarians, rules of civility found in the common law or in statutes regulating public morals, express dominant community norms and thus identity. Restraints on offensive and racist expressions can thus be cast and defended as the product of majoritarian rule-making that reflects prevailing norms such as tolerance and the equal worth of individuals and are enforced for the good of the whole community. Here, the protection of religious feeling may be prioritized over the value of democratic legitimacy, or these legitimacy concerns may simply be seen as a non-issue and ignored altogether (Cram 2009, p. 329).

Those who called for treating religion distinctively remind us that in religion, speech plays a unique role by connecting a person to God positively (prayer) or negatively (blasphemy). It is not "just an opinion". Moreover, religious expression, such as prayer, is often a communal act and thus the community has a direct stake in the content of the speech. Such speech may bring good (blessing) or harm (curse) to others, and thus the others, namely the community, are directly involved in the act of religiously-relevant speech, if only because it is the religious duty of the community to care for its members (Reichman 2009, p. 339). Approximarely 61.3 per cent of the population in Malaysia are Muslims, or about 19.5 million people, as of 2013 (The Pew Research Center's Religion and Public Life Project 2014). All ethnic Malays are Muslims as defined in Article 160 of the Federal Constitution of Malaysia. The Sunni Islam of the Shafi'i school of thought is the official and legal form in Malaysia. The Malaysian authorities have strict policies against other Islamic doctrines including Shia Islam. Al-Arqam, for example, is outlawed.

Thus, Muslims must follow strict guidelines as stated in the *Syariah* law practised in the country. In fact, some religious officials have taken this policy to further the Islamization of society. For instance in August 2004 the Mufti of Perak (the state's top Islamic official) issued a *fatwa* (religious edit) proclaiming that "*Sure Heboh*" open-air concerts (staged at different times in cities around the country) were *haram* (forbidden) under Islamic *Syariah* law. He claimed that the concerts were corrupting the Malay youth, fostering the mixing of the sexes and encouraging Muslims to neglect their religious duties such as praying (Chin 2004).

Although there are many issues with regards to religious expression in Malaysia, this chapter will only examine the perspective of intra-religious expression. First, it will analyse the religious expression model in Malaysia. Next, it will explore the debate on whether Malaysia is a secular or an Islamic state. This debate is essential because it will explain about the practices of freedom of religion and intra-religious expression in Malaysia. Finally, this chapter will go in-depth to study the issues of intra-religious expression. The aim is to enlighten and give an understanding about the realities of intra-religious expression in Malaysia.

Religious Expression Model

In debating on religious expression, it is imperative to understand the exact model of religious expression. What is it about? Why is it so important and controversial? This section will have thorough discussions on the religious expression model and to what extent it is applied in Malaysia and briefly compared it to other places in the world. According to Carolyn Evans (2009, pp. 357–74), there are at least three categories of religious expression: the sacred speech; speech as a religious duty; and forbidden speech.

The first category of religious expression involves sacred expression which might take the form of prayers, rituals, the reading of sacred texts, chants, songs, or spoken elements of meditation. The act of speaking these words is often heavily circumscribed. The person who speaks them, the office of the speaker, the place in which the words is spoken, the language that is used, the precise wording that is used, and the time at which they are spoken may all be prescribed in a form that the believer understands to be unchangeable and divinely mandated. These are not matters for negotiation, critical evaluation, or development over time, even if the reality is that they have in fact been negotiated and developed over time (Evans 2009).

For the state to regulate this area of the sacred, such as to require religions to allow women the opportunity to serve as *imam* (leader) in mass prayers or Friday prayer, for instance in the case of Amina Wadud who acted as *imam* for a congregation of about sixty women and forty men seated together on 18 March 2015, or to mandate gender neutral language in religious ritual, is thus completely unacceptable, since it amounts to a state imposition of conduct diametrically opposed to religious belief. Under this religious model, the secular state has no role in regulating the sacred and no authority recognizable by people who adhere to this model to do so. Therefore, certain sacred practices which would rank very highly are in need of protection.

The second type of religious expression relates to speech as a religious duty or obligation. This type of expression is a duty placed on the speaker either by the requirements of the external deity or by a commitment to a transcendent moral or spiritual order. An example of such expression from an intra-religious perspective, for a Sunni Muslim, is the requirement of proselytism in religion to convert, for instance, a Shia to a Sunni. To attempt to convert others to one's own doctrine or sect of religion is not merely about trying to bring someone else to see the truth and is thus not simply analogous to trying to convince others of the superiority of a particular political, social, or other position. However, for a Sunni Muslim, it is forbidden to leave the doctrine for the other Islamic doctrines. The truth is that speech is an obligation rather than a right. There is no right to relinquish the belief but there is obligation to spread the belief to others (Evans 2009).

The third type of religious expression is forbidden speech. This is speech which is positively dangerous either because it encourages listeners to turn to untrue beliefs or immoral ways or because it is speech which damages the speaker in the saying. Blasphemy, apostasy, heresy, and other religious speech offenses fall into this category. This expression is spiritually dangerous to speakers, even if no one else ever hears them say it and it has no effect on other people. In serious cases, it may even severs the relationship between the speaker and the divine. Such speech is also forbidden because of the effects that it has on others and on the moral and social order. Speeches that deny creationism, argue for the pluralism or equality of people regardless of religion, or promote moral relativism are all types of expression that certain religious speakers have argued to be forbidden because of their corrupting effects on society (Evans 2009). A notable example, as discussed earlier in Chapter 3, is the *Satanic Verses* published in 1988. Written by Muslim-born Indian writer, Salman Rushdie, the *Satanic Verses* was banned and considered to be "blasphemous" in some Islamic societies in Asia because it ridiculed the most sacred symbols of Islam and resorted to profanity and insult to the Prophet Muhammad's family. Muslims may judge that artistic expression should be limited if it allows language that are deemed insulting or hostile to their religion. It would be difficult to argue that this judgement is wrong and that banning this book in these places violates the human right to freedom of expression (Chan 1995, p. 35).

Secular or Islamic State in Malaysia?

The Federal Constitution, according to its Article 4, is the supreme law of the land. It is at the apex of the legal hierarchy, so any acts of parliament or state assembly to the contrary may be deemed unconstitutional. Former Federal Judge Raja Azlan Shah's account on constitutional supremacy in *Loh Kooi Choon v. Government of Malaysia* (1977) particularly stated that:

> [T]he Constitution ... is the supreme law of the land embodying 3 basic concepts: One of them is that the individual has certain fundamental rights upon which not even the power of the State may encroach ... no single man or body shall exercise complete sovereign power, but that it shall be distributed among the Executive, Legislative and Judicial branches of the government (Shah and Sani 2011, p. 658).

Article 3 (1) states that Islam shall be the religion of the Federation, but other religions may be practised in peace and harmony in the Federation. This provision is a product of inter-communal compromises reached in a pre-independence memorandum (hereinafter "Alliance memorandum") constructed by the three main political parties—namely United Malays National Organisation (UMNO), Malayan/Malaysian Chinese Association (MCA), and Malayan/Malaysian Indian Congress (MIC)—in 1956 to safeguard the rights and interests of all communities (Thomas 2006, p. 17).

Scholars have come out with various advanced interpretations of Article 3, primarily connected to its ceremonial, historical and traditional significance (Fernando 2006, p. 249). For instance, Sheridan and Groves (1987, p. 31)[1] and Thomas (2006, p. 29) argued that Article 3 entails the use of Muslim rites in religious parts of federal ceremonies. Thomas (2006, p. 31) suggested that Article 3 gives due regard to the elements and traditions of the Malay states long before the colonial period, i.e., the Sultanate, Islamic religion, Malay language, and Malay privilege. The constitutional ideas of the Malay states stem from the Melaka Sultanate in the fifteenth century, where Buddhist, Hindu and Islamic influences permeated through the systems of law and governance (Harding 1996, pp. 5–6). Shad Saleem Faruqi (2006, p. 1) stressed that:

> the implication of adopting Islam as the religion of the Federation is that Islamic education and way of life can be promoted for Muslims. Islamic institutions can be established. Islamic courts can be set up. Muslims can be subjected to *Syariah* laws in certain areas provided by the Constitution.

Historical evidence suggested that although the Alliance memorandum discussed Islam as a religion for Malaysia, it emphasized that this should not affect non-Muslims' rights to profess and practise their religion, and there is no implication that the State is not a secular state.[2] Chief Justice Abdul Hamid, the Reid Commission member from Pakistan, opined that the provision on Islam as the religion of the State is innocuous (Thomas 2006, p. 19). However, "secular", as intended by the founding fathers, does not connote an anti-religious or anti-Islamic state of governance (Sarwar 2007). The Constitution envisages that *Syariah* laws would govern the personal law requirements of Muslims, but it recognizes that the *Syariah* would not be made the supreme law. Malik Imtiaz Sarwar (2007) argues that unlike the Constitution of Pakistan that entrenches the *Syariah* as the basis of all laws, the Federal Constitution does not accord the *Syariah* law such a status.

These views were espoused by the Supreme Court in the landmark case of *Che Omar bin Che Soh v. Public Prosecutor* (1988). In this case, the accused was faced with a mandatory death sentence for drug trafficking. He challenged the sentence on the basis that the imposition of death penalty for the offence is contrary to Islamic injunction and therefore, unconstitutional and void. The Court reiterated the secular character of the law and governance system, which resulted from colonial Anglo/Malay treaties. It also emphasized that the British establishment of secular institutions separated Islam into the public and private aspects. Islamic law was rendered isolated in a narrow confinement of the law of marriage, divorce, and inheritance only. Despite the foregoing arguments, it is notable that the establishment of a particular religion over the State is not unique to Malaysia. In Norway, for instance, primacy on Christianity means that the king and a majority of the cabinet are required to be members of the state church (Shelton and Kiss 2007, p. 575). In England, the Anglican Church remains at the centre of public policy and receives substantial support from the State (Shelton and Kiss 2007, p. 576).

Ever since Malaysia gained independence from the British in 1957, it has always been maintained that Malaysia is a secular state. Its first Prime Minister, Tunku Abdul Rahman Putra Alhaj, once made a political statement declaring Malaya/Malaysia as a secular state (Sivaperegasam 2011). However, this position changed when Mahathir sparked the debate on "Islamic state" in the 1990s. Mahathir also made a political statement, presumably with the intention of challenging the Malaysian Islamic Party's (PAS) brand of "Islamic state", and unilaterally announced that Malaysia is already an Islamic state. It sparked a controversy and debate within the non-Malay community, who rejected such notion in Malaysia. Mahathir's successor, Badawi, then drastically declared that Malaysia is an Islamic state, but maintained that Malaysia is not a secular or theocratic state. He argued that Malaysia will be ruled by following Islamic principles together with the Parliamentary democratic principles as stated in the Federal Constitution (Lee 2008, p. 48).

Historically, the term "Islamic state" has never been regarded as a political concept before the twentieth century (Khan 1982, p. 74) until Abul Ala Maududi, an Indian Muslim theologian who founded the political party Jamaat-e-Islami, conceptualized the concept in order to differentiate it from socialism and liberal democracy (Kurzman 2002). Maududi (1995 pp. 7–8), in his book *Human Rights in Islam*, argued the type of Islamic state in which is built on the foundations of *Tawhid* (the Unity of God), *Risala* (the prophethood of Muhammad) and *Khilafa* (the caliphate) through the political system that upholds the principles of morality, justice, truth and honesty. Influenced by Maududi, PAS (n.d., p. 4) published *The Islamic State Document* advocating the implementation of Islam as a comprehensive way of life, identifying various major guidelines derived from the vast principles and provisions of the *Syariah* which are to be implemented in the establishment of an Islamic state. The implementation of *Syariah* further provides the cleansing and purification of society. A virtuous and moral society in turn, entitles itself to further bliss and grace from the Almighty, including the alleviating of problems and overflowing prosperity. The implementation of *Syariah*, of which *hudud* (punishment) law is a part of it, provides the much required peace and security as crimes would be reduced to its minimum (PAS n.d., p. 7). PAS accepts parliamentary democracy as a political system, but its intention to introduce *hudud* law has been politicized and triggered several major racial and religious debates on the issue.

Former Prime Minister, Najib Tun Razak, made a statement when he was the deputy prime minister on 17 July 2007 that Malaysia is not a secular state but an Islamic nation with its own interpretation. He said:

> Islam is the official religion and we are an Islamic state. But as an Islamic state, it does not mean that we don't respect the non-Muslims. The Muslims and the non-Muslims have their own rights (in this country). ... We have never been secular because being secular by Western definition means separation of the Islamic principles in the way we govern a country (*Bernama* 2007, pp. 1–2).

The issue sparked criticisms from the opposition and civil society. For instance, Ambiga Sreenevasan, the then president of Malaysia's Bar Council, rejected the notion that Malaysia is an Islamic state. Meanwhile, the Chairman of the Christian Federation of Malaysia, Bishop Paul Tan, said that the use of the term "Islamic state" is unacceptable to Malaysians of other faiths. This reaction is not unexpected as the non-Muslim community has been greatly alarmed by Islamization agenda in Malaysia (Hong 2007).

Pawancheek Marican, a well-known solicitor, argued that "secular" is defined in the Oxford Dictionary as "1. concerned with the affairs of this world; not spiritual or sacred. 2. (of education, etc.) not concerned with religion or religious belief". Therefore, there are two questions that need to be answered: (a) does the situation in Malaysia contemplate with what is in the definition, and (b) whether such interpretation is consistent with the Federal Constitution. The answers to both queries are in the negative (Marican 2009). There are many articles of the Constitution that place Islam in a special position such as Article 74 (4) (the right of the states to pass civil and criminal laws relating to Islam), Article 12 (2) (the right of the government to pass laws to grant financial assistance to

Islamic institutions and for Islamic education), Article 160 (the definition of "Malay", one such requirement of which requires him to be a Muslim), and Article 150 (6A) (the Yang di Pertuan Agong cannot pass laws that touch on Islamic matters when declaring an Emergency). In Malaysia, the constitutional structure is also such that the Islamic law system runs parallel to the civil law system, due to an amendment passed in 1988. The various articles of the Federal Constitution, as described above, have not only epitomize this duality of the constitutional structure, but have also enhanced Islam's special position.

In addition, as mentioned by Marican, the Constitution definitely grants special attention to Islam and envisages *Syariah* laws would be enacted to fulfil the personal law requirements of Muslims, but manifestly recognizes that the *Syariah* would not be made the supreme law. In the landmark case of *Che Omar bin Che Soh v. Public Prosecutor* (1988), the Supreme Court was called upon to determine the meaning of Article 3. The Court stressed that the British colonial in Malaya separated Islam into the public and private aspects, where Islamic law is limited to matters involving marriage, divorce, and inheritance only (Thomas 2006, p. 28). It is only in this sense of dichotomy that the framers of the Constitution understood the meaning of the word "Islam" in Article 3. Scholars like Professor Ahmad Ibrahim also observed that the intention of making Islam the official religion of the Federation is primarily for ceremonial purposes (Thomas 2006, p. 29). Marican submitted that the special status of Islam in this structure is the very antithesis or direct opposite of a secular state. Therefore, he concluded that Malaysia is certainly not a secular state. However, it would not be wrong to give Malaysia the appellation of "a hybrid state" (Marican 2009).

Najib Razak, since he became prime minister in 2009, refused to be drawn into the debate on "Islamic state", by saying on 2 May 2011 that "I do not want to enter into this polemic over what is (an) Islamic state because there are various interpretations of what is Islamic state" (Sani 2011, p. 1). Najib tried to avoid the controversial debate on Malaysia as an "Islamic state" because his ruling party Barisan Nasional (BN) has lost quite a significant number of support from the non-Muslims since the 2008 general election due to the Islamization agenda practised by his predecessors, Mahathir and Abdullah Badawi.

Freedom of Religion and Intra-Religious Doctrine

As mentioned in Chapter 2, Article 11 of the Federal Constitution guarantees freedom of religion, which literally seems comprehensive enough to safeguard this fundamental right for Malaysia's plural society. A citizen has the right to profess, practise and—subject to Article 11 (4)—propagate his religion. Religious groups have the right to manage their own religious affairs or any matters relating to the properties and the establishment of religious institutions. On the surface, Article 11 does not expressly prohibit the conversion of a Muslim, though at the same time it does not explicitly include the right to change one's religion. However, it is suggested that Article 11 can be construed broadly to include one's freedom to relinquish or change a religious belief (albeit with limitations for Muslims under specific religious laws), and even to not be religious (Thomas 2006, p. 34).

The extent of religious freedom in Malaysia is also challenged by restrictions on religious doctrines. As the preceding section demonstrates, states reserve the right to restrict or control propagation of any religious doctrines among Muslims. These limitations affect both the Muslim and non-Muslim communities alike. The first implication of this restriction is that non-Muslims' freedom to practise their religion may be severely curtailed with respect to propagation of their religion to Muslims. There are some state laws and federal laws restricting the right to propagate any religious doctrine or belief among Muslims except for Sunni Islam. One example is Terengganu's "The Control and Restriction of the Propagation of Non-Islamic Religious Enactment" of 1980 (Adil 2007). Meanwhile for the Federal Territories, Article 5 of Syariah Criminal Offence Act 1997 states as follows:

> [A]ny person who propagates religious doctrine or belief other than the religious doctrine or beliefs of the religion of Islam among persons professing the Islamic faith shall be guilty of an offence and shall on conviction be liable to fine not exceeding three thousand ringgit or to imprisonment for a term not exceeding two years or to both.

As a matter of constitutional law, these legislations are rightly constitutional by virtue of Article 11 (4) (Harding 2002, p. 167).

Restrictions on propagation may be linked to concerns of widespread proselytism, conversions, and also non-Sunni religious doctrines among Sunni Muslims (Harding 2002, p. 168). While such restrictions interfere with the right to practise a religion, it is often taken for granted that proselytism itself may be deemed a serious encroachment of religious freedom. If this right is to be meaningful, individuals should be free from any compulsion or undue influence to adopt a particular belief. Thus, conversion resulting from compulsion or undue influence is more problematic than conversion out of one's free will. The implication from Article 11 (4) is that state laws may prohibit the propagation of other sects or doctrines within Islam itself. Mohamed Salleh Abas (1984, p. 45), former lord president, argues that:

> [T]his limitation is logical as it is necessary consequence that follows naturally from the fact that Islam is the religion of the Federation. Muslims in this country belong to the *Sunni* Sect which recognises only the teachings of four specified schools of thought and regards other schools of thought as being contrary to true Islamic religion. It is with a view to confining the practice of Islamic religion in this country within the *Sunni* Sect that State Legislative Assemblies and Parliament as respects the Federal Territory are empowered to pass laws to protect Muslims ...

Thus, state laws may prohibit "deviations" from the Sunni sect. Since Muslims in Malaysia officially adhere to Sunni teachings, non-Sunni schools of thought are outlawed (Adil 2007, pp. 10–11). Although there is no constitutional provision entrenching the position of Sunni teachings among Muslims in Malaysia, certain state enactments such as that of the Federal Territories of Kuala Lumpur, Labuan and Putrajaya provide that Muslims must conform to Sunni teachings, with emphasis on the Shafi'i school of thought. The executive and state religious departments have been fairly active in crackdowns against adherents of other sects. For example, in the 1990s the *Arqam* Islamic group faced persecution by the government. Its leader, Ashaari Muhammad, formed a *da'wah* (the proselytizing or preaching of Islam) group in 1968 which promoted an "Islamic" way of life, in place of a secular one. Its members, through *Aurad Muhammadiah* teachings, believe in self-sufficiency and adherence to Islamic teachings.³ In 1994, this group was labelled by the National Fatwa Council as "deviant" and unlawful. The Ministry of Home Affairs also delegitimized *Arqam* under the Societies Act of 1966.

Meanwhile, between October 2000 and January 2001, the Federal government detained six Shia followers under the Internal Security Act (ISA). Although none of them were charged either in civil or *Syariah* courts, *fatwa* committees in the country, including the one at the federal level, issued a *fatwa* labelling the group as "deviant". In 1984, the Fatwa Committee of the National Council for Islamic Religious Affairs declared that the following Shi'ite schools of jurisprudence, the Ja'fari and Zaidi, were acceptable in Malaysia. In 1996, this decision was revoked. A 1996 *fatwa* by the Fatwa Committee of the National Council for Islamic Religious Affairs stated that Muslims in Malaysia must only follow the teachings of Islam "based on the Sunni doctrine (*Ahl al-Sunnah wa al-Jama'ah*) on creed, religious laws and ethics" (Razak 2013). Thus, the propagation of Shia teachings was banned. This was followed by a series of *fatwas* between 1998 and 2012 issued by various states in Malaysia that placed restrictions on the spread and practice of Shi'ism (Alatas 2014). In addition, the publication, broadcasting and distribution of any books, leaflets, films, videos, and others relating to the teachings of Islam that contradict the Sunni doctrine is prohibited and deemed unlawful (Razak 2013).

In 2010, the authorities detained more than 200 Muslim Shi'ites in Selangor on the ground that the Shia doctrine is a threat to national security (*Jakarta Post* 2010). In early August 2013, two Shi'ites were arrested, followed by another six arrests in September. The Perak Islamic Religious Department (JAIPk) enforcement chief Ahmad Nizam Amiruddin was reported to have said that Shia believers should be eradicated. In March 2014, Perak state religious authorities arrested more than 114 people believed to be Shi'ites. The arrests were carried out while they were commemorating the birth of Siti Zainab, the daughter of Sayyidina Ali, the fourth Caliph of Islam, and the grand-daughter of Prophet Muhammad (Alatas 2014). The government claimed that Shia doctrine allows the killing of Muslims who are considered as infidels—i.e., non-Shi'ite Muslims. However, it is not clear if these threats are actually true or if they are serious and imminent at all.

The Department of Islamic Development Malaysia (JAKIM) has frequently warned Muslims nationwide against liberalism, with an official sermon for the *Aidilfitri* (Aid Mubarak) celebration in early August 2013 warning of a conspiracy by "enemies of Islam" to manipulate them through ideas like liberalism, secularism, pluralism, socialism, feminism and positivism. The recent spotlight on Islamic decrees by Malaysian authorities on its followers as well as on non-Muslims has led to heated debates over the enforcement measures, with some groups deeming certain provisions under religious law to be regressive while others have voiced their concerns over a worrying trend of overt Islamization in a multicultural country (Zurairi 2013a).

Islamist group, Ikatan Muslimin Malaysia (ISMA), denounced the moderate tag, Liberal Muslims, labelling them as "extremists" similar to those resorting to violence. An activist Umar Hakim Mohd Tajuddin argued that the Islamic approach taken by liberal Muslims cannot be afforded the label "moderate", and would threaten the "true" teachings of Islam if allowed to run riot. The effort to put the moderate label on liberal Muslim groups was inaccurate and deviant. In a rallying call to Malaysian Muslims, Umar urged them to be wary of any thoughts that "looked foreign" and backed by those fond of Western ideas, alleging that the teachings could potentially threaten the position of Islam in Malaysia. He was actually referring to ISMA's attacks on the Coalition of Malaysian NGOs (COMANGO), which was involved in the recent human rights peer review against Malaysia in October 2013. ISMA said that there was no room for lesbian, gay, bisexual and transgender (LGBT) rights or religious freedom in Malaysia, as it lobbied Putrajaya to ignore the proposals put forth by the local human rights activist coalition in Geneva. ISMA Deputy President Aminuddin Yahya called COMANGO's recommendations as an affront to the religious sanctity and the sovereignty of the Federal Constitution for insisting on religious freedom and LGBT rights and also on the right of Muslims to be an apostate and pressing for the removal of Malay privileges (Zurairi 2013b).

In Malaysia, liberal Islam is defined in the context of racial politics among Malays, Chinese, and Indians. Malaysian liberal Muslims show their critical stand against *Syariah* laws that do not conform to Malaysia's constitution and pluralism, and are opposed to the politicization of Islam and the discriminative policies toward women and religious minorities. Malaysian liberals define and work for religious freedom and civil law that is just for all citizens, an increasingly popular attempt that critics, including the Islamic scholars councils, see as heretical, secular, and Western (Ali 2012).

Therefore, intra-religious expression is subjected to the rules imposed by the Federal Constitution and state constitutions that protect the practices of Sunni Islam. In the following sections, this chapter will further explore the issues of intra-religious expression such as public speech, publication and broadcasting, blasphemy and dress code. These issues will be discussed in turn.

Public Speech

Public speech is closely monitored by the religious authority. Other doctrines are treated in hostility because they are considered as threatening the Sunni Islam practice in Malaysia. As reported by a news online portal, *The Malaysian Insider*, in one Friday sermon entitled *"Virus Shia"* on 29 November 2013, JAKIM declared that Shia Muslims propagated beliefs such as encouraging sodomy, celebrating the Karbala on the 10th of *Muharam* (the first month in the Muslim calendar), defending the practice of *mutaah* (contract marriage), questioning the sanctity of the Sunni branch of Islam and declaring themselves as the true Sunni. These might upset many Shia Muslims and are perceived as promoting hatred against the Shia community in Malaysia and abroad. According to JAKIM, the Fatwa Council in 1996 had declared Shia as forbidden or *haram* in Malaysia and made it compulsory for Malaysian Muslims to only follow the teachings, customs and beliefs of the Sunni branch of Islam (Azizuddin 2013b). Perhaps, this is due to the State's concern about the spread of Shia in Malaysia, besides responding to the conflict between the Sunni and Shia in the Middle East. Furthermore, on 3 December 2013 during his speech at the UMNO general assembly, Deputy Prime Minister Muhyiddin Yassin urged the Federal Constitution to be revised to include a provision to protect the Sunni doctrine in Malaysia.

As regards the state jurisdiction, Article 74 (2) of the Federal Constitution reads:

> Without prejudice to any power to make laws conferred on it by any other Article, the Legislature of a State may make laws with respect to any of the matters enumerated in the State List (that is to say, the Second List set out in the Ninth Schedule) or the Concurrent List.

Further, under Item 1 of the State List, Schedule 9 of the Federal Constitution, this power shall be evolved under matters pertaining to:

> ... Islamic law and personal and family law of persons professing the religion of Islam, the control of propagating doctrines ..., and the determination of matters of Islamic law and doctrine and Malay custom.

With regard to Malaysia's constitutional supremacy, states have the power to make laws subject to Article 74 (1) and the State List of the Federal Constitution. However, such powers cannot violate other provisions laid out in the Constitution. For example, state legislative assemblies may pass laws relating to religious issues as illustrated by the judgments, *Che Omar Che Soh v Public Prosecutor* (1988),[4] *Mamat bin Daud v Government of Malaysia* (1988),[5] and several others. The power then vests to the Majlis Agama Islam Negeri (State Islamic Council), *muftis* (state religious heads), and the *Syariah* court. Recently, much publicity has been given to issues pertaining to states' *Syariah* criminal enactments, particularly those underlining that a *tauliah* (qualified approval) is required before one can propagate Islam publicly or conduct talks on religious issues. Thus, in *Fathul Bari bin Mat Jaya & Anor v Majlis Agama Islam Negeri Sembilan & Ors* (2012), the Court of Appeal affirmed that:

> It was commonly accepted that deviant teachings were an offence against the precepts of Islam. Therefore, there was merit in the respondents' contention that, by necessary implication, the teaching of Islam without a *tauliah* could similarly be construed an offence against the precepts of Islam.[6]

In this case, the petitioner contended that the state legislature had exceeded its legislative authority by enacting Section 53 (1) under which any person engaged in the teaching of religion without a *tauliah* from the Approval Committee, except for members of his family at his place of residence, was guilty of an offence punishable by a fine, imprisonment, or both. However, the Federal Court accepted the term "precepts of Islam" to cover the three main domains of creed or belief, law, and ethics or morality, and that such precepts were derived from *al-Quran* and the *Sunnah* as contended.

In another case, a former *mufti* of the state of Perlis, Mohd Asri Zainul Abidin, was arrested on 1 October 2010 by the Selangor State Department of Religious Affairs (JAIS) and police personnel for giving a religious lecture to more than 500 people without obtaining any kind of authorization from the Selangor state religious department. On 18 October 2009, Abidin was charged under Section 119 (1) of the Selangor Islamic Religious Administration Enactment 2003. It was argued that Abidin is widely known for his outspoken and liberal approach to Islam, which has caused different opinions on certain issues between him and other Islamic religious institutions such as the National Fatwa Council (SUARAM 2010, p. 72). Similarly, JAIS officers also detained a local entertainer Bob Lokman, a PAS activist, in October 2011 while he was speaking at a *surau* for giving a religious speech without accreditation. JAIS had made an announcement in September 2011 that it would not issue accreditation to any politician to give religious talks or lectures at *suraus* or mosques in Selangor (Centre for Independent Journalism 2012, p. 102).

Therefore, it is patently obvious the government is attempting to monitor liberals in the country, particularly by deeming liberal Muslims deviant. In response to PAS leader, Nik Abduh Nik Abdul Aziz's comment about curbing liberalism, the Minister in charge of Religious Affairs Jamil Khir Bharom stated:

> The government made its stance against liberalism clear in a 2006 declaration, during the 74th National Fatwa Council's discussion. Cooperation between religious authorities and security agencies will be increased to monitor deviant beliefs (Yunus 2016, p. 1).

Moreover, he said that the government would even consider censoring publications to control the spread of deviant beliefs nationwide. However, his statements did not go unchallenged. Indeed, former minister, Mohd Zaid Ibrahim, argued that Jamil should be charged under Section 124 of the Penal Code for activities detrimental to parliamentary democracy (*Free Malaysia Today* 2016).

Publication and Broadcasting

As mentioned by Ahmad Murad Merican (2005) in the previous chapter, Islam is portrayed by the print media as monolithic. The only legitimate faith in Malaysia and for the Malays is from the teachings of Sunni Islam and Shafi'i school. Muhammad Raqib Mohd Sofian, Rizki Briandana, and Azman Azwan Azmawati (2018) concur with Merican after undergoing a study on the *Sinar Harian* newspaper. They collected a three-year sample from the years 2013 to 2016 consisting many controversial cases of Shia Muslims in Malaysia which included banning books on Shia's ideology and several raids by the authorities on Shia's gathering. They concluded that *Sinar Harian* supported the existing status quo and labelled Shia as illegal, misguided, and harmful. *Sinar Harian* was corresponding to the reality of the government's policy and Shia Muslims were denied any space to explain about their issues and beliefs in the newspaper. The authors also believed that the Media Prima, which owned the *New Straits Times*, *Harian Metro* and *Berita Harian*, and the Utusan Group, which was responsible for *Utusan Malaysia* and *Kosmo*, were very hostile towards Shia Muslims as these print media were controlled by UMNO who promoted the agenda prosecuting Shia doctrine and its followers.

The same print media was also utilized to support the ruling government against other political parties. Religious issues were highlighted during the election by the print media. Since one of the main opposition parties was PAS, religious issues were among the most debatable issues in the parties' campaign during the election especially for the Malay-Muslim communities. For instance in the 2008 general election, the daily coverage of *Utusan Malaysia* was mainly focused on the debate between BN and PAS where it favoured the former and disfavoured the latter. The opposition party, PAS, was negatively portrayed as an orthodox and extremist party. Among other headlines criticizing the opposition were "*PAS dicabar masuk konsep negara Islam dalam manifesto pilihanraya*"

[PAS challenged to include the concept of Islamic state in its manifesto], 23 February 2008; "*Fatwa Hadi ditegah agama*" [Hadi's *fatwa* forbid by the religion], 29 February 2008; "*Politik balas dendam tersasar dalam Islam*" [The politics of revenge is unIslamic], 21 February 2008; "*PAS tidak konsisten dalam perjuangan-Alwi*" [PAS inconsistent in its struggle—Alwi], 29 February 2008; and "*PAS guna mimbar hentam BN*" [PAS uses sermon to condemn BN], 5 March 2008 (Azizuddin 2009). In the 2013 general election, BN was portrayed as a protector of Islam as seen in these columns in the *Utusan Malaysia*: "*BN konsisten perjuang Islam*" [BN struggles consistently for Islam], 24 April 2013; "*Saya tidak akan korbankan agama untuk politik- Najib*" [I will not sacrifice religion for politics—Najib], 26 April 2013; "*Pilih UMNO, BN selamatkan umat Islam*" [Choose UMNO, BN to save Islamic community], 26 April 2013; and "*Agenda pembangkang hakis Islam*" [Opposition agenda diminish Islam], 3 May 2013 (Azizuddin 2013c).

Moreover in 2012, a total number of six books were banned from publication namely, *Allah, Liberty & Love: Courage to Reconcile Faith & Freedom* and its Malay language translation by Irshad Manji; *Where Did I Come From?*, by Peter Mayle; *Penghantar Ilmu-ilmu Islam*, by Murtadha Muthahhari; *Dialog Sunnah Syi'ah*, by A. Syarafuddin Al-Musawi; and *Tafsir Sufi Al-Fatihah Mukadimah*, by Jalaluddin Rakhmat. The book by Irshad Manji was banned under Section 7 (1) of the Printing Presses and Publications Act 1984 (PPPA) and gazetted on 29 May 2012. According to Deputy Home Minister Abu Seman, the book was believed to contain elements that can shake Muslims from their faith, Islamic teachings and elements which insulted Islam. JAIS confiscated seven copies of Manji's books from Borders bookstore and charged Borders store manager, Nik Raina Nik Abdul Aziz, under Section 13 of the Federal Territory Syariah Offences Act 1997 for distributing the book. JAIS also raided ZI Publications office and confiscated copies of Manji's books under Section 16 (1)(a) or (b) of the Religious Publications Offences against Islamic Law (SUARAM 2013, p. 23). The ban on the book has since been lifted following a High Court ruling on 5 September 2013. Under Section 16 of the Perak Criminal (Syariah) Enactment 1992, it is an offence to possess items on Shi'ism including books, audio-visual materials and posters (Farid 2014).

Meanwhile, *Noah*, a film loosely based on the prophet venerated by Muslims and Christians, has been banned in Malaysia on 4 April 2014 because the movie is believed to cause anger and distress if shown in Malaysia. The Home Ministry's Film Censorship Board (LPF) division chairman, Abdul Halim Abdul Hamid, said that the decision was made after the board viewed the film during a private screening together with officials from JAKIM. The main reason for the ban, according to Abdul Halim, was *Noah*'s depiction by Hollywood actor Russell Crowe. Islam forbids visual depictions of any prophet. The film is said to be based on the biblical story of *Noah*'s Ark and has already been banned in several Islamic countries including Egypt, Bahrain, Qatar, the United Arab Emirates and Indonesia (Shazwan 2014).

Blasphemy

For some cases, it is unclear whether they are inherently blasphemous or are a form of dissent against the religious authority. On 4 February 2002, several groups led by the Muslim Scholars Association of Malaysia (MSAM, *Persatuan Ulama Malaysia*) submitted a memorandum to the Conference of Rulers urging action against several individuals who are alleged to have insulted Islam in their writings. Those named in the memorandum included the Malaysian Human Rights Commissioner and the leader of a NGO Sisters in Islam Zainah Anwar, *Malaysiakini* and *New Straits Times* columnist Farish A. Noor, former *The Sun* columnist Akbar Ali, writer Kassim Ahmad, University of Malaya researcher Patricia Martinez, and lawyer Malik Imtiaz Sarwar. They were accused of blasphemy by insulting Islam, the Prophet, belittling verses in the *Quran* and *Hadith*, and questioning the intellectual role of Muslim religious scholars or *ulama*. At first, MSAM lodged a police report on 25 January 2002 against a business weekly *The Edge* writer, Farish Noor, for allegedly insulting Islam in an article published on 3 December 2001. In the paper, MSAM President Abdul Ghani Samsudin accused Noor of insulting the Prophet and the sanctity of the religion by belittling the

Quran and *Hadith* (Loone 2002). For instance, in the interview, Noor replied to the questions on the role of the *ulama* and interpretations in the *Quran* as follows:

> That option is only for down and out and unemployable people like me. There is a desperate need for Malay Muslims to break free from the hegemonic grips of both the *ulama* and the state by reclaiming Islam for themselves. Islam is a discourse and all discourses are open, contested and plastic. If I can contribute in any way to keeping the doors to *ijtihad* (personal interpretation) open, I will do it. The danger of not doing is so great (Loone 2002, pp. 1–2).

Zainah Anwar was accused of blasphemy when she said in the *Utusan Malaysia* on 26 September 2000:

> Islam is not owned by the individual or any groups who claim that they are *ulama*. Thus, any interpretation on Islamic sources such as *Quran* is not solely the domain of the *ulama* (MSAM 2002, p. 4).

The Sun columnist Akbar Ali was said to have ridiculed and disparaged the *ulama* in his articles by referring to them as "men who dislike shaving" and that the "turbans of the *mufti* (religious leader) are too tight and therefore not enough oxygen is getting into their brains" (MSAM 2002, p. 2).

What began as a religious issue, however, turned into a sensational political theatre when several UMNO members responded to the issue and criticized MSAM because of its close links with the opposition party, PAS. For instance, Mustapa Muhamad, Executive Director of the National Council of Economic Action, supported the writers and said: "There is nothing wrong if their opinions do not go against the *aqidah* (faith) and Islam. Difference of opinion is normal in Islam" (MSAM 2002, p. 42). Furthermore, Zainuddin Maidin, Parliamentary Secretary for the Ministry of Information, said: "Their (the writers) writings can improve the image of Islam that has been damaged by the frozen-minded and fusty orthodox scholars. Their (the writers) thoughts are respectable, through them people see the true Islam" (MSAM 2002,

p. 43). The support from several UMNO members was a surprise, even to the secular-liberal NGOs themselves, because the ruling government, particularly during Mahathir's leadership, had never shown much intention of allowing free speech, or any space for dissent. In this regard, UMNO support was understandable because Mahathir himself has been the favourite target of MSAM and other Islamic bodies' wrath. The PAS Selangor website, for example, has a section dedicated to a collection of speeches, utterances and remarks made by the prime minister and several other cabinet ministers considered to have insulted Islam (Maznah 2002, p. 6). Clearly, this issue has become a political contestation between two strong Malay-based parties, UMNO and PAS.

The MSAM's memorandum triggered a confrontation between Islamic NGOs, supported by the Islamic party PAS, and secular-liberal NGOs, supported by the nationalist party UMNO, on the issue of free speech, especially on the boundary of free speech with respect to Islam. In my view, if Malaysia believes in a democratic system which encourages freedom of speech as well as freedom of religion, there should be discussions in a civil and peaceful manner between the MSAM and those writers as this issue involves Islam and the sensitivities surrounding it. Freedom of speech should not be sacrificed on this issue, but all parties should show a sense of social responsibility in discussing such a sensitive matter. Through dialogues, parties can seek peaceful resolution, avoid hyper-partisan deadlocks and achieve some compromise.

The recent case was that of a former political and social activist Kassim Ahmad being charged with committing the offences at a seminar in Putrajaya on 15 and 16 February 2014. He pleaded not guilty in the Syariah High Court on 27 March 2014 to insulting Islam and not complying with religious authorities. On the first count, he was alleged to have tabled a script of his speech entitled "Speech for the National Political Conference to Determine the Direction of Malaysia over the next 30 years", which insulted Islam by criticizing Islamic practices. On the second count, he was alleged to have tabled the same script which was deemed insulting or not in compliance with religious authorities, defied the order issued by the Yang di-Pertuan Agong as the head of the Islamic religion as well as the *fatwa* issued by the *mufti*. Kassim was charged under Section 7 (b) and Section 9 of the Syariah Criminal Offenses (Federal Territories) Act 1997. He faced a fine of up to RM3,000 or a jail term of up to two years, or both, upon conviction (*The Malaysian Insider* 2014a). He was later acquitted and discharged by the *Syariah* court over charges of insulting Islam and defying Muslim authorities. Judge Azzeman Omar made the order following the withdrawal of the charges after the Syarie prosecuting officer agreed with the decisions of the Court of Appeal and Federal Court. Both the Court of Appeal and the Federal Court had ruled that Kassim's arrest and prosecution were invalid. The appellate court ruled that Kassim's arrest on 26 March 2014 at his house in Taman Kulim Perdana, Kulim, Kedah was illegal as it was not in accordance with the Kedah Syariah Enactment. It also ruled that Kassim, being a resident of Kedah, was not obligated to a Federal Territory "*fatwa*" because he was not arrested in a Federal Territory (Maizatul 2017).

Dress Code

The manifestation of Islam in everyday life seems to be growing day by day in Malaysia, due to the fact that it is taken to reflect the religiousness and piety of individuals and society (McIntyre 2006). It is also the easiest to regulate as it is the physical and external expression of faith. The assertion of the form of one's dressing as an expression of that faith is found in the case of *Hajjah Halimatussaadiah binti Haji Kamaruddin* v. *Public Services Commission Malaysia & Anor* (1994). The applicant, a clerk at the office of the Perak State Legal Adviser, was dismissed from her work for wearing *purdah*, a form of dressing which covers all parts of the body except the eyes. This was said to be in contravention of the dress code for civil servants. One of the issues before the Supreme Court was whether the circular which prohibits the wearing of such attire has infringed her constitutional right to practise her religion. It was held by the Supreme Court that such prohibition does not affect her constitutional right to practise her religion and that wearing *purdah* has nothing to do with her constitutional right to profess and practise her religion. It was held that wearing *purdah* is not a requirement in Islam and is not specified in the *Quran* (Abdullah 2007, pp. 264–89).

In *Meor Atiqulrahman bin Ishak & Ors* v. *Fatimah bte. Sihi & Ors* (2000), the applicants challenged the principal of the school and the authorities with regard to the prohibition on *serban*, a form of headgear worn by the boys. The boys were suspended from school for their refusal to abide by the ruling. The argument for the primacy of Islam found favour in this case. The trial judge refused to abide by the decision in *Che Omar*. The judge was of the view that Islam occupies a special position under the Constitution and is the primary religion in Malaysia. Islam is therefore, according to the judge, above other religions. He surmised that, Islam being a complete way of life, is a universal religion which is acceptable by all other religions. Article 3 is to be given a "proper interpretation" by extending it beyond rituals and ceremonies (Abdullah 2007).

The decision in *Meor Atiqulrahman bin Ishak & Ors* v. *Fatimah bte Sihi & Ors* (2000) was overturned by the Court of Appeal but the appellate court did not seize the opportunity to address the trial judge's pronouncements on Article 3 of the Federal Constitution. The Federal Court recently affirmed the Court of Appeal's decision and had no difficulty in accepting the position that it is for the civil courts to determine whether the limitation on the practice of a religion is constitutional. It was stated, albeit *obiter*, that "whether we like it or not, we have to accept that Malaysia is not the same as a Malay State prior to the coming of the British. She is multi-racial, multi-cultural, multi-lingual and multi-religious" (CommonLII 2006).

When the issue of cross-dressing hit the headlines, the pendulum shifted. In *Muhammad Juzaili bin Mohd Khamis & Ors v State Government of Negeri Sembilan & Ors* (2015),[7] all three appellants were Muslim men diagnosed with the medical condition— "gender identity disorder" (GID). As a result, for many years, the appellants had expressed themselves as women by displaying feminine mannerism and wearing women's clothes and makeup. Indeed, they contended following such a lifestyle felt natural.

Justice Mohd Hishamuddin Mohd Yunus held that:

We hold Section 66 of the Negeri Sembilan Syariah Criminal Enactment 1992 as invalid and unconstitutional with Articles 5 (1), 8 (1), 8 (2), 9 (2) and 10 (1)(a). The appeal is therefore allowed (Zurairi 2014, p. 1).

The coram, which included Justices Aziah Ali and Lim Yee Lan, made an unanimous ruling that Sharia law contravened constitutional provisions guaranteeing personal liberty, equality, freedom of movement, and freedom of political speech. Further, it stressed that while the state was empowered to enact laws involving matters of Islam, these laws must not contravene the supreme law of the land, i.e. the Federal Constitution. The particular issue in question concerned Section 66 of the Negri Sembilan Syariah Criminal Enactment 1992 (which criminalized cross dressing) under which the men had been repeatedly charged. Judge Hishamuddin described Section 66 as "degrading", "oppressive", and "inhuman", stating that the provision deprived the appellants of their dignity. He also lashed out at the Seremban High Court for declaring the law as necessary to prevent homosexuality and the spread of HIV regardless of the medical reasons behind transgenderism (Zurairi 2014).

However, on 8 October 2015, the Federal Court overturned the Court of Appeal's decision stating that the respondents had made a grave error in failing to follow specific procedures laid out in Clauses (3) and (4) of Article 4 of the Federal Constitution in their challenge of Section 66.[8] In other words, proceedings without proper jurisdiction or power to hear a case must be deemed null and *void ab initio*. Therefore, the judges concluded the Court of Appeal had no jurisdiction to declare the law unconstitutional, maintaining that the three transgender men had used the wrong legal procedure to start their action (Suparmaniam 2015).

Private Speech

The term "private speech" is synonymous with "non-political speech". Non-political (also unpolitical or apolitical) is defined in the Oxford Dictionary as a subject matter that is neither related to nor motivated by politics. A country which acknowledges freedom of political speech as enshrined in its constitution, such as Malaysia, should therefore not ban non-political artistic work, whether books, songs, paintings, or movies, unless deemed detrimental to national security or public morality under Article 10 of the Federal Constitution. Despite this, according to the *Encyclopedia of Censorship* (Green and Karolides 2014), over the past decade, the Malaysian Home Ministry has banned books for containing religious, sexual, or profane contents.

Under Section 2 of the PPPA, a publication is defined as: (1) any document, newspaper, book, or periodical; (2) any written or printed matter; (3) anything capable of suggesting words or ideas; or (4) any audio recording. Further, regarding "undesirable publications", Section 7 (1) of the PPPA states:

> If the Minister is satisfied that any publication contains any article, caricature, photograph, report, notes, writing, sound, music, statement or any other thing which is in any manner prejudicial to or likely to be prejudicial to public order, morality, security, or which is likely to alarm public opinion, or which is or is likely to be contrary to any law or is otherwise prejudicial to or is likely to be prejudicial to public interest or national interest, he may in his absolute discretion by order published in the Gazette prohibit, either absolutely or subject to such conditions as may be prescribed, the printing, importation, production, reproduction, publishing, sale, issue, circulation, distribution or possession of that publication and future publications of the publisher concerned.

Thus, this provision allows the Home Minister to ban any publication that he or she thinks fit, if such materials contain any element that could potentially affect public or national security.

Section 8 lists the punishments for the offence in Section 7 (1). Section 8 (1) states that any person, who without lawful excuse, is found in possession of any prohibited publication shall be guilty of an offence and liable to a fine not exceeding RM5,000 upon conviction, suggesting that any person who buys, reads, or keeps undesirable publications may be charged, convicted, and fined. Under Section 8 (2), any person who prints, imports, produces, reproduces, publishes, sells, issues, circulates, offers for sale, distributes or has in his possession for such purpose any prohibited publication, shall be guilty of an offence and on conviction, be liable to imprisonment for a term not exceeding three years or to a fine not exceeding RM20,000, or both. This provision applies solely to the publishers of undesirable publications.

Religious-themed books banned in 2014 by the Home Ministry include *Akhirnya Ku Temui Kebenaran* by Dr Muhammad Al-Tijani Al-Samawi, *Agama Politik Nalar Politik Islam* by Ahmad Vaezi and Ali Syahab, *99 Wariat Imam Ja'far Ash-Shadiq Lentera Ilahi* by Imam Ja'far Ash-Shadiq and Rahmani Astuti, *Saling Memberi Saling Menerima* by Sayyid Mahdi As Sadr and Ali Bin Yahya, *Fatwa-Fatwa 2 Soal-Jawab Seputar Muamalah Ahlulbair* by Ayatullah Al-Uzhma Imam Ali Khamenei and Mubsin Labib, *Teladan Abadi Ja'far Shadiq Sang Mahaguru* by Husain Nahrawi, *Teladan Abadi Hasan Askari Tumpuan Kaum Papa* by M Ilyas and Hasan Al-Habsyi, *Teladan Abadi Husain Syahid* by Abdullah Beik, *Fatimah Az-Zahra & 9 Keturunannya Yang Mulia* by Tarikuddin Bin Haji Hassan, *Imamul Muhtadin Ali Bin Abi Thalib* by HMH Al-Hamid Al-Husaini, *Meniti Titian Kebenaran* by KhairIzzah, and *Memories Of Muhammad: Why The Prophet Matters* by Omid Safi (*Malay Mail Online* 2014).

In 2016, five books were banned: *The Teachings of the Quran* by HU Weitbrecht, *Bahaullah and the New Era and Introduction to the Bahai Faith* by JE Esslemont, *Detik-Detik Pembongkaran Agama: Mempopulerkan Agama Kebajikan Menggagas Pluralisme-Pembebasan* by Nur Khalik Ridhwan and Sirsaeba Alafsana, *Jalan Yang Lurus: Kita Harus Meneroka Jalan Ini* by Kassim Ahmad, and *Tabut: Penjelasan Tentang Segala Sesuatu* by Abdul Kahar Bin Ahmad Jalal (Azlee 2016). These books were written to propagate ideas relating to the non-Sunni Islamic doctrine such as Shia, Bahai, Liberal Islam, etc., and were banned for interrupting the religious faith of believers of the Sunni doctrine (as embraced by the majority of Malay Muslims in Malaysia).

In addition, the ministry has also banned a number of movies from being broadcast in the country including: *The Raid 2: Berandal* (2014) (banned for violent content); *Race 2* (2013) (banned for showcasing the underworld of Turkey); *Banglasia* (2013) (banned for depicting the sarcasm of Bangladeshi foreign labourers thought to be overcrowding Malaysia); *The Wolf of Wall Street* (2013) (banned for nudity); *The Dictator* (2012) (likely banned for the lead actor's habit of harassing and offending politically correct groups); and *The Girl with the Dragon Tattoo* (2011) (banned for nudity) (Casey Lee 2014). Meanwhile, local film *Dukun* (2007) which was based on a true story by Dain Said—depicting a high profile crime which caused the death of politician, Mazlan Idris—was banned by the Film Censorship Board of Malaysia (FCBM) for being controversial and for the possibility of causing offence to the relatives of the victim.

Section 26 of the Film Censorship Act 2002 governs the banning of movies:

> If the Minister is of the opinion that the exhibition, display, distribution, possession, circulation or sale of any film or any film-publicity material would be contrary to public interest, he may, in his absolute discretion, by order published in the Gazette, prohibit the exhibition, display, distribution, possession, circulation or sale of that film or film-publicity material.

Thus, any domestic or international movie thought to affect the public negatively may be withdrawn from circulation. In addition, the media is also prohibited from publishing materials considered to violate public interest. In 2006, the National Fatwa Council (NFC) of Malaysia forbade Muslims from engaging with black metal music because it was deemed to encourage Satanism, rebellion, and incite hatred among people. However, after a period of consideration, the ban was lifted and changed to counselling sessions.

Another form of private expression that has faced censorship is the Dikir Barat. Dikir Barat is a musical form from the state of Kelantan characterized by competitive groups singing in the local dialect. Performed with or without percussion accompaniment, the uniqueness of this form of expression lies both in its competitive setting and its dance movements. Most lyrics are written spontaneously to suit the occasion. The leader of the group or the lead singer is known as the *tukang karut* and it is this person's ability to create "up-to-date" lyrics that will help to increase a group's reputation. One particularly popular *tukang karut* (singer) in Kelantan, Shahima Edayu Akma Mohd Alwi or "Rosalinda", was charged by the Syariah court for wearing a sexy dress while performing at the Felda Aring Enam in 2014. As a result, she was fined RM1,000 for behaviour deemed to be overtly against Islamic teachings and for promoting immorality (*The Rakyat Post* 2014). Another form of private expression under fire is that of "cross-dressing" while performing Dikir Barat. Mohd Hafiz Jeffri or "Kajol" was charged for his female and sexy appearance while performing in April 2011. He accepted the charges and paid the RM1,000 fine but appealed on the prison penalty. The Syariah court in Tanah Merah, Kelantan accepted his appeal, suspending it to one year of good behaviour (Muthiah and Raman 2012).

In Malaysia, those charged with (political and non-political) defamation can be guilty of both civil and criminal offences. Criminal defamation is covered under Chapter 21 (Sections 499–502) of the Penal Code while civil cases are governed by the Defamation Act 1957. Three criteria must be reached before a charge of defamation can be bought: (1) a defamatory statement must have been made; (2) the statement must mention or identify the claimant (or the individual being defamed); and (3) the statement must have been circulated to a third party.

Defamation cases are often subjective, full of innuendo, ambiguous, and linguistically murky. As such, the cases themselves are often sensitive and may continue for extended periods of time. Another challenge is that defamation laws in Malaysia are antiquated. As Salleh Buang (2015) pointed out, the Malaysian Defamation Act 1957 strongly resembles England's Defamation Act 1952. However, whereas the English statute has been revised several times, Malaysia's defamation law has never been updated. According to Salleh Buang (2015), defamation cases should only succeed if two prerequisites are met: (1) defendants must be able to show attempts were made to verify facts before publishing, writing, or saying the statement in question; (2) the published material must and should be a matter of public interest.

One example of a political defamation case was *Jahara Hamid, Muhamad Yusoff Mohd Noor, Omar Abdul Hamid and Shabudin Yahya*, where four BN MPs and Penang State Assemblymen claimed that Penang State Executive Councillor, Afif Bahardin, defamed them in a public speech on 17 April 2014. Afif spoke in front of an estimated 4,000 people claiming that all four BN lawmakers participated in a fraudulent transaction involving the sale of the Royal Malaysian Air Force (RMAF) base in Butterworth to a crony company. Judicial Commissioner, Lim Chong Fong, said on 29 April 2016 that the accusation was a serious one with the potential to damage the plaintiffs' political image, especially as it had been said in front of so many people. Thus, he awarded each BN member RM70,000 in exemplary and general damages (*Malay Mail Online* 2016).

By contrast, Maunsell Sharma & Zakaria Sdn Bhd had sued Utusan Melayu (M) Bhd for RM50 million for libel in 2006. This is an example of a non-political defamation case in which Maunsell Sharma & Zakaria alleged that Utusan Melayu published defamatory words in two one-page articles on 9 and 10 February 2006 by saying "there were cracks in the highway and these were caused by flaws in the engineering design of the highway" (*The Star Online* 2006b). Accordingly, Maunsell Sharman & Zakaria sought an injunction, an apology, and damages. So far there is no report especially in the media that indicates the outcome of this case.

Clearly, it is difficult to differentiate between public/political expression and private/non-political expression because, based on the cases above, private speech is often politicized for political gain. Most defamation cases relate to issues of religion or morality as defined by the practice of Sunni Islam in Malaysia. Hence, the division between public and private expression is rather blurred in Malaysian society. Most importantly, the term "public ... morality" in the Constitution needs to be more clearly defined taking into account the country's diverse multicultural, multireligious, and multiracial population. Through education, deliberation, civil society engagement, the involvement of families, and the use of role modelling, the government should construct and implement policies to ensure individuals, families, and communities promote positive moral behaviours (*Malaysiakini* 2005).

Conclusion

Religious expression in Malaysia is allowed only if it is in line with the concept of common good as accepted by the state and religious authority. Malaysia only follows the teaching of Sunni doctrine, thus all Islamic practices must not deviate from the Sunni teachings especially from the Shafi'i sect. This is definitely protected by the Constitution as Islam is a religion of the country, but other religions are allowed to be practised by their followers. Not only is propagation not allowed by non-Muslims to convert Muslims in Malaysia, non-Sunni are forbidden to convert Sunni into non-Sunni doctrines. Therefore, the practices of Islam in Malaysia are considered somewhat restrictive as compared to other Muslim countries.

The argument of this chapter is that Malaysia is unique in its practice of Islam as the religion of the Federation. Currently there is a debate on whether Malaysia is still a secular state or it is becoming an Islamic state. Several prominent scholars and practitioners agree that Malaysia has a combination of civil and Islamic laws being practised together and now Malaysia is exactly a hybrid state. However, the actions, policies and politics of the government and Islamic religious authorities in Malaysia seem to suggest that Malaysia is already becoming an Islamic state. This can be seen from the practices of intra-religious expression in Malaysia ranging from the issues of public speech, publication and broadcasting, blasphemy and dress code.

Many restrictions are imposed on the practice of Islam even though some of them are more political rather than protecting Sunni Islam. For instance, this chapter mentioned earlier about the "*Sure Heboh*" open-air concerts being considered un-Islamic. Later, the organizer, private television station TV3, changed the name to "*Jom Heboh*" with an almost similar concept like the previous one, but reducing the elements of Western culture and promoting family activities, businesses and government messages. However, no criticism was levelled at the programme on whether it was Islamic or not. It is debatable whether "*Jom Heboh*" complies with Islamic teachings, but the authority seems to be content with it.

This chapter suggests that instead of prosecuting those who act against Islamic teachings in Malaysia, dialogues and intellectual discourse should be encouraged in a civil and productive manner. In this way, many problems and criticisms toward the government and religious authorities can be resolved. By taking actions against religious hatred and hate speech, Islam will be protected by the government. Promotion of true moderation in Islam should be encouraged in the public domain.

Notes

1. L.A. Sheridan and Harry E. Groves (1987) explained that the intention in making Islam the official religion of the Federation is primarily for ceremonial purposes.
2. The White Paper issued by the British Government on 14 June 1957 containing the constitutional provisions for an independent Malaya, reiterated that a declaration of Islam as "the religion of the Federation . . . will in no way affect the present position of the Federation as a secular State" (Thomas 2006, pp. 18–19). "Although Article 3 names Islam as the religion of the Federation, it has until recently always been agreed that this provision does not in any sense establish an Islamic state, but merely provides for the religious nature of state ceremony" (Harding 2010, p. 506).
3. By 1994 it was estimated that *Arqam* ran forty-eight small residential communities throughout Peninsular Malaysia. The settlements were complete with their own schools and health clinics. The total number of its members was estimated at about 100,000 with middle class Malay professionals forming the majority. Most of its male members were normally dressed in turbans and long green robes while female members covered their faces entirely (Adil, 2007: 11).
4. Che Omar Bin Che Soh v. Public Prosecutor [1988] 2 MLJ 55.
5. Mamat bin Daud & Ors v. Government of Malaysia [1988] 1 MLJ 119.
6. Fathul Bari Mat Jahya & Anor v. Majlis Agama Islam Negeri Sembilan & Ors. [2012] 1 CLJ (Sya).
7. Muhamad Juzaili Bin Mohd Khamis et al. v. State Government of Negeri Sembilan et al. Civil Appeal No. 01-498-11/2012.
8. Raus Sharif PCA referred to *Abdul Karim bin Abdul Ghani v Legislative Assembly of Sabah* (1988), which read: "Article 4(3) and (4) of the Federal

Constitution is designed to prevent the possibility of the validity of laws made by the legislature being questioned on the ground mentioned in that article incidentally. The article requires that such a law may only be questioned in proceedings for a declaration that the law is invalid. The subject must ask for a specific declaration of invalidity." See Abdul Karim Bin Abdul Ghani v. Legislative Assembly of Sabah [1988] 1 MLJ 171.

5

EXTREME EXPRESSION AND RADICALIZATION

Introduction

This chapter explores the link between extreme religious expression and radicalization, which can lead to acts of terrorism. There is no doubt that religious expression is essential for any religion, including Islam. However, religious expression can also be detrimental if it is manipulated for violent purposes. It can radicalize innocent people into extremists for certain illegitimate and illegal causes. Article 20 (2) of the International Covenant on Civil and Political Rights (ICCPR or "the Covenant") codifies the duty of the state to prohibit advocacy of religious hatred and to provide assistance in resolving these difficulties (Temperman 2011, p. 109). However, this chapter will explore further than religious hatred expression.

In the UK parliamentary debate on 17 January 2006, the government paid attention to the role of free speech in propagating violent radicalization:

> We should not ignore the contributory role that radical texts and extremist pamphlets have in radicalisation. They serve to propagate and reinforce the extremist and damaging philosophies which attempt to justify and explain the motivations of terrorists. We should not

underestimate the role that such literature can have in radicalising vulnerable and susceptible young people, particularly changing Muslims from law-abinding members of the community to potential terrorists (Choudhury 2009, p. 465).

Sara Savage and Jose Liht (2009, p. 504) concur with the UK government that speech that explicitly incites racial or religious hatred or glorifies or incites terrorism rights comes under the authority of the government, policing, and legislative bodies. In other words, any attempt to radicalize people for the purpose of luring them into terrorism are illegal and will be dealt with by the authority. As announced in Queen Elizabeth's speech on 18 May 2016, the UK "Counter-Extremism and Safeguarding Bill" is expected to codify the definition of extremism identified in "vocal or active opposition to fundamental British values including democracy, the rule of law, individual liberty, mutual respect and tolerance of different faiths and beliefs, as well as calling for the deaths of members of the armed forces" (Shepherd 2017, p. 63). The Bill also imposes a range of mainly civil measures directed towards eliminating allegedly dangerous extremist speech from public dialogue.

In Malaysia, the same concern was expressed by the authority. In fact, the royalty reminded people not to incite any hate speech that brings violence in the society. Sultan Nazrin Muizzuddin Shah in his speech delivered in the Perak's Maal Hijrah celebration on 1 September 2019 warned of the dangers of hate speech in Malaysia. He described hate speech as a ticking time bomb if allowed to be manipulated without any action taken by the government. Sultan Nazrin said:

> These excessive provocations between races and religious groups are a threat to our country. Placing dolls and hurling pork at mosques, placing of a cow's head at a Hindu temple and spreading false news on social media will spark more hatred among each other. These disgraceful acts and hate speech need to stop immediately. It's not healthy, as it puts the country in a dangerous situation. The more they let emotions take control of their judgment, the more shallow their minds get. It seems that whenever an accident happens on the road, changes to the school curriculum or mistakes made when flying the flag, these are being described as a racial or religious issue. We need to wake up and do something about it (Aqilah 2019, p. 1).

Sultan Nazrin reminded everyone, especially leaders and politicians, to stand for moderation and disregard radicalization, reasoning and brotherhood so that people of various races could live in peace and harmony in Malaysia. He was concerned that hatred religious speech could incite radicalization and terrorism. This chapter elaborates on religious or Islamic expression that was utilized in Malaysia to radicalize Muslims into terrorism. In a case study, this chapter shows that religious expression can go to the extreme and this serves as a reminder to the Malaysian authorities to counteract religious expression that radicalizes Muslims and legitimizes the acts of terrorism. Savage and Liht (2009) said that extreme speech is most strongly "activated" under totalist or extremist group conditions, thus terrorism-prevention strategies are a key opportunity to detect and identify potential "hot spots". According to Bhikhu Parekh (2005–6, p. 214), for example, the word hate in hate speech "implies hostility, rejection, a wish to harm or destroy, a desire to get the target group out of one's way, a silent or vocal and a passive or active declaration of war against it". Thus as a case study, this chapter examines extreme religious expression used by the notorious Islamic State and the Levant (ISIL) in Malaysia.

Southeast Asia has seen many groups that can be considered as extreme, aggressive and radical such as Al-Qaeda, Jemaah Islamiah (JI) and Hizbut Tahrir. However, the most extreme, aggressive and radical movement is a group called ISIL. This chapter will focus on ISIL as a case study to examine how they utilized extreme religious expression for recruiting and radicalizing Muslims into terrorism. Another name for ISIL is the Islamic State (IS) or Islamic State for Iraq and Syria (ISIS). In Arabic, it is known as *Al-Dawla Al Islamiya fi al-Iraq wa al-Syam* (Daesh), which is about the Islamic state in Iraq and "al-Syam", which refers to Syria and the surrounding areas (Dearden 2014).

ISIL had managed to attract a number of supporters from Malaysia to join them in Syria and Iraq. The supporters were willing to travel from their country to join this "holy war" or *jihad*. ISIL militants had effectively used the social media to recruit supporters and fighters to join them. The ability of ISIL to operate its mission via the social media such as Twitter, Instagram, Tumblr, Youtube etc. proved that they were able to use current technology which contributed to the increase in the number of supporters. Famous videos of the beheading of American freelance journalist James Foley on 19 August 2014, *Time Magazine* journalist Stevan Sotloff on 2 September 2014, and Allan Henning on 3 October 2014 had gone viral on the Internet which depicted the merciless and cruelness of the ISIL group. Apart from these three western victims that were widely reported, there were also at least seventeen Iraqi journalists who had been executed by the ISIL militants (Henley 2009). Ever since the spread of the so-called jihadist movement attempting to revive the caliphate system, Malaysians who joined ISIL have been identified.

The Malaysian authority had detained more than 250 suspected militants from 2013 to 2017, including some who allegedly planned attacks in the country. The only attack done by ISIL in Malaysia was a grenade blast at a bar in a suburb outside Kuala Lumpur in June 2016 which injured eight people (*Associated Press* 2017). Besides, several radical groups who were previously linked to Al-Qaeda had re-emerged and declared its allegiance to ISIL. Among the group was *Katibah Nusantara*, a "dedicated Southeast Asian military unit" under ISIL and the Mindanao-based radical Islamic terrorist group, Abu Sayyaf, which was active in Southern Philippines and East Malaysia and waged war with the Philippine army in Marawi, Southern Philippines after it overtook the town (*Agence France-Presse* 2017). For instance in Sabah, Abu Sayyaf gunmen kidnapped two Malaysians, a fish breeder Chan Sai Chuin on 16 June 2014 in Kunak and a marine police constable corporal Zakiah Aleip on 12 July 2014 from a police post in Mabul Island (Vanar 2014). Also in July 2014, Abu Sayyaf had vowed its allegiance to ISIL and Abu Bakr (Baghdadi), the leader of ISIL, through an oath of loyalty (Nadaraj 2014). The resurgence of Abu Sayyaf threatened not only the citizens in the Philippines but also endangered Malaysian communities, particularly those in eastern Sabah. In its movements, Abu Sayyaf had been enormously involved in kidnapping, bombing and other attacks against civilians in the Philippines. Recently, Abu Sayyaf was believed to have recruited and trained new fighters in their military base and then sent them to fight with ISIL in Iraq and Syria (*Asian Pacific Post* 2014).

Malaysia has also been awakened by the emergence of four new terror organizations known as BKAW, BAJ, DIMzia and ADI (known only by their acronyms) (*Straits Times* 2014). These groups were believed to be operating mainly in Selangor and Perak on a mission to establish a "super" caliphate system called *Daulah Islamiah Nusantara*, which comprised several states in Southeast Asia, including Indonesia, Malaysia, Singapore, Southern Philippines and Southern Thailand (*The Malaymail Online* 2014b). These groups aggressively embarked on recruiting new members and struggled in pushing their agenda ahead. Although the four groups operated independently, they actually subscribed to the same salafi "Jihadi" ideology as that embraced by ISIL. The salafi "*Jihadi*" justifies bloodshed for its divine purposes (Holbrook 2014).

Theory of Radicalization and Counter-Radicalization

Tinka Veldhuis and Jørgen Staun (2009) discuss the absence of clear and universally accepted definitions of radicalization:

> Although radicalisation has increasingly been subjected to scientific studies, a universally accepted definition of the concept is still to be developed. Nevertheless, faced with pressure to tackle radicalisation, policy makers have developed a few definitions. Definitions of radicalisation most often centre around two different foci: (1) on violent radicalisation, where emphasis is put on the active pursuit or acceptance of the use of violence to attain the stated goal, and (2) on a broader sense of radicalisation, where emphasis is placed on the active pursuit or acceptance of far reaching changes in society, which may or may not constitute a danger to democracy and may or may not involve the threat of or use of violence to attain the stated goals (Veldhuis and Staun 2009).

In general, radicalization is a process involving either an individual or group whereby they are indoctrinated to a set of beliefs supporting the acts of terrorism. This can be manifested in one's behaviour and attitude. Although radicalism does not equate to terrorism, radicalism typically precedes terrorism (Sageman 2004; Silber and Bhatt 2007).

On the theory of radicalization, which is relevant in explaining youth involvement in terrorism, is the theory of moral disengagement. In the process of radicalization, an individual's sense of morality becomes reversed, making committing terrorism a moral obligation instead of a forbidden crime (Rahimullah, Larmar, and Abdalla 2013, pp. 19–35).

Albert Bandura (1990) outlined a model that explains this transformation. Bandura argued that while moral standards can be strong, they can also be changed through disengagement. Moral disengagement can be influenced by many factors, including the background of individuals which made them receptive to extremist ideology (Travis 2008).

Meanwhile, John Horgan suggests six key factors that may contribute to an individual's involvement in radicalism and terrorism:

1) having an "emotional vulnerability" (feelings of anger, alienation or disenfranchisement), often linked to feelings of being culturally uprooted or displaced and searching for spiritual guidance.
2) being dissatisfied or disillusioned with mainstream political or social protest as a method to produce political change.
3) identifying with the suffering of Muslim victims globally or having personally experienced victimization.
4) having the conviction that violence against the state and its symbols can be morally justified (and this conviction can be "fine-tuned" by a religious figure).
5) gaining rewards from being a member of the group/movement (such as status, respect, and authority over other members).
6) having close social ties and contacts with people experiencing the same set of issues or having some involvement with terrorism through family or other associates (Horgan 2005, pp. 105–6).

It is clear that with all these factors, the personal marginalization and Western double standards in foreign policy are believed to play a crucial role. Individuals often join radical groups for political or religious reasons when searching for moral empowerment. Sageman (2004) who studies about Jihadists found that there are some common patterns just prior to joining the terrorist groups such as being "socially and spiritually alienated and probably in some form of distress". Therefore, these individuals are willing to go to the extreme to prove their moral ground based on religious argument. They have no problem in believing that violence should be paid with violence even in the name of religion.

In this modern age, radicalization is made possible during the recruitment process. This process becomes easy when the Internet is utilized. The Internet, which is cheap and easy to access, has a facilitating and enabling role in maintaining network contacts and reinforcing ideological messages (Christmann 2012, p. 30). However, face-to-face human contact remains crucial in recruitment and in driving radicalization to violence.

Radicalization is related to the ideology of the terrorists. This ideology has a big influence on the shift towards radicalism. According to the International Crisis Group (ICG) (2007), the Salafi movement, particularly the jihadist version (as opposed to the reformist version) opposes the West's oppressive military and political presence in Muslim lands and hence advocates for armed resistance. Members of the Wahhabi movement, while separating themselves from the Salafist, share the Salafist's extreme intolerance for "infidels" or non-Muslims (Schwartz 2007). The Salafism manages to attract many young Muslims to its ideology and struggles because of Muslims' strong connection with the value of *ummah* or brotherhood. This contributes significantly to radicalization. If an individual possesses a strong connection to the Muslim *ummah*, he/she is deeply empathic of the suffering of his/her "brothers and sisters" in Islam around the world. These sufferings often occur at the hands of western governments, either directly or indirectly such as in Iraq, Afghanistan, Bosnia, and Chechnya. Therefore the people who support and elect these governments are also guilty and are legitimate targets for attack (Rahimullah, Larmar, and Abdalla 2013).

To overcome the radicalization of youth, there should be strategies for effective counter-radicalization and de-radicalization in counterterrorism. It is not easy to explain why some individuals join terrorism while others do not as terrorists come from a wide variety of backgrounds (Horgan 2005). Lorenzo Vidino (2009) argues that in counter-radicalization as well as counterterrorism, attempts to dismantle terrorist networks are similar to playing a game of "whack-a-mole" and that governments should take steps to mitigate radicalization to stop people from becoming terrorists. He goes on to argue that anti-radicalization programmes should vary from "convening interfaith meetings to creating government-funded Muslim magazines and TV channels, from promoting lectures of Muslim clerics exposing the theological flaws of al Qaeda's ideology (Salafism) to mentoring projects and professional development seminars" (Vidino 2009, pp. 61–75).

The success of counter-radicalization is measured by the effectiveness of counterterrorism programmes, for example an increase in the amount of community engagement to target and mentor individuals who are susceptible to being recruited into terrorism. But it is difficult to prove that these programmes are able to prevent youth from involving in terrorism. The government counterterrorism programmes should also offer terrorists a pathway out of terrorism by facilitating disengagement and rehabilitation (Rineheart 2010). It is obvious that there should be a mechanism to stop people especially the youth from joining terrorist movements, for example by putting in place preventive laws on terrorism, monitoring the social media particularly jihadists' propaganda websites and countering the spread of ideology such as Salafism. With these approaches, the youth can be prevented from joining terrorist activities.

ISIL Media Propaganda

The ISIL has a vast propaganda machine which sends over 90,000 social media messages every day. A major method is getting the large Islamist publishers in the region to distribute pamphlets, newsletters, magazines, and periodicals advocating for ISIL's ideology, which is to establish a global caliphate rooted in the early years of Islam (Chalk 2015). These materials are available for less than one US dollar, making them easily accessible to the general public. Another important recruitment tactic comes in the form of social media, which has been formative in connecting militants across borders. Facebook, in particular, has been found to connect Indonesian and Malaysian militants to ISIL recruiters. Elsewhere on the Internet, other ISIL members have mastered Twitter and hashtags to spread their messages (Institute for Policy Analysis of Conflict 2014). Additionally, Islamic extremists that have been part of the security environment in Southeast Asia for decades amplify the message of ISIL by contributing to ISIL's social media campaign and assisting ISIL with translation and other media-related recruitment methods (King 2015).

In fact, ISIL has its own news agency called Amaq, which communicates with the global audience (Gotbaum 2016). ISIL also has an official online journal called *Dabiq*, which is named after a northern Syrian town featured in eschatological traditions as one of the battlefields (Ahmad Fauzi 2016). From late 2015 onwards, both Malaysia and Indonesia are targeted by ISIL operations and have been regularly mentioned in *Dabiq*. ISIL sympathizers are encouraged to commit their macabre deeds in any place where ISIL's foes are present, instead of emigrating to Syria and Iraq if circumstances do not permit them to travel:

> As for the Muslim who is unable to perform hijrah from dārulkufr to the Khilāfah, then there is much opportunity for him to strike out against the kāfir enemies of the Islamic State. There are more than seventy crusader nations, tāghūt regimes, apostate armies, rāfidī militias, and sahwah factions for him to choose from. Their interests are located all over the world. He should not hesitate in striking them wherever he can. In addition to killing crusader citizens anywhere on the earth, what, for example, prevents him from targeting Rāfidī communities in Dearborn (Michigan), Los Angeles, and New York City? Or targeting Panamanian diplomatic missions in Jakarta, Doha, and Dubai? Or targeting Japanese diplomatic missions in Bosnia, Malaysia, and Indonesia? (Ahmad Fauzi 2016).

Since July 2014, ISIL has used social media, propaganda, and recruitment videos released by its media wing, Al-Hayat Media Center, to persuade Indonesians, Filipinos, and Malaysians to travel and join the group in Syria and Iraq. The sheer number of Indonesians and Malay-speaking foreign fighters has been enough to form its own fighting unit in Syria, known as Katibah Nusantara. Formalized in September 2014, through a series of *baiah* (pledge of allegiance), Katibah actively recruits in the region, provides a social platform for recruiting, settling in and connecting with other ISIL members, as well as tutorials for logistical and tactical training (*TRENDS Research & Advisory* 2017).

As reported by Reuters, a video produced in June 2016 entitled "Toghut" (sinners against the teachings of Allah) shows a Malaysian ISIL fighter in Syria, along with two other ISIL combatants decapitating three captives. The Malaysian terrorist, identified as Mohd Rafi Udin from Negeri Sembilan, threatened attacks against Malaysian police in the twenty-minute video. The jihadist said in Malay that those fighters who could not go to Syria should travel to the Philippines and fight there. Udin called on jihadists to unite under the leadership of Abu Abdullah, a Philippine extremist leader of Abu Sayyaf militant group, who swore allegiance to ISIL in January 2016. Abu Abdullah, also known as Isnilon Hapilon, was on the FBI's most wanted list with a bounty of US$5 million (RM20 million) on his head. Ayob Khan Mydin Pitchay, director of the Malaysian Police Counter-Terrorism unit, called the latest propaganda video a threat: "We are preparing for potential attacks within six months by two sources, Khatibah Nusantara in the Philippines, and central ISIL" (*RT* 2016).

Besides Abu Sayyaf militant group and Katibah Nusantara, authorities are also worried that more extremist organizations in the region might now unite under Abdullah's command. Just like Abu Sayyaf, Abu Dujana Brigade, Abi Khabib Brigade, Jund Allah Brigade, and Abi Sadr found in the region have also pledged their allegiance to ISIL and its self-proclaimed "caliph", Abu Bakr al-Baghdadi, ISIL's caliphate.

The ISIL has published a local language publication to recruit many more new jihadists in Southeast Asia. The publication called *al-Fatihin* (means the Conquerors in Arabic) was launched on 20 June 2016 in the holy fasting month of Ramadan, with the tagline: "The newspaper for Malay-speaking migrants in the Islamic State". The articles, bringing updates from Iraq and Syria, were mainly written in the Indonesian language, which is comprehensible for many Malay speakers in Southeast Asia. Apart from serving these jihadists, *al-Fatihin* also seeks to target its supporters in Malaysia, Indonesia, Brunei, Singapore, southern Thailand and southern Philippines—areas that overlap with the territory of a Southeast Asian caliphate. Two days after the newspaper was launched, ISIL released a video declaring the Philippines as its territory and called for Southeast Asian jihadists to travel to the Philippines if they could not go to Syria. Recent terrorist attacks in Indonesia and Malaysia have been blamed on ISIL supporters with links to Indonesian and Malaysian jihadists in Syria (Kwok 2016).

However, since 2016, the extremists have shifted their focus to Southeast Asia, where the group has in the past two years stepped up its propaganda campaign and bragged about its child soldiers from the Malay Archipelago. As ISIL loses ground in consolidated territories, there are growing fears that the group will venture overseas, encouraging

ISIL-inspired "lone wolf" attacks. There are also mounting concerns that Indonesian and Malaysian fighters may return home equipped with training and combat experience, harnessed further by staunch ideological beliefs. They may use social media for their propaganda campaign and showcase their attacks in local soils. This chapter will study how ISIL uses media/social media to commit acts of terrorism in Malaysia.

Concerns over Malaysians' Involvement in ISIL

There are several cases demonstrating that ISIL influence has been gaining ground in Malaysia and these involved the local youths. This includes a case where one Malaysian citizen, Ahmad Tarmimi Maliki, aged twenty-six, said to be Malaysia's first ISIL suicide bomber. As reported by the media, a military vehicle driven by Ahmad Tarmimi and carrying explosives managed to kill twenty-five Iraqi soldiers including himself after attacking Iraq Special Forces headquarters in Anbar (Regencia 2014). According to a report by the *Straits Times* (2016, p. 1) on 18 December 2016, "the number of Malaysian suicide bombers who have carried out strikes in Syria for ISIS (ISIL) to nine".

In 2014, three Malaysian women in their twenties travelled to the Middle East as "comfort women" for the ISIL fighters. It is believed that they had offered themselves in sexual comfort roles (*jihad Al-Nikah*) to ISIL fighters to allegedly boost their morale (Lee Shi Ian 2014). However, the Malaysian government later argued that there was no clear proof to suggest that they were "comfort women". Apart from these cases, an estimated forty Malaysian citizens have flown to Syria to fight with ISIL against the Syrian President Bassar Al-Assad's regime (*The Star Online* 2014a).

So far, ISIL employed several methods to lure Malaysians, especially the youth, to join *jihad* in the Middle East. Among them are using propaganda to recruit students to join their struggle and funding the trips and activities.

The Strategy of Recruiting

ISIL recruits a lot of volunteers. The strategy of ISIL so far is to use social media for recruitment, targeting mainly at students. Recently, there are shocking news that ISIL recruiters are also targeting a fourteen-year-old schoolboy to fight alongside militants in Syria. According to Ayob Khan Mydin Pitchay, the Principal Assistant Director Senior Assistant Commissioner, "We found that among those targeted by the recruiter was a Form Two (14 years old) student. The recruiter was communicating with this boy through Facebook, coaxing him to join IS (ISIL) in the war-torn country (Syria)" (*Today Online* 2014, p. 1). The best method for recruiting volunteers is through social media like Facebook and WhatsApp. Ayob said that teenagers are targeted as they are easily misled and manipulated and the recruiter could use and misinterpret Quranic verses to legitimize the objective of fighting against the authorities in Syria. Other example is that of Syamimi Faiqah, aged twenty, a former student of the International Islamic University College, Selangor who had left for Syria on 4 October 2014 to join ISIL after being drawn to it via Facebook (*Today Online* 2014).

In order to combat ISIL, the police made the decision on 15 October 2014 to shut down pro-ISIL websites used to recruit Malaysians. About twelve locally registered websites used by militant recruiters targeting Malaysians were shut down in 2012. These websites had glorified several terrorist groups, including Al-Qaeda, and were known to be responsible for convincing a number of Malaysians to join militant activities. The police now work with the Malaysian Communications and Multimedia Commission to monitor sites which are not only used to recruit but also promote terrorism and extremist beliefs. Other recruitment tools used are Yahoo Messenger and WhatsApp (*The Malaysian Insider* 2014b). However, it is not an easy task to combat ISIL online because the ISIL members from Malaysia actively update their activities in the Middle East for the local audiences. For instance, Muhamad Wanndy Muhamad Jedi, aged twenty-five, used Facebook to upload a video onto Abu Hamzah Al Fateh's Facebook account on 22 February 2015, depicting a beheaded man in Syria. However for the actions depicted in the video, there were a mix of strong support and indifference in the comments thread. The earlier picture of the dead man captured the conversation surrounding it and showed Muhamad Wanndy explaining that he was present when the beheading occurred, and that militants had fired fifty rockets from the same site earlier. He further thanked all those whom he claimed had helped him change, and "dedicated" his journey to Harakat Ilmu Wal Dakwah @ HIDD and friends detained under the Special Offences (Security Measures) Act (SOSMA). Muhamad Wanndy was in Syria with his wife Nor Mahmudah. He was believed to have gone to Syria with her in January 2015. It was understood that Muhamad Wanndy was a member of the new wing of Malaysian and Indonesian militants identified as "Majmu'ah al Arkhabiliy" (Tam 2015, pp. 1–2). Recently, the Malaysian Police confirmed that Muhammad Wanndy had been killed in an attack in Raqqa, Syria on 29 April 2017 (*Aljazeera* 2017).

The police also managed to arrest a militant recruiter, a former civil servant, and a housewife on suspicion of links with the ISIL terror group. The man was detained on 19 March 2015 while he was returning to Malaysia from abroad. The housewife was detained at the Kuala Lumpur International Airport (KLIA) as she was about to travel to a neighbouring country for Syria. Meanwhile, Dr Mahmud Ahmad (a former university lecturer, also known as Abu Handzalah) and Mohd Najib Husen (a sundry shop owner), both aged thirty-six years old, were suspected of recruiting youth for ISIL as well (Farik 2015). According to Khalid Abu Bakar, Inspector-General of the Police, the police had launched a full-scale investigation through the Counter Terrorism Unit to find out if a National Service trainer, who was arrested on 17 December 2015 for attempting to join the ISIL terror group, had influenced National Service (NS) trainees while he was a trainer in Pahang. Police were also looking into whether there were other militant elements in NS camps (Jayamanogaran and Prakash 2014).

ISIL also targets students of institutions of higher learning in Malaysia (*Today Online* 2014). For instance, the police nabbed two students of higher learning institutions. One was a woman aged twenty-seven years old who was married to an ISIL militant via Skype, and was about to leave for Syria to join ISIL on 24 December 2014. The female suspect was a student at a private institution in the Klang Valley. The second suspect, who was arrested in KLIA on 28 December 2014, was a male student aged twenty-two years old of a public university in Perlis. Both were sympathetic to ISIL struggle after watching ISIL's propaganda videos on YouTube (Hariz 2015). Therefore, local public and private universities are frequently monitoring students' activities in order to prevent students from being recruited by ISIL. Rais Yatim, president of the International Islamic University Malaysia (IIUM), said: "The management and staff of the university's security division should check on students' background and curb the increasingly aggressive actions of militant groups in enticing the young through Facebook" (*Malaysiakini* 2014, p. 1).

Furthermore, the Malaysian police managed to detain at least ten people associated with ISIL during multiple raids across Malaysia on 20 August 2015. Among those arrested were six security forces personnel, a kindergarten teacher, and a former interior designer (Kaplan 2015). However, it is still a huge task by the authority to stop any new recruit from joining ISIL. This is even after a video appeared online in April 2015 of several young Malay-speaking Malaysian and possibly Indonesian boys attending religious classes and participating in weapons training in what is believed to be an ISIL-held territory in Iraq or Syria (Kaplan 2015).

Funding

Some Malaysians have gone to the extent of taking personal loans up to RM20,000 from banks and moneylenders in order to join ISIL in the Middle East (*The New Paper* 2015). It has emerged that according to the Special Branch's Counter-Terrorism Division (SB-CTD), the former National Service trainer, aged thirty years old, who was arrested, had taken out a RM20,000 loan. A source from the police said:

> Investigation papers on at least five Malaysian fighters, who were stopped from going over, showed that they had not only disposed of most of their properties, but had also applied for loans, some up to more than RM100,000. Malaysians heading for Syria and Iraq to fight with the ISIL have been taking out bank loans to fund their journey and life there (Farrah and Hariz 2014, pp. 1–2).

Police also had detained two ISIL sympathizers, aged twenty-three and twenty-eight, who worked at a government agency in Kuala Lumpur for channelling funds to new recruits who were planning to travel to Syria to fight alongside ISIL. They were detained on 27 November 2015 under the Security Offences (Special Measures) Act 2012 (SOSMA) (Prakash and Daniele 2014). Noor Rashid Ibrahim, Deputy Inspector-General of

Police, said that the police reportedly investigated a shop in Bandar Baru Bangi for selling militant-themed merchandise on whether profits from the business were utilized to fund ISIL activities. This is a serious matter because the shop could at the same time spread propaganda on behalf of the ISIL (*The Star Online* 2015).

According to the *New Delhi Times*, Malaysia is now at a greater risk of having its youth involved in ISIL as the growth of Muslim-dominated politics has allowed more room for "radical Islam" to spread. This weekly paper argued that although Malaysia is a multireligious country, it manages to keep peace by "appeasing" the local Muslim conservatives. Now there are growing calls for the implementation of *hudud*—a strict Islamic penal code—and increase debates on Islam's role in Malaysia, making the Southeast Asian nation more vulnerable to the ISIL group. Malaysia is giving room for the growing radical Islamic influence through mosques and other organizations, which in turn is having an adverse impact on the youth in Malaysia. Malaysia is particularly vulnerable to extremism due to the existence of radical-leaning political parties and the aggressive ISIL recruitment drive of locals by organizations such as Jamaah Islamiah and Kumpulan Mujahidin Malaysia (*The Malaymail Online* 2015). However, the main problem is also that, according to Ahmad El-Muhammady, a panel member of the Royal Malaysia Police Rehabilitation Programme for terrorist detainees, Malaysians youths in particular who join or support the ISIL believe that it is an honour to be part of the ISIL group (*Free Malaysia Today* 2015). Meanwhile, Akhbar Satar, Director of HELP University's Institute of Crime & Criminology, opined that

> religious departments needed to play a bigger role in the long term to enlighten the people, especially youths, of the true meaning of Islam and what ISIL, which propagates jihad, is all about. Religious departments, like the Department of Islamic Development Malaysia (JAKIM) for example, should go to schools and institutions of higher learning to explain further what ISIL and Jihad were (*Free Malaysia Today* 2015, pp. 1–2).

The anxiety is that if there is no monitoring and engagement of the youth by the government, this will stir the growth of homegrown terrorists who will threaten Malaysian security. All incidents occured have shown that ISIL threats are becoming real in Malaysia. Serious actions should be taken to combat them.

Efforts in Combating ISIL Threats in Malaysia

The assessments of the degree and character of the threat posed by the ISIL in Malaysia might suggest several strategies for combating it. The biggest battle is to counter ISIL ideology. Fighting against ideology is nevertheless a complicated and difficult mission. In this matter, Malaysia needs to come out with various strategies and initiatives to combat the ISIL ideology. This includes monitoring of social media by picking out contents used to recruit and exploit young Malaysians to join the ISIL movement and detained those behind it (Nadaraj 2014). ISIL has been using online media, particularly social media, as its tools for exporting its influence to the global audience. Through this strategy, the government has at least shut down the main source of ISIL's medium of expansion. In this case, censorship against a terror group like ISIL is justifiable for security reasons, but this should not be a slippery slope to justify any other restriction on social media and free expression by the government.

ISIL ideology has in other aspects successfully inspired many radical Islamic movements in Southeast Asia. Recently, many movements sharing the same ideology, such as the threat of Abu Sayyaf in eastern Sabah, have been operating aggressively and are expected to threaten national security. In this case, Malaysia is currently taking pro-active precaution measures to curtail the movements from expanding to eastern Sabah. According to Hishammuddin Hussein, Malaysia's minister of defence, the government had spent RM6 billion to increase

> the defence and security in Sabah, especially the Eastern Sabah Security Command, the airport runaway in Lahad Datu (to accommodate landings by the military aircraft C-130), improving the airforce base in Labuan (for the Hawk fighter jet and acquiring high-capability control radar), and establishing two Forward Operational Bases in the form of sea bases (intended to fight off threats, especially at sea exit points—but also functioning as command centres, intercepting and blocking routes,

surveillance, inspection points and enforcement for control) (*Esscom Times* 2014, p. 1).

In order to prevent Malaysian citizens from going to Iraq and Syria, the Malaysian government works closely with the Interpol and intelligence agencies to monitor the movements of Malaysians travelling to these two countries via transit countries (Fazleena 2014). Apart from that, the Malaysian government has also come out with regional initiatives which called for regional cooperation in Southeast Asia to prevent the threats from getting a foothold in this region. Regional cooperation and intelligence sharing are important to halt the movements from advancing. Hishammuddin Hussein claimed that: "We cannot work in isolation. We need to work with our friends and our neighbours" (*The Star Online* 2014b, pp. 1–2). Hishammuddin strongly requested for greater cooperation particularly on regional intelligence sharing as this is important to detect and combat an increasingly mobile and global threat. The exchange of intelligence between neighbouring countries is pivotal in combating the growing threat of the ISIL influence in Malaysia. Particularly, Malaysia, Indonesia, the Philippines, Thailand and Singapore have experiences of dealing with terrorists and extremist movements in the past. Aside from neighbouring countries, information gathered from other countries such as the United States, which is already dealing with the ISIL in the Middle East, might prove to be useful in assisting Malaysia on the actions needed to combat against terrorism.

Meanwhile, in Kuala Lumpur on 15 September 2015, the Malaysian authorities have also arrested Ardit Ferizi, a twenty-year-old Kosovo citizen and Malaysia-based hacker, who was accused by the Malaysian authorities and the US Justice Department of hacking and stealing the personal information of US military members. According to the US government,

> Ferizi was accused of hacking into the computer system of a company in the US and stole personally identifiable information of more than 1,000 US service members and federal employees. He later allegedly gave that information to several ISIL figures, including a prominent propagandist for the group namely Junaid Hussein, a British hacker who was active

on social media recruiting Westerners to join ISIL (Perez, Shoichet, and Bruer 2015, p. 1).

The arrest of Ferizi was a collaborative effort between the authorities from the United States and Malaysia.

In order to counter people such as Ferizi, Home Minister Ahmad Zahid Hamidi, at a meeting with US Secretary of State John Kerry in Washington on 10 October 2015, confirmed that a Regional Digital Counter-Messaging Communications Centre would be set up in Kuala Lumpur. The Centre would take the battle against ISIL in the cyberspace with the United States assisting Malaysia in three aspects namely training, operations and equipment. Kerry and Zahid also jointly signed the Homeland Security Presidential Directive No. 6 (HSPD-6) stating the commitment of Malaysia and the United States to share information of 86,000 potential and suspected terrorists in the United States particularly and in various countries (*Straits Times* 2015). Ferizi was extradited to the United States and was sentenced to twenty years imprisonment by the US Court on 23 September 2016 (*Associate Press* 2016).

Prime Minister Najib Tun Razak tabled a nineteen-page White Paper entitled "Towards Handling Threats of Islamic State" in Parliament on 26 November 2014. He proposed a new law to be enacted as a strategy to combat ISIL's threats. He said:

> The involvement of Malaysians in militant activities using the name of Islam has tarnished the country's image and affected the sanctity of Islam. These militants, who are equipped with military expertise, logistics and capability to make explosive materials, will be able to make individual attacks, from IS (ISIL) cell groups in Malaysia and establish a network with militants in the region, if action is not taken (*The Sun* 2014, pp. 1–2).

The White Paper also intended to strengthen present laws such as the Prevention of Crime (Amendments and Extensions) Act 2013 (POCA), SOSMA, and the Penal Code to specifically tackle militant activities. Therefore, the Special Measures Against Terrorism in Foreign Countries Act and the Prevention of Terrorism Act (POTA) were tabled in the Parliament. POTA, for instance, would allow authorities to detain suspects indefinitely without trial. It will create a five-to-eight member Prevention of Terrorism Board to make decisions on detention or restriction orders as well as a Registrar containing fingerprints and photographs of persons detained. On the other hand, the Special Measures Against Terrorism in Foreign Countries would enable authorities to seize travel documents of citizens or foreigners believed to be engaging in or abetting terrorist acts. Several amendments to existing laws would also tighten restrictions in this regard. For example, a proposed amendment to the penal code would make it an offense to receive training from terrorist groups and other perpetrators (*The Malaysian Insider* 2015a, p. 1).

POTA was passed by the Parliament on 7 April 2015 and all bills will be enforced by the end of 2016. However, there is also a concern whether the restrictions could be too harsh and undermine human rights (*The Diplomat* 2015).

Until January 2017, the Malaysian authorities have charged 122 suspects, including several women. They were sixty-two militants who had been found guilty under several laws. Furthermore, there were thirty-eight people that had been detained under POCA and eighteen people under POTA. For instance, the High Court sentenced Yazid Sufaat and Muhammad Hilmi Hasim to seven years in jail in accordance to Section 130M of the Penal Code on 27 January 2016. Both detainees pleaded guilty to an alternative charge of omitting information relating to terrorist acts (*The Malaymail Online* 2016). The National Fatwa Council (Islamic Council) had also listed "ISIL as a terrorist group and the deaths of Muslims due to ISIL activities cannot be categorized as martyrdom" (*The Sun* 2014, pp. 1–2).

There is a concern that ISIL uses religious expression to spread its influences and to call for new recruits in waging war against the government and people. Current Malaysian Defence Minister Mohamad Sabu on 24 April 2019 urged for greater alertness against the threat of ISIS on the Internet because even after the defeat of ISIL in Iraq and Syria and terror attacks in Sri Lanka, the battleground in cyberspace still continues. According to Mohamad (Mering 2019, p. 1), "Cyber-attacks can be very complicated to deal with and requires totally new doctrine for us to counter it effectively. Cyber defence is not about physical strength, but wit and sharpness. We need new types of soldiers, one with sound knowledge in information technology."

In an effort to counter the narratives of ISIL propaganda in the cyberspace, the Malaysia government needs its cyber defence capabilities to be enhanced by working together with other countries in a cyber defence network. For instance, the Malaysia police have initiated the Counter Messaging Centre (CMC) to monitor the use of social media by ISIL and any terror groups in order to stop the spread of their radical ideology and to counter their narratives and rhetoric. The Ministry of Defence has also formed the Cyber Defence Operation Centre (CDOC) to reduce this non-traditional security threat. For Mohamad, there are two ways to deal with the ISIL threat: first, promoting a better understanding of various religions and strengthening the firearms control. He explained:

> With deeper understanding about religions, we can eliminate misjudgment and avoid resentment and hostility. Virtual caliphate and cyber-attacks require us to have a better control over the cyberspace ... Threats posed by Daesh (ISIL) are now greater due to the advancement of technology. Combating terrorism requires better cooperative security strategies in various forms, be it hard or soft approaches ... There is no 'one size fits all' in terms of violent extremist or terrorist profile, set of motivations, level of radicalisation and extremism, and their trajectories. Similarly, counter terrorism responses and solutions. It is fundamental that we be united to fight against terrorism effectively (Mering 2019).

Similarly, Anwar Ibrahim argued that freedom of expression must then become secondary to the right to dignity and freedom from harassment or vilification on account of ethnic or religious differences. For Anwar, "Terrorists are murderers. And they will continue to kill and maim not just to do battle against freedom of speech, but against generally the free world, including Muslims" (*The Malaysian Insider* 2015b). Clearly, ISIL has tarnished the image of Islam by using the Islamization agenda as part of its struggles. ISIL opted for violence because of its failure to understand Islam wholly. Anwar urged all Muslims to return to true Islamic teachings and to reject the narrative from ISIL (*The Malaysian Insider* 2014c).

Conclusion

Extreme religious expression glorifing terrorism definitely goes beyond the principle of free speech. Eric Barendt (2009, p. 447) explained lengthly about the free speech principle and its incompatibility with speech encouraging terrorism. He argued that:

> We should first distinguish from expression of general encouragement, or of a defence, of terrorism, the expression of a strong imperative to someone about to detonate a bomb or pull a trigger ('Kill him' or 'Slaughter these infidel'). The latter is so closely linked to the violent act that it should be characterized as conduct or action, rather than speech, and so falls altogether outside of freedom of speech principle. The expression is communicated immediately before act, perhaps as an instruction to start it, so it seems right to treat it as part of the conduct itself.

Barendt's argument is in line with John Stuart Mill (1991, p. 62) who once argued:

> An opinion that corn-dealers are starvers of the poor, or that private property is robbery ... may justly incur punishment when delivered orally to an excited mob assembled before the house of a corn dealer, or when handled about among the same mob in the form of a placard.

It is clear that radicalizing people for terrorism goes beyond the principle of free speech and this should be restricted legally. ISIL clearly uses extreme religious expression to glorify terrorism and manipulate people to join its violent activities.

The violence against civilians and innocent people by ISIL that has been widely published on the Internet since August 2014, indicates that this extremist group poses a global threat to the international community. ISIL's goal of restoring the caliphate system suggests that the group is concerned about pursuing political power and this contradicts with Islamic teachings. It clearly shows that the act of ISIL could be referred to as crimes. The growing number of foreign fighters joining ISIL from around the world shows that this extremist group is capable of pursuing its goals strategically and deliberately. As for now, the major concern for Malaysia is to counter the spread of ISIL ideology, especially among Malaysian youths as social media is ISIL's effective tool for recruitment and gaining influence (Azizuddin 2016).

So far the threats of ISIL in Malaysia are manageable and relatively under control. However, the actions of previous extremist movements in Malaysia and others in Southeast Asian countries have shown that the threat of the ISIL movement is real and should not be taken lightly as it can harm regional and national security. Therefore, cooperation among countries is the key to combat this issue. Efforts should be made to involve all stakeholders including civil society to increase their awareness of the potential threat of this extremist movement. Thus, religious expression needs to be managed properly by the authorities, otherwise it can be manipulated for subversive activities such as radicalism, extremism and terrorism.

6

NEW MALAYSIA UNDER PAKATAN HARAPAN

Introduction

According to Prime Minister Najib and his predecessors, Malaysia's culturally diverse population is the main reason additional restrictions have consistently been placed on the population's civil liberties. Thus, under the banner of "national security", the government limits freedom of speech to safeguard race relations and to ensure national stability. Further, while democracy as a political ideal is still sought after, restrictions are imposed on political processes to protect other fundamental values. Unlike the West, it is not so much the restriction of freedom of speech that is being questioned in Malaysia but the government's domination of the channels of political expression which it uses to weaken the opposition and eliminate criticism. Thus, the main problem in Malaysia lies in the ruling government's willingness to exploit the country's fragile political situation for its own ends by routinely suppressing dissent and criticism from political opposition, non-governmental organizations (NGOs), and the public.

However, Prime Minister Najib has rebuffed such claims, saying, on the contrary, his government is open to criticism. While denouncing opposition leaders and foreigners, whom he blamed for spreading falsehoods and fake news, Najib said that the media has a duty to:

> fight to the last this tide of fake and false news that threatens to turn truth into a purely subjective matter, with little relation to the actual facts ... The government of Malaysia will be on your side ... All we ask in return is the opportunity to remind you to rely in your reporting and sourcing—in whichever country that may be—not on rumours, not on unsourced anonymous quotes, and not on invented propaganda, no matter how persuasively it may be presented, but on verified facts. We have no fear of the facts: for they are undisputed. For the future of newspapers, both in print and online, to be as healthy as we all want and need it to be, I am sure (*Channel News Asia* 2017).

Najib even argued that "free speech is thriving in Malaysia", compared to other nations in the region, before going on to blame the false and fake news tyrannizing social media now plaguing the country.

Unsurprisingly, many have criticized Najib's comment that "free speech is thriving in Malaysia". For example, an NGO called Article 19 declared that it was astonished with the statement because it was in stark contrast with "the repressive laws and policies facing Malaysians who wish to exercise their rights to freedom of speech, opinion, or expression, particularly on issues deemed sensitive to the ruling government, with hundreds arrested and charged during his term". In particular, Article 19 was concerned that Najib seemed to blame "foreign activists" for fabricating the notion of "crackdowns on free speech in Malaysia". In fact, not only "foreign activists" but many local civil society organizations, independent journalists, and members of the public have criticized the government for the dismal state of free speech in Malaysia (Article 19, 2017).

It must be said that in his first term as prime minister (2009–13), Najib (2017, p. 1) did demonstrate a willingness to support freedom of political speech by amending the Printing Presses and Publications Act 1984 (PPPA) and abolishing the Internal Security Act (ISA) and the Emergency Ordinance (EO), and he indeed continued to remind people of these early policies:

> We recognize the vital role that newspapers play in free societies, and my government has opened up the space for the democratic scrutiny

they rightfully bring to bear. We eliminated the bans on opposition party newspapers; we removed the annual renewal requirement for printing licences from the 1984 Printing Presses and Publications Act; and we opened up the Home Ministry's authority to block, allow, or revoke licences to judicial review.

However, since the 13th General Election in 2013, Najib has imposed more restrictions on freedom of expression by introducing such laws as the Prevention of Terrorism Act (POTA), the Security Offences Special Measures Act (SOSMA), and by retaining and strengthening the Sedition Act. As a result, many have condemned the prime minister for regressing, rather than progressing, toward complete democratization. His actions have gravely impeded those opposing his rule, both from within and outside his party, preventing them from competing equally in the political arena. Najib's use of the Sedition Act has been especially prevalent, with politicians, artists, human rights defenders, lawyers, journalists, students, academics, and members of the general public investigated, arrested, and even charged for expressing opinions deemed detrimental to the country. As mentioned in Human Rights Watch's forty-page report, *Deepening the Culture of Fear: The Criminalization of Peaceful Expression in Malaysia*, "the government's use of broad, vaguely worded laws to criminalize peaceful speech and assembly" is worrying and raises questions about the future of freedom of political speech in Malaysia. As such, Human Rights Watch urged "the Malaysian government to cease using criminal laws against peaceful speech and protests, and to bring its laws and policies into line with international human rights law and standards for the protection of freedom of speech and assembly" (Hunt 2016, p. 1).

Hence, it is obvious that the government limits the right to freedom of speech, not simply to protect national security against hate speech as Najib has claimed, but to insulate it from criticism and to preserve its political power and self-interest. Local civil society groups are particularly sceptical of the future of these rights in Malaysia, pointing to the current government's continued policies to regulate and suppress freedom of political speech. For example, the decision to ban the G25 book, *Breaking the Silence: Voices of Moderation—Islam in a Constitutional Democracy* (for promoting liberalism and pluralism)—even though the book was published in 2015 without any issue—has been questioned.

Freedom of expression is vital for democracy and denying constructive and peaceful expressions will only hamper the democratic process and democratization.

On this matter, Malaysia seems to have regressed rather than progressed. The chairman of Malaysian Human Rights Commission (SUHAKAM), Razali Ismail, explained that freedom of opinion and expression formed the foundation for every democratic society because exercising such rights "are indispensable conditions for the full development of a person" (*The Star Online* 2017). Accordingly, he urged the government to ratify the International Covenant on Civil and Political Rights (ICCPR) because unless legitimate democratic values are allowed to flourish and the government displays political will to promote and implement such rights, there appears little hope for the future of freedom of political speech in Malaysia.

Najib, however, made a surprise move on 1 March 2018 (two months before the 2018 general election) when he launched the National Human Rights Action Plan (NHRAP), demonstrating Malaysia's commitment to guarantee and safeguard human rights. He said that this is in line with the agenda and vision of the National Transformation 2050 (TN50) initiative, which has gathered the people's views, feedback and aspirations to ensure the success of its implementation. The NHRAP document, according to Najib, was developed in accordance with UN international standards. It outlined five key thrusts:

1. The first is civil and political rights, with the prime minister citing as example the abolition of the Internal Security Act 1960 and the formation of the Peaceful Assembly Act 2012 during his tenure. The abolition of the mandatory death sentence for convicted drug traffickers under Section 39B of the Dangerous Drugs Act 1952 has elicited praise from the European Union.
2. The second thrust is economic, social and cultural rights which included the rights to basic needs, education and cultural practices.
3. The third is the rights of vulnerable people which focuses on five groups, namely women, children, the disabled, senior citizens and refugees. For example, the government introduced the Sexual Offences against Children Act 2017, which led to the establishment of the first Court on Sexual Crimes against Children, not only in Malaysia, but also in Southeast Asia.

4. The fourth thrust is on human rights among the Orang Asli and the natives of Sabah and Sarawak.
5. The fifth is Malaysia's international obligation relating to human rights (*Free Malaysia Today* 2018).[1]

It seems that this was the last attempt by Najib to boost his image, particularly abroad, before the general election. Unfortunately, it is too late. Najib was never able to see the implementation of NHRAP when his government called for the dissolution of parliament on 6 April 2018 paving way for the next general election.

Malaysia held its 14th general election (GE14) on 9 May 2018 as declared by the Election Commission of Malaysia. This is the first time that three coalition parties, namely Barisan Nasional (BN), Pakatan Harapan (PH) and Gagasan Sejahtera (GS) competed with each other to rule Malaysia for the next five years. Prime Minister Najib Razak, who led BN, aimed for a second mandate since 2009. However, he was challenged by his former mentor and also the longest serving prime minister for twenty-two years in Malaysia, Mahathir Mohamad. Amid the scandal surrounding Najib regarding the 1Malaysia Development Berhad (1MDB) issue, Mahathir formed the PH and collaborated with his former political foe, Anwar Ibrahim, to run against Najib. It was a comeback for Mahathir after retiring in 2003. The PH was formerly called Pakatan Rakyat (PR) when it coalesced with the Malaysian Islamic Party (PAS). However, PAS decided to leave the coalition and formed another coalition with smaller parties and NGOs because of policy disagreements over *Syariah* law and Malay unity (Azizuddin 2015). The PAS-led coalition was named Gagasan Sejahtera.

The outcome of GE14 was that an opposition alliance led by Malaysia's former ruler Mahathir Mohamad had won a majority in parliament, a shock victory that ends the ruling BN coalition's sixty-year grip on power. The PH won 113 seats—one more than required for a simple majority—and the BN had 79 seats in the 222-member parliament. Bridget Welsh, a Southeast Asia expert at John Cabot University in Rome, Italy attributed the opposition's surprising gains to Mahathir. Welsh argued: "The person who has made this happen is Mahathir. He has been a significant game changer. He made people feel that a transition of power is possible ... This is a repudiation of Najib's government from all walks of life from the very rural northern states to the more industrial southern coast" (*Aljazeera* 2018). The opposition was also sweeping state elections, including Johor state where the dominant Malay party was founded. BN's rout was made possible by a "Malaysian tsunami", in which all major ethnic groups turned out to vote against the ruling coalition. John Sifton, Human Rights Watch's Asia advocacy director, said: "Nothing less than a historic political earthquake is under way in Malaysia right now" (*Aljazeera* 2018). The new PH promises to uphold freedom of political speech in Malaysia.

Mahathir has obviously sent a signal that he will uphold free speech in a "New Malaysia" under the PH government. For instance, Mahathir instructed the police not to prosecute a man who was arrested for insulting him (Ramzy 2018). During the campaign period, PH released a manifesto pledging to review and potentially abolish regulations that undermine free speech (Palatino 2018). These included the Sedition Act 1948, Prevention of Crime Act 1959, Prevention of Terrorism Act 2015, Communications and Multimedia Act 1998, and the Anti-Fake News Act 2018. Deputy Minister in the Prime Minister's Office, Hanipa Maidin, reiterated the commitment of PH to repeal repressive laws but asked for patience as the government prepares for broader reforms in the bureaucracy: "I only hope the people can be a little more patient with us, just as we have been very patient with BN over the past 60 years. … This is because there is far too much damage left by the previous regime for us and for you. This is not an excuse, but a sincere request from us" (Palatino 2018). Another official affirmed the intention of the government to remove controversial laws such as the Anti-Fake News Act, the Universities and University Colleges Act (UUCA), and SOSMA. Tommy Thomas, who was appointed as Malaysia's new attorney general in 2018, said that repealing "oppressive laws" is one of the government's first legal priorities. He specifically named the fake news law and a national goods and services tax, adding that: "the list of such laws is pretty long". Thomas also declared his support for free speech by saying that: "I am happy for everybody to criticize me; it's part of free speech. … In fact, I'd rather listen to criticism than praises" (Ramzy 2018).

Global Civil Society Alliance (CIVICUS) (2018) welcomes the acquittals of three people who have been charged under the draconian Sedition Act. For example, political cartoonist Zulkiflee Anwar Ul

Haque (Zunar) has been on trial for nine tweets he posted following a controversial court ruling in 2015, upholding the conviction and five-year prison sentence of opposition leader Anwar Ibrahim. Zunar's satirical cartoons have been sharply critical of the previous BN government. Moreover, human rights lawyer Surendran had been charged with sedition in 2014 for comments he made in a YouTube video, criticizing Prime Minister Najib Razak while parliamentarian Sivarasa Rasiah was charged in 2015 for his claims of a political conspiracy between the government and the judiciary against Anwar (Ramzy 2018).

The Malaysian Communications and Multimedia Commission (MCMC) has used broad powers to block websites reporting on the 1MDB corruption scandal, including the UK-based Sarawak Report and regional news outlet, The Asia Sentinel. The MCMC decided to unblock the Sarawak Report and The Medium on 17 May 2018 (Article 19, 2018). In his address to the 73rd United Nations General Assembly on 28 September 2018, Mahathir has pledged that Putrajaya will ratify all remaining core UN instruments related to the protection of human rights. However, Putrajaya will not accept calls for lesbian, gay, bisexual and transgender (LGBT) rights and same-sex marriage. Mahathir said that LGBT rights and same-sex marriages would remain unacceptable to Malaysians, despite their acceptance elsewhere in the world (Jamny Rosli 2018). At the same time, the government condemns any harmful attack or discrimination against these groups.

Hate Speech

Mahathir gave a statement in the wake of the riots in the vicinity of the Seafield Sri Maha Mariamman Temple in USJ 25, near Subang Jaya, on 26 and 27 November 2018 (*Daily Express* 2018). He said: "No one can act as one likes in violation of the law and cause anxiety among the people and chaos in the country." It is not the intention of the government to punish anyone blindly but democracy has its limits and everyone must understand these boundaries. Mahathir emphasized again that the incident is not racial or religious in nature but a criminal act which should not be given any room to ruin the inter-racial relations in the country. The government will not hesitate to take firm actions against those who try to challenge the country's laws. Mahathir said that his government has pledged not to impose any barrier to news reporting and communications but this freedom must be treated with responsibility and not be used to exploit circumstances that may lead to inter-racial breakups and disharmony. The riots on 26 and 27 November 2018 near the temple resulted in the death of a firefighter Muhammad Adib Mohd Kassim—the Coroner's Court on 27 September 2019 ruled that Adib's death was a result of a criminal act—, while several other people were also hurt, twenty-three cars torched and public and private property damaged. The police had arrested thirty people to assist in the investigation into the riots. This incident raised concern about hate speech and how Malaysia should have a tougher law to eliminate hate speech.

Salleh Buang (2019) said:

> Free speech is the freedom to voice out our thoughts and expressions without restrictions, whilst hate speech is the abuse of this freedom to harm others, or speech intended to cause violence. Put differently, free speech means we can say whatever we want. Hate speech is when we say things that are offensive or harmful, targeted at a particular person or group of people.

In July 2018, Minister in the Prime Minister's Office, Mujahid Yusof Rawa, proposed three new laws to criminalize hate speech—the Anti-Discrimination Act, the National Harmony and Reconciliation Commission Act, and the Religious and Racial Hatred Act. So far, there are no new developments to the proposal. In September 2018, Communications and Multimedia Minister Gobind Singh Deo stated that there is a need to push ahead for laws on hate speech. He said that such laws must have an "extra-territorial reach" to facilitate the prosecution of persons who reside abroad. Gobind was referring to a "turban remark" by a London-based blogger against a senior Bukit Aman officer, Amar Singh, which he regarded as an attack against, not only the officer, but also the entire Sikh community (Salleh 2019).

Thousands rallied at Dataran Merdeka, Kuala Lumpur on 8 December 2018 to celebrate the government's decision not to ratify the United Nation's International Convention on the Elimination of All Forms of Racial Discrimination (ICERD). In late November 2018, before the ICERD rally, the National Patriots Association (Patriot) president, Brigadier-General (Rtd) Mohamad Arshad Raji urged the police to monitor all hate speeches and messages pertaining to the ICERD rally. He was concerned about incendiary speeches and messages on social media that may lead to chaos.

Many do not know that by ratifying ICERD, Malaysia would have a mechanism to eradicate hate speech. Japan enacted its Hate Speech Act in May 2016 but it has no punitive provision (Salleh 2019). The law was passed to comply with ICERD. At the international level, there are two UN conventions containing provisions relating to hate speech. One is the International covenant on Civil and Political Rights (ICCPR) which states in Article 20(2) that, "Any advocacy of national, racial or religious hatred that constitutes incitement to discrimination, hostility or violence shall be prohibited by law." The second one is ICERD which states in Article 4(a) that all state parties "shall declare an offence punishable by law all dissemination of ideas based on racial superiority or hatred, incitement to racial discrimination, as well as all acts of violence or incitement to such acts against any race or group of persons of another colour or ethnic origin" (Salleh 2019).

According to Salleh Buang (2019), Malaysia has unfortunately never ratified ICCPR and has recently declared that it will not ratify ICERD. So, where does that leave us? To counter hate speeches, the police invoke Section 504 (intentional insult to provoke a breach of the peace) and Section 506 (criminal intimidation) of the Penal Code. For hate speeches via social media, Section 211 of Act 588 (dealing with offensive content) can be considered.

Recently, there are two cases which stirred a debate among politicians and civil society activists. First is the case of human rights lawyer and activist Fadiah Nadwa Fikri who was summoned by the police in July 2018 for questioning the role of monarchy in politics in her blog. Fadiah is now under probe for posting an allegedly seditious content online. The police are investigating her under Section 4 (1) of the Sedition Act 1948 and Section 233 of the Communications and Multimedia Act 1998. The Centre for Independent Journalism (CIJ) condemned the investigation and advised the police and the government to stop using draconian laws while the Parliament is considering the repeal of these measures (Palatino 2018). Second, on 26 December 2018, the police arrested Azwanddin Hamzah, president of a right-wing NGO called Jaringan Melayu Malaysia (JMM), after he threatened to attack a police station during a rally in

Klang, Selangor. The police also confirmed that Azwanddin would be investigated for making insults against Minister in the Prime Minister's Office P. Waytha Moorthy and Primary Industries Minister Teresa Kok. Azwanddin had uttered a derogatory term on Waytha Moorthy, and accused Kok of being involved in the temple riot and had links to the developer (Salleh 2019).

Furthermore in blasphemy cases, a Malaysian was sentenced to more than ten years' jail and three others were charged over insults against Islam and the Prophet Muhammad on social media on 9 March 2019. All four were charged under laws against causing racial disharmony, incitement, and misusing communication networks. The sentence is believed to be the harshest of such penalty on record in the Muslim-majority country. The Inspector-General of Police, Mohamad Fuzi Harun, said in a statement that the person, who was not identified, had pleaded guilty to ten charges of misusing communication networks. The offence carries a maximum penalty of one year in jail or a fine of up to RM50,000 (US$12,228) or both. Minister in charge of Religious Affairs, Mujahid Yusof Rawa, said that the Department of Islamic Development Malaysia (JAKIM) had set up a unit to monitor writings and communications insulting Islam and Prophet Muhammad. His ministry would not compromise on any acts insulting the religion and called for punishments against those found guilty of such acts (*New Straits Times* 2019). In fact, Zamri Abd Razak, a fifty-two-year-old part-time photographer, pleaded guilty in the Sessions Court to two counts of insulting the Hindu religion on his Facebook page. He was charged under Section 233 (1)(a) of the Communications and Multimedia Act, which carries a maximum RM50,000 fine, maximum one year's jail or both (Chow 2019). Hence under the PH government, any racial and religious motivated hatred and abuse will be punished by law. Insulting any religion is an offence under Malaysia's laws.

In another case, Wan Ji Wan Hussin, an Islamic preacher, was sent to prison on 9 July 2019 after the High Court rejected his appeal for making seditious remarks, publishing religious words deemed insulting against Sultan Sharafuddin Idris Shah of Selangor on his Facebook account, wanji.attaaduddi, on 5 November 2012. He was charged under Section 4 (1) of the Sedition Act 1948. He was initially sentenced to nine months imprisonment in April 2018 by the Sessions Court, but the sentence was increased to twelve months by High Court judge Abdul Halim Aman on 9 July 2019. Critics of the Sedition Act rallied after Wan Ji and criticized the PH government who pledged to repeal the law. Prime Minister Mahathir told the Parliament on 11 July 2019 that his administration is committed to repealing the law and replacing it with another suitable legislation (Chong 2019).

Inculcation of Islamic Values Continued

Since the end of GE14, the narrative of Islam is dominated by UMNO and PAS. Both parties collaborate in order to face PH and at the same time accuse PH of moving away from protecting Malay interests and Islam in the country. The narrative brought by UMNO and PAS dominated the campaign period in at least three by-elections namely Cameron Highland, Semenyih and Rantau, where all three were won by BN candidates defeating the PH. Prior to those by-elections, there were four by-elections namely Sungai Kandis, Balakong, Seri Setia and Port Dickson, which were won by the PH candidates, including Anwar Ibrahim who made a comeback in Port Dickson. Salahuddin Ayub, the minister of agriculture and agro-based industry and deputy president of Amanah Party, claimed that:

> Malays fear that Islam is no longer relevant under the PH government, yet many did not talk about the failure of Tabung Haji or Felda. Did this happen under PH or what? ... You want to blame Pakatan Harapan because Islam is supposedly eroded under our administration? We are only seven months in compared to 60 years (of BN and Perikatan administration) (Dzulkifly 2019).

Salahuddin condemned the opposition UMNO and PAS for spreading religious and racial hatred to weaken the PH government.

Mahathir dismissed claims that PH will not safeguard Islam. He reiterated that the government will not do anything contrary to Islamic teachings, given that Islam is the country's official religion as embodied in the Federal Constitution. He further said that there are leaders who claimed to be upholding Islam but acted against tenets of the religion instead. He argued that: "We know that there are many who claim that they supposedly protect Islam but we find that their actions are contrary to Islam … We will not hesitate to administer in accordance with Islam and (we) will prove why their policies and stance are not in accordance with the true Islam" (Tham 2018).

Muhyiddin Yassin, home minister and president of BERSATU Party, supported Mahathir's view by saying, as reported by *Bernama*, that:

> Those wild speculations (from UMNO and PAS) have been proven wrong. The Malay rulers are still heads of religion in their respective States, JAKIM still exists and it is quite impossible for the law allowing LGBT culture and same-sex marriage to be passed by the Parliament when the majority of the members are Muslims who adhere to the practice of the *Sunnah Wal Jamaah* (Sunni Islam) (*The Edge Markets* 2018).

He explained that UMNO and PAS were daydreaming if they thought they could win the next general election by spreading lies based on religious sentiments.

What is interesting is that Mahathir reinstated his commitment to uphold his policy of the Inculcation of Islamic Values, pioneered by him. In his meeting with thirty-seven Muslim scholars in the Prime Minister's Office on 31 July 2018, he said that he will continue with the policy and will make sure that the PH government implement Islamic practices in Malaysia according to Islamic teachings from the al-Quran and Sunnah. Among those present in the meeting were the Mufti of Federal Territory Zulkifli Mohamad al-Bakri, Perlis Mufti Mohd Asri Zainul Abidin, Fellow and Lecturer of Islamic Centre in the Faculty of Theology, University of Oxford, United Kingdom, Muhammad Afifi Al-Akiti, famous preacher Habib Ali Zaenal Abidin Abu Bakar Al-Hamid, Minister in the Prime Minister's Office Mujahid Yusof Rawa and Deputy Minister Fuziah Salleh. Mahathir also shared the government's aspiration of making Malaysia as the model of contemporary Islam following its "*Rahmatan Lil 'Alamin*" brand of Islam, which means "blessings to all creations" by putting such a philosophy into practice in their daily routines (Saifulizam Mohamad 2018).

The PH government's stance on the policy caused concerns among some segments of society who worry that the PH will move away from a moderate to a hardliner stance in order to win the hearts and minds of the

Malay Muslims. Tawfik Ismail, who was a member of parliament (MP) for Sungai Benut between 1986 and 1990, claimed that Mahathir's Inculcation of Islamic Values caused deep divisions between the different races and even within the Muslim community. He asked PH to stake its position on the matter. Tawfik also took PH to task for its alleged lack of firmness in opposing PAS President Abdul Hadi Awang's tabling of a private member's bill to amend the *Syariah* Courts (Criminal Jurisdiction) Act 1965, which was intended to arm the *Syariah* courts with greater powers. He argued:

> It was deeply disappointing that the Malay and Muslim MPs in Pakatan did not stand up against Hadi … If Pakatan MPs cannot uphold their oath to defend the constitution, then there is little to choose between Barisan Nasional and Pakatan (PH) … The battle for the Malay vote and, at the moment, the fear of going against the *ulama* version of Islam by both sides is a disappointment to progressive Malays as well as other ethnic groups (Sheith Khidhir 2018).

When it comes to Islam in Malaysia, Chandra Muzaffar (2018) argued that a more formidable challenge facing PH is to develop a perception of Islam among Muslims and non-Muslims that

> it is an inclusive, universal religion capable of fulfilling its role as the ultimate reference for guiding values and principles in a multi-religious society where it is constitutionally recognised as the religion of the federation. This is a role it will not be able to play as long as Islam is projected as an exclusive faith over-emphasising form over substance and preoccupied with a punish and prohibit (2P) approach towards the practice of the religion.

However, Mahathir also continued to reassure Malaysians that Islam will be protected under the PH government and there will be no discrimination against any other religion as long as he is in power (Tham 2018). Muhyiddin also proposed the setting up of an Ummah Consensus Council comprising representatives of government and non-governmental organizations to contribute to the development of the *ummah* in Malaysia. Fuziah Salleh, deputy minister in the Prime Minister's Office, in her opening speech at the 61st International al-Quran Recital and Memorisation Assembly at Kuala Lumpur Convention Centre (KLCC) on 15 April 2019, reconfirmed that Malaysia promotes Islamic values and culture through the message of *"Rahmatan Lil 'Alamin"* and the *Maqasid Syariah*, by saying: "It is translated through one's actions and superior personality, and thus forms a model of a multi-racial Islamic country that can be emulated by the outside world" (*Bernama* 2019a).

The concept of *Maqasid Syariah* is elevated into the national administrative policy. It is the primary key to protecting, benefitting, preventing harm and damage, and is the main thrust in all aspects of administration. Mujahid said that the effort is part of the initiative to allocate responsibility to religious agencies to implement the seven strategic plans which will make Malaysia a model (or *manhaj Malizi*) of progressive and inclusive Islamic administration by 2025. The seven clusters are law and justice; education and human development; *dakwah* and media; socio-economics; *haj* management and *halal* certification; mosque management; and *Maqasid* research and culture.

The PH government is also reviewing several existing acts under the *Syariah* courts, including the *Syariah* Courts (Criminal Jurisdiction) Act (or RUU355), in order to strengthen Islamic institutions. Fuziah Salleh, deputy minister in the Prime Minister's Office, mentioned in the Parliament: "In relation to the *Syariah* Courts (Criminal Jurisdiction) Act and other relevant laws, we are looking at them in more detail and … we are committed, ready to amend the act in empowering the *Syariah* Courts as a whole." Among efforts to uplift the court's position are harmonization between *Syariah* and civil laws, the competence of *Syariah* judges and prosecutors, governance as well as infrastructure of the *Syariah* courts (*The Star Online* 2018b). These are part of the institutional reforms planned by the PH government after it took over power in 2018.

The PH government also tries to differentiate the public space from the private space from the perspective of Islam. This is clear in the case of *khalwat* (close proximity). Mujahid has also indicated an end to the middle-of-the-night vice raids by religious authorities investigating reports of *khalwat* or other alleged wrongdoings in the personal space. He believes that what Muslims do behind closed doors is none of the government's business, by saying:

> Let's say you commit something within your personal, individual sphere—I will not interfere. For example, consumption of alcohol is

wrong for a Muslim, but if you consume it within your sphere, then as part of the government, I will not interfere. My concern is what goes on in public that encroaches on sensitivity, legality or criminality. Only then does the government come in, not because we want to be moral police but because we want to secure the public sphere. This issue of enforcement on *khalwat* has been misused and exploited in some cases. It is important that they (enforcement officers) do not interfere with the individual sphere (*Malaysiakini* 2018).

He clearly condemned the breaking down of doors to arrest *khalwat* offenders and expressed hope it would be a thing of the past. Regarding the enforcement, Mujahid said that such raids are under jurisdiction of the state religious authorities. Therefore, he will engage with the various religious agencies to convince them to adopt the stance of the federal authority.

Malaysia, according to Mujahid, rejects both kinds of extremism—religious and liberal extremisms which radicalize people and pose a danger to the nation (Fakhrull 2019). For him, it is a real challenge dealing with the extremists. The government has no choice but to contain those acts of extremism. Mujahid explains that freedom of expression should not be used to insult the Prophets or any religion. As mentioned earlier, a unit under JAKIM will monitor all media and blasphemy cases. He also condemns terrorists' attacks committed by the Islamic State and the Levant (ISIL) such as the attacks in Sri Lanka in April 2019. He urges people to remove any prejudice so that Malaysians can live in harmony together. He also calls for more interfaith dialogues among Malaysia's different religious communities to seek common ground and to counter the rise of extremism (Shazwan 2018). Mujahid wants to use his role as a minister to serve as a bridge between the different faiths in the country. He also plans to change negative perceptions by some Malaysians, particularly non-Muslims, on departments such as JAKIM and its role within the government. It is imperative that religious harmony could be achieved through dialogues, outreach, and engagements. It is obvious that the PH government is trying to find different but effective approaches to overcome the ethnic and relations tensions in Malaysia.

The PH government also realizes that JAKIM had previously overstepped its boundaries in enforcing Islam and as mentioned by

Mahathir in 2018, this made it necessary to assess and review the roles and functions of JAKIM. One significant step taken by the PH government is the closure of Institut Kajian Strategik Islam Malaysia (IKSIM, Institute of Islamic Strategic Research Malaysia). The institute was set up in 2012, supposedly to redress the LGBT issue which threatened the creed (*akidah*) and faith of Muslims. According to Maznah Mohamad (2019), IKSIM was formed with the approval of JAKIM and the State Islamic Religious Councils as a company, rather than a government agency, and was headed by the then de facto Minister of Islamic Affairs, Jamil Khir Baharom. IKSIM was also funded by *zakat* funds from the Federal Territories Religious Council (MAIWP), to the tune of RM10 million (US$3.4 million) in 2018. Prominent academic and legal expert Shad Faruqi wrote about a booklet which IKSIM had produced declaring that secularism, liberalism and cultural diversity could undermine the Islamic agenda, while asserting that the country should not be obliged to protect other religions. The group subsequently lodged a police report against Faruqi in reponse. In 2018, IKSIM urged a *fatwa* to forbid Muslims from voting for the Democratic Action Party (DAP) in the 2018 general election, allegedly because the party was anti-Islam. IKSIM used to label current PH Minister Mujahid Rawa and other Muslim opposition politicians as supporters of liberalism, pluralism and LGBTs (Maznah 2019). Maznah (2019, p. 3) argued: "It is difficult not to associate the formation of IKSIM with the political agenda of UMNO, which may have used this anti-liberalism and anti-secularism narrative to dissuade Muslims from voting for the then-opposition."

However, the concept of "*Rahmatan Lil 'Alamin*" is not short of criticisms. The government has to explain to the public about the concept because many people, Muslims and non-Muslims alike, do not fully understand it. The chairman of National Dakwah Council (MDN) Mahmood Zuhdi Abd Majid stressed on the need for the explanation to avoid the concept being recklessly interpreted based on one's own views (Siti 2018). He suggested to Mujahid to establish a group to explain the concept and to give the people a better understanding.

Many people are also concerned that this concept would put Islam on the same level as other religions. The notion of universal tolerance and acceptance which derives from a Quranic verse, must still be accepted with caution and does mean being "apologetic" to the extent of compromising on Islamic principles against non-Islamic activities and practices (Maznah 2019). For instance, Perlis Mufti Mohd Asri Zainul Abidin, in his lecture in Alwi Mosque, Kangar in Ogos 2019, explained that he does not want the concept to be used for the purpose of justifying the protection of the rights of the non-Muslims only, as the Muslims need to be protected as well. Kamilin Jamilin, a lecturer from the Universiti Sains Islam Malaysia (USIM), concurs with Asri and says that the existing concept is actually *"Rahmatan Lil Kafirin"*, which protects the non-believers only (Ahmad Sanusi Azmi 2019). There are anxieties among Muslims that the policy favours the non-Muslims, and not the Muslims. This requires further public deliberation by the government to raise awareness among the public about this policy.

Undoubtedly, UMNO and PAS also politicize this issue and criticize this concept. UMNO claimed that it can be used for vote-baiting and for promoting the freedom of "deviant" groups such as Syiah, Qadiani, and LGBTs. PAS, as usual, maintained that the PH government appears to be trying to protect the rights of non-Muslims over that of the Muslims. It also reminded the minister to ensure that the Muslim faith is based strongly on faith, rather than anything else (Maznah 2019).

The PH government has had some backlash not only from the conservatives, but also from the liberals, on this issue. For instance, on 17 July 2018, Mujahid was quoted as saying that the LGBT community has the same rights as Malaysians and should not be discriminated. But on 8 August 2018, portraits of LGBT activists were removed from the George Town Festival on the orders of Mujahid. He said that the portraits of activists Nisha Ayub and Pang Khee Teik were removed as they were promoting LGBT activities, which are not in line with the PH government's policies. On 10 March 2019, Mujahid reaffirmed his stand against the gay lifestyle, saying that the government remains strongly against the LGBT lifestyle, which will never be allowed in Malaysia (INSAP 2019).

It is clear that *"Rahmatan Lil 'Alamin"* manages to spur some intellectual debates, even though it is still tentatively accepted by sceptical Islamic factions (Maznah 2019). Overall, the PH government does make some efforts to strengthen the Islamic agenda in the country. The federal government raised the allocation for Islamic development by RM13 million in 2019 from the previous year. This includes an additional RM50 million to religious schools not under the administration of state or federal governments, RM25 million for registered religious (*pondok*) schools, and RM150 million for mosque and surau repairs (Maznah 2019).

Islam and Education

Clearly, the best way to spread these agendas is through education, particularly Islamic education. However, Mahathir believes that the students must not only learn about religion, but also other subjects such as mathematics, science, geography and history. Moreover, the teaching of mathematics and science should be in English. He explained:

> I have talked to the people who are now in the process of changing the (national) education policies and stressed that the national schools have become religious schools ... that's what has happened. The Chinese and the Indians won't go to the national schools. (It is) because four periods in a day, they are teaching Islam, which is fine, but do you want the Malays only to know Islam and nothing else (*Bernama* 2018)?

Prime Minister Mahathir said that Malaysia's national school curriculum is outdated and will be overhauled because currently there is heavy emphasis on Islamic subjects instead of subjects such as the English language that could land the students good jobs in the workforce.

There are also hundreds of Islamic schools called *tahfiz* and *madrasah* that attract young Malays. Mahathir said that he wants to reduce the teaching of subjects related to Islam in the national schools. He said:

> We are going to change the timetable and curriculum in the schools. We will still study religion, but not all periods in one day, maybe one or two periods in a week ... If we want to progress, Malaysians must be well-educated, not only in reciting the Quran, but also in other languages. If we don't, we are going to be very backward (*Straits Times* 2018).

Mahathir's views to revamp the education system are not based on his belief about education in Malaysia. His views are supported by many scholars and practitioners who study about the education system in Malaysia.

For instance, Azmil Tayeb of Universiti Sains Malaysia, who has done a comparative study of Islamic education in Malaysia and Indonesia, claimed that neither the syllabus for national schools nor the one used in the JAKIM-approved programme called "*Kafa*", incorporates the teaching of such democratic values as openness and respect for diversity. An academic has alleged that officially sanctioned Islamic education in Malaysia is not effective in cultivating values that are considered desirable in Islam. Azmil found that both the school and "*Kafa*" syllabi are heavy on the teaching of rituals and avoidance of sins which made them superficial. Moreover, the teaching in schools tends to encourage rote memorization and give a narrow interpretation of Islam. According to Azmil:

> It does not encourage critical thinking and the development of analytical skills ... It teaches students how to perform religious duties, but does not impart the meaning of what it is to be a Muslim, especially in a multi-ethnic society like Malaysia ... There's no opportunity to really study the Quran, to get into the deeper meanings (Ainaa Aiman 2019).

The "*Kafa*" programme, which teaches duties that Islam requires of adherents as individuals and members of communities, is regulated by JAKIM and the state Islamic authorities. The classes are usually held in the afternoon or evening at dedicated centres, but sometimes in the mosques or suraus. In 2016, there were more than 19,000 students at "*Kafa*" programme centres in the Federal Territories of Kuala Lumpur, Labuan and Putrajaya. The students may choose to sit for the Kafa Evaluation Examination to earn a certificate. The subjects studied include Islamic Sciences, Arabic, Quranic Studies, Islamic History and Islamic Manners. *Kafa's* main function is to supplement Islamic Education in non-religious public schools, which many Muslim parents see as inadequate. Azmil criticized the Malaysian syllabus for teaching what he called "extreme behaviour", such as killing apostates, beating disobedient wives, and polygamy. Therefore, he recommended a revision of the Islamic Education syllabus for national schools to include components on comparative religion, arguing that this will cultivate understanding of other religions and cultures (Ainaa Aiman 2019).

Besides, Noor Azimah Abdul Rahim (2019), the chairman of Parent Action Group for Education Malaysia, argues that in the national primary schools, Bahasa Melayu (Malay language) and the English language are each allocated 168 hours or 15 per cent of total hours. Islamic Education (Pendidikan Islam)/Moral (PI/PM) gets 126 hours, or 11 per cent of total hours. If *Tasmik* (learning to recite Quran) is included, that is an additional 42 hours, or 15 per cent of total hours—equivalent to Bahasa Melayu and the English language. For mathematics, primary schools are given 126 hours or 11 per cent of total hours, and science, 84 hours or 7.5 per cent. A sensible student once asked why PI/PM needs to be given equal emphasis as Bahasa Melayu and the English language when it is not a subject tested in the UPSR (Primary School Evaluation Test). In national secondary schools, the time given for Bahasa Melayu remains at 168 hours or 12 per cent of total hours, while that for the English language reduces to 126 hours or 9 per cent. For national lower secondary schools, the time given for PI/PM increases to 146 hours or 11 per cent, while mathematics and science get 126 hours, or 9 per cent each. At upper secondary schools, English, PI/PM, modern mathematics, additional mathematics, physics, chemistry and biology are each given 126 hours or 9 per cent of total hours.

Effectively, in primary schools, Bahasa Melayu, English language and PI/PM are given equal number of hours. At lower secondary level, Bahasa Melayu takes the lead with PI/PM in the second place, while English, maths and science are third. At the upper levels, Bahasa Melayu stands in the pole position, with English, PI/PM, maths and science getting equal number of hours. It is no wonder that the prime minister feels that national schools are not attractive especially to parents. Mahathir says that if parents want their children to have a religious education, there is an option. A student can opt to take the minimum six SPM (Malaysia Assessment Certificate, for secondary school) subjects on top of three—Education on Al-Quran and As-Sunnah, Education on Syariah law and Advanced Arabic. Incidentally, after SPM, not all students from religious schools decide on a career of theology. Therefore, moving forward, reforms need to be carried out to Malaysia's education system.

The latest controversial issue about *Khat* emerged in August 2019, in which a concern was raised among the non-Muslim communities about alleged PH government policy of Islamization. The government denied this. The Education Ministry announced that *Khat* will be taught to Year Four students in Chinese and Tamil vernacular schools as part of the Malay language syllabus beginning in 2020. The decision caused an uproar among the local Chinese community, which is known to be protective of its mother tongue education. Chinese educationists through the United Chinese School Committees' Association of Malaysia, or Dong Zong, questioned the rationale behind introducing *Khat*, which is usually associated with Islam, adding that it will not help the students enhance their Malay language skills. Later, the Cabinet said that *Khat* will only be an elective subject in the Malay language curriculum (*Channel News Asia* 2019). Mahathir condemned Dong Zong for allegedly instigating negative racial sentiments and expressed surprise at the outbursts over this issue. He said that the matter had actually been decided in 2012 and the topic was included in a school textbook. He further explained: "*Khat* will be taught as an arts subject. Calligraphy. This was decided by the then government in 2012. I do not know why it is an issue now … Nobody made noise back then. This is no different than what was (discussed) before" (Syed Umar Arif 2019, p. 1). Mahathir saw this issue as an attempt by the opposition to weaken the PH government.

Religious Publications

The PH government seems more open to a variety of religious book publications. It welcomes many critical, analytical and intellectual debates even though sometimes they may trigger political and religious controversies. The PH government, unlike the previous BN government, tries to stop any attempt to silence reasoned and critical voices and opinions. This is clear in several cases where the PH government fulfils its promises to uplift ban on book publications. For instance, the High Court had lifted the ban order imposed on the book *Breaking The Silence: Voices of Moderation—Islam in a Constitutional Democracy* by G25 on 9 April 2019. Earlier on 29 October 2018, Attorney General Tommy Thomas had withdrawn the government's bid to appeal against the Court of Appeal's 11 January 2018's decision to set aside the Home Affairs Ministry's ban on three books written by academic Mohd Faizal

Musa under the pen name Faisal Tehrani. On 9 January 2018, the G25 was granted leave to apply for a judicial review of the ban on the book. In the G25 book's judgment, Judge Nordin Hassan made the decision after allowing a judicial review application to challenge the ban order and set aside the then home minister's decision in banning the book. Justice Nordin said that the minister must show the basis of his decision to ban the book as stated in the order by saying: "It is not mentioned in the affidavit of the minister, except that the ministry relied on the opinion of the Department of Islamic Development Malaysia (Jakim)" (*The Star Online* 2019a). The G25 members, represented by lawyer Malik Imtiaz Sarwar, had sought for a certiorari under Order 53, Rule 8 (2) of the Rules of Court 2012 to nullify the ban order which was signed by the respondent, Senior Federal Counsel Jamilah Jamil. The book, published in December 2015, was declared illegal by the Home Ministry on 27 July 2017.

In the Faisal Tehrani (Mohd Faizal Musa) case, Attorney General Tommy Thomas wrote in a letter dated 23 October 2018 saying:

> Having read the written representations on behalf of your client and taking into consideration his role as an academician, author of academic and creative books and articles, a scriptwriter and poet, I have decided that the Government of Malaysia will not proceed with its Motion for Leave to Appeal to the Federal Court against the decision of the Court of Appeal in the above-mentioned proceedings … Further, I will also advise the Ministry of Home Affairs to remove books written by your client from its Prohibition Order List (Chong and Chin 2018).

Thomas noted that the three books, *Karbala*, *Ingin Jadi Nasrallah* and the award-winning *Tiga Kali Seminggu* were compilations of short stories and poems that were previously published elsewhere including in *Utusan Malaysia* and its weekend edition *Mingguan Malaysia* as well as *Milinea Muslim*, *Dewan Sastera* and *Dewan Budaya* as far back as 2000 "without any evidence of the occurrence of actions prejudicial to public order and security". He added that his decision was based on the fact that thousands of copies had been printed and sold before the ministry banned it and in all that time, the books had not jeopardized national harmony. Mohd Faizal argued that the ban is a violation of Articles 8 (1) and 10

(1)(a) of the Federal Constitution that deal with equality under the law and the right to freedom of speech and expression, respectively. Thus, he saw the decision as a symbolic victory over Malaysia's struggle for freedom of expression and thought. Earlier, the High Court dismissed his bid for a judicial review in August 2016, but a three-judge panel at the Court of Appeal chaired by Justice Zaleha Yusof ruled in Mohd Faizal's favour in January 2018. Zaleha said the judges had read the disputed books and found that they were love stories, adding that they could not understand the reason for the ban. She added that the ban was illegal as the ministry had not followed the provisions under Subsection 7 (1) of the Printing Presses and Publications Act 1984 (Chong and Chin 2018). On 18 September 2019, the Home Ministry had lifted the ban through an order gazetted on a book entitled *Assalamualaikum (May Peace Be Upon You): Observations on the Islamisation of Malaysia* by former minister Zaid Ibrahim. The book was originally published in 2015 and launched by Mahathir Mohamad. The previous BN government banned the book in December 2017, saying it was "likely to be prejudicial to public order, as well as public interest, and is likely to alarm public opinion" (*Malaysiakini* 2019).

However, the decision to uplift the ban on books does not apply to all, but rather, selected books. In several cases, the Courts continue to impose bans on the books for some specific reasons. For example, the High Court on 22 April 2019 upheld the previous government's ban on three books published by the Islamic Renaissance Front (IRF), saying it is satisfied with the former home minister's reason in imposing the ban. The three books are *Islam Tanpa Keekstreman: Berhujah Untuk Kebebasan*, a Malay language translation of a book by Turkish academic Mustafa Akyol, as well as two volumes from a series edited by IRF director Dr Farouk Musa. The three books were published in 2012, 2014 and 2016. In his judgment, Judge Nordin Hassan explained that the contents of the book are likely to be prejudicial to public order and interest and may alarm public opinion because they are not in line with *Sunni* Islam and can cause confusion among Muslims in Malaysia. In its submission, IRF had called for the ban to be quashed on the grounds that then Home Minister Ahmad Zahid Hamidi acted beyond his powers because matters of Islam should not come under the federal government. Putrajaya has no jurisdiction to regulate issues related to religion, which is a violation of the Federal Constitution, and Section 7 of the Printing Presses and Publications Act 1984. Farouk Musa argued that he fears the court decision will only encourage the authorities to control books on Islamic topics and the minister of home affairs has the absolute discretion in banning books that do not conform to the version endorsed by Islamic authorities like JAKIM. It is believed that IRF will appeal against this decision by the High Court (Kaur 2019). On 13 February 2020, the Appeal Court decided finally to lift the ban on those three books. Obviously, lifting the ban on religious publications is not a straightforward decision. It involves many considerations and the current government should establish clear guidelines on the types of books which are permitted to be published, and the types which are not.

Recent Developments under the PH

The PH government faces many challenges in dealing with the issues of Islamic administration and *Syariah* laws. For instance in September 2018, the Kuala Terengganu Syariah High Court had ordered two women aged thirty-two and twenty-two to be caned six times each in front of 100 witnesses for attempting to have lesbian sex. This issue is controversial because not all agree to canning as a method of judgment. The PH government sees judgment not as a form of punishment but rather a process of education to rehabilitate those involved back to the true teachings of Islam. Punishment does not solve the problem. In responding to this case, Mahathir said that the Cabinet is of the view that the caning of the two women because of their "extraordinary relationship" does not reflect the true face of Islam and justice. He explained:

> We know this is the first case involving the two women and usually in such a case we need to give them advice and not whip them until the whole nation knows about it. This gives Islam a bad name. The Cabinet is of the view that consideration should be given to those involved based on the circumstances. In Islam we can initially give them a lighter sentence and advice them about their wrongdoing (*The Sun Daily* 2018).

He further said that it is important to show that Islam is not a cruel religion. Laws that humiliate people are not the way to promote Islam. The main concern here is on how Islam is portrayed: it is not a religion of no compromise or no consideration.

Meanwhile on other issues of religious expression, Mujahid said that this matter is serious and has asked the Selangor Islamic Religious Department (JAIS) to investigate a forum and the launch of a book on 13 April 2019 about Muslim women who have given up wearing the *hijab* or *tudung* (headgear). The book, *Unveiling Choice*, by human rights activist Maryam Lee, was launched at an event at Gerakbudaya in Petaling Jaya, which was followed by a forum on "Malay Women & Dehijabing". It tells a story of Muslim women who once wore the *hijab* in public but later gave up the habit. The preface in the book says the author has "neither the need nor the intention to make a case against the *hijab*", while a blurb for the forum states that *hijab* dialogue is scarce in the Muslim world, "but a few Malay women are seeking to reclaim their identity and rejecting the *hijab*" (*MSN* 2019). So far there is no action taken by JAIS on this case.

Now, there are many criticisms against the government on the issue of Islamic affairs. The PH government is accused of abandoning Islamic agenda. For instance, Muhyiddin as the home minister refuted the allegation made by Mufti of Perlis Mohd Asri Zainul Abidin on Facebook saying that the status of Islam is "unsafe" under the PH government. Muhyiddin explains: "The status of Islam as the religion of the Federation as enshrined in the Federal Constitution will not change." His ministry also takes a serious view on the issue of blasphemy against Islam, Prophet Muhammad and the monarchy institution on social media. He said: "stern action had been taken by the police so far in regard to the issue, with eight out of the 53 cases investigated had been charged in courts" (*The Sun Daily* 2019).

Asri's criticism is also related to the case of an Indian Muslim preacher by the name of Zakir Naik, one of the most controversial cases so far dealt by the PH government. In August 2019, Naik ignited outrage in Malaysia after suggesting the expulsion of ethnic Chinese minorities. Previously, he also drew a huge public outcry for commenting that Hindus in the Southeast Asian country have "100 times more rights" than the Muslim minority in India, and that they support the "prime minister of India and not the prime minister of Malaysia". Naik was granted a permanent residency in Malaysia by the previous BN government and has been living in Malaysia since 2016 (Chew 2019a). In an interview with Turkish international news channel TRT world, Prime Minister Mahathir argued that Naik's extreme views are a threat to the country's racial and religious relations. However, it is difficult to extradite him because no other country wants him. On 28 June 2019, Foreign Minister Saifuddin Abdullah said that Malaysia will not extradite Naik to India, his home country, to face money-laundering charges despite receiving an extradition application from India (*The Star Online* 2019b). Naik was also accused of disparaging other people's faith and associating himself with Muslim terror organizations. He denied all these accusations. However, Malaysian police has given nationwide orders banning Naik from delivering public talks in the interest of national security. Police is investigating Naik after at least 115 police reports were lodged against him. Many leaders of political parties including PAS have reminded Naik not to touch on Malaysian politics during his lectures (Chin 2019).

Minister Mujahid in September 2018 criticized Naik's combative style of propagating Islam, which puts down other beliefs. He argues that Zakir Naik's preaching approach is not suitable for Malaysia by saying: "We don't want a debate that ridicules others. We need a more intellectual and composed method of Islamic propagation without the need to ridicule other religions." However, after personally meeting Naik on 13 March 2019, Mujahid changed his stance and said: "His experience in *dakwah* (preaching) throughout the world is an inspiration for us to continue preaching work. May Allah strengthen his preaching efforts to guide people to recognise Islam" (Lipi 2019, p. 1). This invites criticisms against Mujahid from Latheefa Koya, Executive Director of Lawyers for Liberty.

There is no doubt that Naik is very popular among Muslims even though he is known for making controversial and provocative statements ruffling people living in multi-religious countries like India and Malaysia. Many instances during his public lectures, Naik made disparaging remarks on other religious books but the Holy script of the Muslims as inauthentic and contain nothing else but fallacious teachings. This method employed by Naik can cause polarization and disharmony within society. There are Muslims who also feel that Naik should not get himself entangled in controversies by belittling other religions, but rather focus on the beauty, tolerance and values preached by Islam (Schwartz 2015). I agree with Maziah Mustapha and Mohd Abbas Abdul Razak (2019, p. 82) who studied about Naik's method of preaching. In their words, they urged:

1. In order to be more successful as a preacher, Naik has to employ diplomacy and persuasion. He has to be more lenient towards his questioners during public lectures.
2. Naik should avoid disgracing his questioners by asking provocative questions on their religions and practices in the midst of a vast Muslim audience.
3. He has to give equal opportunity for the questioners to articulate their ideas and not to intrude or make fun of them when they are giving their opinions.
4. Naik should not pester his non-Muslim questioners to change their faith at public forums. He has to respect their opinions and give them ample time to ponder over his explanations, suggestions or invitations to embrace his religion.
5. He has to overcome his over-reactionary character, high pitch and mentality of always wanting to win in a debate. What will be ideal for him is to present his case and leave it to the judgment of his audiences.

The Malaysian government monitors Zakir Naik closely and forbids him from giving any public lecture, except in religious rituals. However, by refusing to deport Naik to face justice in his home country India, the PH government continues to receive many criticisms including from the leaders and supporters of its own party.

Conclusion

Overall, based on the cases mentioned above, we can see that the PH government embraces religious freedom. In fact, the PH government allows more religious issues to be debated in public than in previous governments, unless those issues are too sensitive to be discussed in public or are considered deviant from the Islamic teaching of *Sunni* Islam in Malaysia. Furthermore, some restrictions can still be imposed if those religious expressions, whether through attire or books, do not comply with the public order subscribed by *Sunni* doctrine. However, based on several judgements by the courts, the PH government has yet to show clear and different guidelines, rules and regulations on how to practise Islam. No announcement is made on this matter. Thus far, the PH government follows the existing practices and guidelines. Having said that, it is clear that the PH government is giving more space for intellectual and academic debates on the issue of religion. As argued earlier, the concept of *"Rahmatan Lil 'Alamin"* will become the main policy to govern Islam including religious expression in Malaysia. The best way to implement the policy is for the government to explain the concept to both the Muslims and non-Muslims in Malaysia so that they can better understand and adhere to it. Although it remains to be seen how this policy will be implemented, I believe that the PH government will be more moderate in its approach, and move away from the hardliners' stand employed by the previous governments. Unfortunately after the collapse of PH government on 23 February 2020 due to the resignation of Mahathir and the formation of a new Perikatan Nasional (PN) government, we will never know the full extent and impact of Islamization policy under PH government.

Note

1. Following the launch, Najib announced three mechanisms to kick off the NHRAP. One of which was the creation of a smartphone application to obtain feedback from the people on the implementation of the plan. This facility encouraged more effective public participation in the implementation of the NHRAP and its improvement from time to time. Second, the government also agreed to set up a high-level committee to monitor the implementation of the NHRAP. And third, the government also agreed to appoint appropriate impartial individuals, from among civil society organizations and academicians, to gather and analyse the public feedback on the implementation of the NHRAP. Najib hoped that these efforts will boost the performance and image of the country, especially in terms of economic development and efficient and credible governance, to enable Malaysia to become a high-income advanced economy and be among the twenty best and most advanced countries in the world by 2050 (*Free Malaysia Today* 2018).

7

CONCLUSION: SEEKING FOR A GENUINE FREEDOM OF RELIGIOUS EXPRESSION

Introduction

This book examines the Islamization policy and the roles of Islamic bureaucracy in enforcing the policy of religious expression. Overall, religious expression in Malaysia is limited to the practices allowed by the *Sunni* doctrine. As Islam is the religion of the Federation and the jurisdiction of Islam is under the state authority, the Islamic bureaucracy has the authority to interpret Islam. In Western Liberals' perspective, theoretically there are two schools of thought imposed upon religious expression—one is very hostile to religious expression because their intention is to protect the non-believers, and the other is open to all views including religious expression. In Malaysia, the societal belief, constitution and legislation must subscribe to *Sunni* beliefs even though this is not mentioned at all in the Federal Constitution, but is mentioned in the state's Islamic law. Thus, Chapter 1 traces the historical and contemporary background of freedom of expression in Malaysia. As freedom of expression is enshrined under Article 10 of the Federal Constitution, there have been many restrictions imposed against that freedom which were sometimes based on religious arguments and practices. No doubt that the right to legitimate religious expression is also protected by the Federal Constitution, but not hate speech.

Chapter 2 outlines the Islamization policy which was started in the 1960s but became the official policy of the country in the 1980s during the administration of Prime Minister Mahathir Mohamad. During this period, several permanent federal and state religious bodies, such as JAKIM and Syariah courts, were established to promote Islam. In fact, Mahathir also introduced Islamic banking, securities, and insurance laws. Besides, he attempted to increase the power of Islamic legal authorities in the Federal Constitution. Thus, Mahathir's Islamization policy was called the Inculcation of Islamic Values in Administration. This was continued by the policies of Mahathir's successors—Abdullah Ahmad Badawi's *Islam Hadhari* and Najib Razak's *Wasatiyyah*.

Through these policies, the government provided support for the expansion of the Islamization policy. Islamization would not be successful without the human capital produced by the government to administer the policies. Thus, many Islamic education institutions were established to offer courses in Islamic studies and Islamic laws. In order to promote Islam, the government spread the good aspects of Islam to Muslims and non-Muslims alike via the media. Islamization is effective when Islam can be enforced on Muslims. The enforcement of Islamic laws can be clearly observed on the issue of moral policing such as in the case of close proximity. Recently, the *Syariah* index, which was officially launched on 10 February 2015, is the next step of the government's Islamic agenda. It is obvious that Islamization has become one of the main agendas for the government to implement in Malaysia's multi-ethnic society.

The best way to understand the issue of Islamic religious expression in Malaysia is to divide the discussion into two aspects—inter-religious expression and intra-religious expression. Chapter 3 offers the observations on inter-religious expression in Malaysia. There are many restrictions on religious expression including in publications, on hate speech, and blasphemy. The inter-religious expression is controversial because it involves the issue of religious freedom and the relations between Islam and other religions, particularly Christianity. The recent case of the "Allah" issue is crucial to religious expression. The word "Allah" can only be used by Muslims and not the non-Muslims, even though Christians in Sabah and Sarawak and the Sikh community have used "Allah" to refer to their gods for generations. To resolve this issue, the government allows the non-Muslims to use "Allah" except in Herald publications. It is clear that religious freedom and religious expression are very sensitive in the race relations in Malaysia. The government is seen trying to protect political stability and racial harmony in Malaysia. There should be efforts made to ensure religious expression can be practised in harmony. Perhaps, an inter-faith organization could be set up to promote understandings between various faiths that exist in Malaysia.

Chapter 4 discusses about intra-religious expression. Most Muslims in Malaysia follow the teachings of *Sunni* doctrine from the *Shafi'i* sect. Propagations by non-Muslims and non-*Sunni* Muslims to *Sunni* Muslims are prohibited. The practice of Islam in Malaysia is restrictive as compared to other Muslim countries. Other doctrines such as Shi'ism and Liberal Islam are considered deviant from Islam in Malaysia. This shows that pluralism in religion does not exist in Malaysia.

This chapter also debates on the issue of whether Malaysia is an Islamic state or a secular state. It supports the argument that Malaysia is a hybrid state, which is a combination of an Islamic state and a secular state. The reason is that Islam occupies a special position in Malaysia's constitution but at the same time, Malaysia's legal system is based on the British common law system. So far, Muslims are allowed to practise *Syariah* law, which only covers civil law. The implementation of intra-religious expression in Malaysia is very complex. This chapter examines on several issues such as public speech, publications and broadcasting, blasphemy and dress code.

It is obvious that religious expression in Malaysia is limitedly practised, subject to Islamic teachings as interpreted by Islamic bureaucracy based on the teachings of *Sunni* Islam. This is the result of Islamization policy as propagated by the government since independence. Future research and publications can explore this topic further, especially with regard to the implementation of *Syariah* index, the expansion of Islamization policy and the expansion of the power of Islamic bureaucracy. Islam is always a hot topic in Malaysia. The more we observe the public sphere, the more we understand about political Islam in Malaysia as shown in the practice of religious expression.

Although Malaysia is very strict in the practices of Islam, some evidences show that some practices are political and must align with the government policy and agenda. Based on the study of intra-religious expression, it is obvious that there are many restrictions and limitations in practising intra-religious expression in Malaysia. It is legitimate to restrict religious hatred and hate speech for national security reasons. However, this gives the opportunity for the government and religious authorities to limit intra-religious expression which also includes expression considered non-threatening to national security but not in line with the *Sunni* doctrine and Islamic beliefs in Malaysia.

Chapter 5 argues about extreme religious expression in Malaysia through a case study of the Islamic State and the Levant (ISIL). It shows that the international community was shocked by the online videos of incidents involving members of the ISIL gruesomely beheading western journalists. The violent methods used by ISIL militants were considered crimes and contradicted with Islamic teachings. ISIL managed to attract many supporters and sympathizers including Malaysians to join them in Iraq and Syria. As a Muslim-majority country, the influence of ISIL in Malaysia is considered as a threat to national security and stability. The concern now is the spread of ISIL extreme ideology especially through social media to Malaysian youth. If this fails to be contained pre-emptively, it can result in terrorism activties which can harm Malaysian society. It is clear that ISIL utilizes religious expression in their recruitment strategies in Malaysia and manages to attract Malaysians to join them. The chapter observes the efforts taken by the Malaysian government to counter the ISIL threats both online and offline.

Since 9 May 2018, Malaysia has for the first time voted the opposition Pakatan Harapan (PH) as the Federal government replacing Barisan Nasional (BN). Chapter 6 explores the politics behind the success story of PH winning the general election. Clearly, the PH government faces huge challenges in establishing Islam as the religion of the Federation. The biggest challenge is religious hate speech. The government has put up some measures to overcome this. It also introduces the concept of *"Rahmatan Lilalamin"* as the main policy to govern Islam and ethnic and religious relations. It seems that the PH government will continue the policy of Inculcation of Islamic Values. Moderate Islam will be propagated through reforms in the education system. This book also contains several relevant cases in the context of religious expression. The last chapter, Chapter 7, summarizes the discussions in the previous chapters. It is imperative to say that religious expression is crucial in Malaysia.

The implementation of religious expression needs to take into consideration the multiracial and multireligious society that exists in Malaysia. Promoting civility must be encouraged but spreading hatred between religions should be avoided. All Malaysians should respect each other even though we embrace different religions. It is essential that all Malaysians understand the Constitution which states the best practices for religious expression. With a political transformation that happened after the 14th General Election in 2018, clearly practising and regulating religious expression is becoming more challenging with the United Malays National Organisation (UMNO) and Malaysian Islamic Party (PAS) collaborating and using Malay rights and religious issues to condemn the PH government. Hate speech against other ethnic groups and within the Muslim community in Malaysia will cause the government to safeguard racial harmony in the country. Therefore, the success of Malaysia in the future is dependent on whether the current government is able to bring people together and get them to respect each other for the common good. This is something the current Perikatan Nasional (PN) government, led by new Prime Minister Muhyiddin Yassin, cannot afford to ignore. Unity among Malaysians and within the Muslim community will depend on the practice of religious expression. I believe that the PN government is aware of this and will tackle this issue wisely.

Future Challenges for Political Islam

In an interview with Prime Minister Mahathir Mohamad on 11 March 2019 at the Prime Minister's Office in Putrajaya, I asked him about political Islam and religious expression, he said:

> In our country, we have this political party (without mentioning name of the party) which claims that the people who are not in the party are not Muslim. So then there is now a new condition attached to becoming a Muslim. Apart from your enunciation of the declaration of faith '*Lailahaillallah Muhammadarrasul*' (There is no god but Allah, and

Muhammad is his messenger), you must also say "I am a member of this party", then only you become Islam. Which is totally wrong because the whole world cannot be a member of that party and yet they are very proud to say they are Muslim, they are practising Islam, every now and again they shout 'Allahu Akhbar' (Allah is great). I mean you are doing something wrong and then you link it with Islam, that is wrong. That is what is happening to the Muslim world today because it is not the religion. The religion is perfectly good. It is a very moderate kind of religion, very concern about the welfare of the *Ummah*. Every time you talk you say '*Bismillahhirrahmanirrahim*' (In the name of Allah The Merciful, The Compassionate) and then you cut off his head. Is that right? Cannot be right, you see, but these are people who say they are doing things for Islam and this is what Daesh (ISIL) is doing, you know. Where before, Muslims were not fighting Muslims. They simply say that they are Islam. They simply cut off people's head. They kill people. They commit acts of terror against Muslims in order to set up Islam. Doing all these things (are) forbidden by Islam, in the name of Islam. So that is where we are lost now because we don't believe the teaching of Islam. We believe in our leader in our *Imam* and that kind of thing. If you read the Quran, you will find that all the behaviours promoted by Islam are very good, very clear. If you follow, you will succeed but you don't follow. That is the problem.

It is clear in Mahathir's view that Islam is being manipulated and politicized by certain groups to justify suppression of other fellow Muslims and non-Muslims who disagree with them in issues such as religious expression. Mahathir urges for a change of this mentality and promotes what he claimed as the correct behaviours according to Islamic teachings.

James Chin (2019) argues that the Islamization of Malay society for the past four decades has totally transformed the Malay political landscape. Political Islam is now the only game among the Malay polity. Today, after decades of indoctrination and state-supported Islamization, there is no political space to even hold a considered discussion about the place of Islam in Malaysian political life. It is taken for granted that Islamic beliefs must be above all other opinions. In the era of "Old Malaysia" (*Malaysia Lama*) under the BN government, national Islamization policy has four objectives (Azizuddin 2018). The first is to make Islam a special religion with state sponsorship. The second is to make *Sunni* Islamic teaching—the dominant sect of Islam in the world—the teaching for all Muslims in Malaysia. The third is the empowerment of the Islamic bureaucracy through the Administration of the Islamic Law Act. The final is to give legitimacy to the ruling BN party for championing Islamic issues such as constitutionally protecting Islam as the religion of the Federation in Malaysia. UMNO knows that as long as it favours a strict interpretation of Islam, conservative Muslims and PAS will be on BN's and its side. Meanwhile, PH had no clear Islamization policy prior to the 14th General Election in 2018. However, they did not copy the previous BN government's Islamization policy. Instead, they introduced the *"Rahmatan Lil 'Alamin"* policy to bring prosperity to all races and religious communities.

However, the PH government realizes the reality that they face. As reported by the *South China Morning Post* (Chew 2019b), social media was used to incite racial tension in Malaysia in order to undermine the current Malaysian government. This trend becomes prevalent especially after the 14th General Election in 2018. In one recent posting on Facebook, a Chinese-looking man was seen setting fire to the Malaysian flag. This ignited strong emotions and was shared more than 5,500 times with angry responses particularly from the Malay-Muslim netizens. The truth is that the man in the picture was not a Malaysian Chinese. He was a retired Filipino policeman burning a Malaysian flag in Manila as a protest against Malaysia and the then president of the Philippines for his handling of the Sabah issue. The photo was actually taken in 2013. In addition, many fake images of the Malaysian flag were circulated online including speeches by controversial Indian Muslim preacher Zakir Naik were utilized to stoke racial and religious sentiments to undermine the PH government (Chew 2019a). Kadir Jasin, media adviser to Prime Minister Mahathir, said: "There was a need for authorities to act decisively against people who misuse social media, including closing down sites and arresting people for inflammatory posts" (Chew 2019b).

One might wonder why racial and religious slurs are used to undermine the PH government. This is to create fear among Muslims, in particular, as well as non-Muslims to weaken and work against the current government. This is because in the 14th General Election, most of the Malays voted for BN and PAS rather than the PH party. A Merdeka

Centre study shows that the Malay vote was evenly split between PH, BN and PAS. The research shows that 65–73 per cent of the Malay votes went to either BN or PAS, which means that about 70 per cent of the Malay voting populace did not support PH and voted within racial and religious lines (*Straits Times* 2014). Mahathir also recognizes the fact that he is facing a declining Malay support and an opposition out to paint his government as "un-Islamic", while also struggling to deal with massive debt inherited from the previous government amid a slowing economy. According to Ahmad Awang from the progressive Islamic Amanah party, preachers have been telling their congregations that the current government is "anti-Islam" and "liberal", which is an anathema to conservative Muslims. He said: "They (opposition preachers) have been using the mosques, surau (a small Muslim place of worship) to fan religious and racial sentiment (by preaching) that the current government discriminates against Islam, is anti-Islam, and wants to get rid of Islam" (Chew 2019b). This is clearly an attempt to prevent Malay-Muslims from supporting the PH government.

For the opposition PAS and UMNO, they have to collaborate and step up efforts to lure Malay-Muslims to support them against the PH government. They believe that by collaborating, but not merging, they can defeat the PH government with the Malay votes alone. P. Ramasamy (2019), deputy chief minister of Penang, argues that the signing of the political charter between PAS and UMNO might represent an important milestone for both. Ramasamy (2019) further said:

> Having been arch political enemies for the greater part of the post-independence era, the very act of UMNO and PAS coming together might be a new phase in the evolution of Malaysian politics. The signing of the charter is not a political amalgamation of the two parties into one entity; amalgamation might be a long way away or might not happen. Although both the parties, with different sets of ideologies, have come together for the sole reason of opposing Harapan, their inner differences might be hidden for some time. Even if the desperate UMNO wants to merge with PAS, I seriously doubt that PAS would want to merge with UMNO, considering UMNO's history of corruption and abuse of power. PAS is no embodiment of virtue, either. The party's universalistic notion of Islam free from the encumbrances of race and nationalism, has been long abandoned under its present leadership. The increasing attacks by

PAS (and UMNO) leaders against the DAP is an example of the narrow sectarian pursuits meant to attract Malay-Muslim support.

The main challenge for the PH government was to overcome the narrative circulated by UMNO and PAS that the PH government did not protect Islam. With the collapse of PH government and the formation of PN government on 29 February 2020 consisting of splinter groups from Bersatu and PKR together with UMNO-BN, PAS and several political parties from Sarawak and Sabah, it seems that the hardliners won the narrative battle. They are said to form a Malay-Islam centric government. However, the reality is that Malaysia is a multi-religious country. Therefore, the best narrative needs to be found and this can be in the form of a concrete policy in championing Islam and winning the hearts and minds of the Muslims without discriminating and distancing the non-Muslims in this multireligious Malaysian society.

Future Challenges for Religious Expression

There is no doubt that states, but not the federal government, have jurisdiction for Islamic affairs. There are limitations to the roles of the federal government including JAKIM to function and administer Islamic affairs. We can see that many policies and practices of Islam continue as usual under the PH government just like in the previous governments. This is because the religious authorities and bureaucracy are still the same and they impose similar policies like before without any interference from the federal government. For instance, the police in Johor and Selangor raided private functions by *Shia* Muslims on 9 September 2019, arresting foreigners in a continued crackdown on followers of the second largest Islamic branch deemed deviant by Islamic authorities. As reported by *Free Malaysia Today* (2019), there were at least two dozens officers from the Johor Islamic Affairs Department (JAINJ) who arrived accompanied by the police at a private function in Kempas, where adherents were attending a ceremony to mark *Ashura* or the death anniversary of Hussein, the Prophet Muhammad's grandson, who is a central figure in *Shia* Islam. Eight people were arrested, including one Yemeni and two Singaporeans. They were investigated under Section 9 of the Johor Syariah Criminal Offences Enactment for violating the order of the Sultan, Mufti as well as *fatwa*, which carries a RM3,000 fine and one-year jail sentence.

Meanwhile in Selangor, JAIS Bandar Sunway raided a private function in Bandar Sunway attended by Pakistani Muslims to mark *Ashura* and a *Shia* centre in Gombak on 6 September 2019 detaining twenty-three people (*Free Malaysia Today* 2019). State Islamic authorities have declared its teachings as "deviant", with sermons in Selangor frequently condemning its followers as heretics. Mosques in Selangor have been instructed to deliver a sermon attacking *Shia* Muslims for Friday congregations on 6 September 2019, in what critics have slammed as a fresh round of hate speech by authorities targeting religious minorities. The sermon, prepared by JAIS ahead of an important *Shia* occasion the following week, describes *Shia* Muslim beliefs and practices as "heinous", "nonsense", "deviant", and "nauseating". Ahmad Farouk Musa, a prominent critic of Islamic authorities, said that the sermon is equivalent to hate speech against religious minorities (Koya 2019). The latest arrests and sermons marked a move from a past policy which allows foreigners to follow *Shia* Muslim practices in private, an assurance given in 2013 by then Minister in charge of Islamic Affairs Jamil Khir Baharom. In fact, the PH government in Selangor headed by the Menteri Besar Amirudin Shari backed the arrests and sermons. The Minister in charge of Islamic Affairs Mujahid Yusof Rawa in November 2018 agreed that no one should be persecuted for their beliefs, including Muslims who follow *Shia* teachings, which Islamic authorities in Malaysia labelled as "deviant". He said that the line must be drawn when it comes to hate speech against *Shias*, despite a 1996 *fatwa* banning Muslims from practising the second biggest denomination in Islam (Augustin 2018). However, in the recent event, Mujahid declined to comment on the Friday sermons prepared by JAIS, which attacked *Shia* Muslims (Fadli 2019).

On other issues, High Court Judge Nordin Hassan ruled on 27 August 2019 that the *fatwa* issued by the Selangor *fatwa* committee and gazetted by the Selangor government in 2014 is in order. Therefore, the *fatwa* declaring Sisters in Islam (SIS) as a deviant organization for subscribing to "religious liberalism and pluralism" still stands. Justice Nordin also ruled that the High Court does not have the jurisdiction to rule on the case based on Article 121 (1A) of the Federal Constitution where such matters should have been referred to the *Syariah* court (Yatim 2019).

Furthermore regarding dress code, in September 2019 Terengganu through Sukan Terengganu (SUTERA) showcased the *Syariah* compliant sportswear in thirteen sports participated by both men and women athletes. The attention during the event was definitely on the women athletes who participated in all the events including sepak takraw, petanque, volleyball, tennis, badminton, volleyball and cycling, except football. During the five-day event, the athletes showed no sign of discomfort from wearing tight track bottoms and slightly oversized t-shirts. State Chairman for Youth, Sports and Non-governmental Organization Wan Sukairi Wan Abdullah said that the introduction of dress code or *Syariah* compliant sportswear is in line with the state government's policy of prioritizing Islam in its administration, which will only be enforced in 2020. Terengganu is now under the PAS's rule (Rosli 2019). Whether this dress code will be followed by other states or not, only time will tell. Similarly, the Kelantan state government has held a *Syariah*-compliant bodybuilding competition titled "The Mr Awang Selamat Kelantan" since 2016. The participants covered their bodies from the navel to the knees (*Bernama* 2019b).

One crucial point to make here is about *tauliah* (accreditation), which is applicable in all states. For instance, Section 11 of the Syariah Criminal Offences (Federal Territories) Act 1997 (Act 559) mentions that "any person who teaches or professes to teach any matter relating to the religion of Islam without a *tauliah* (accreditation) … shall be guilty of an offence". Shad Saleem Faruqi (2017) argued that the *tauliah* is clearly in conflict with Article 11 (4) of the Federal Constitution and all statutes empowering universities and schools. Faruqi was referring to the case of Turkish Islamic intellectual Mustafa Akyol who was detained by the Federal Territories Islamic Affairs Department (JAWI) on 24 September 2017 after giving a talk on Islam without prior accreditation from the relevant Religious Teaching Supervisory Committee. Faruqi argued that Mustafa was not "teaching" but merely taking part as a panelit in a forum. "Teaching" is not synonymous with "propagating" because a teacher may teach criminology but is not propagating criminal conduct. Moreover, the words "any matter relating to the religion of Islam" cover the whole range of Islamic thought. Regarding university autonomy, he said: "If section 11 is to be interpreted literally, then any lecturer of Islamic theology, law, economics, banking, commerce, history, good governance and philosophy or any participant in a seminar or workshop on any aspect of Islam must first obtain a *tauliah* or risk a RM5,000 fine or three years' jail!" (Faruqi 2017). The PH government has not intervened on this matter. When some critics commented on how Zakir Naik who managed to obtain a *tauliah* for his talk, Mujahid responded that Putrajaya will not interfere on this issue as it is under the state jurisdiction. The federal government can only decide on the qualifications of Naik or other scholars to deliver talks in public gatherings (Nur Hasliza 2019).

Overall, there is not much change in terms of the practices of Islam and religious expression under the "New Malaysia" era. The constraint is not so much about the PH government not wanting to interfere in Islamic affairs which are under the state's jurisdiction. For instance, there is the case of *Shia* raids in Johor and Selangor where both states are clearly under the rule of the PH. There is no doubt that the Sultans and religious authorities have the power and play significant roles in the practices of Islam in their respective states.

The PH government also realizes that it does not want to lose the support of the Malay-Muslims if they interfere in Islamic affairs, drastically change the policy of Islamization, and transform the practices carried out by state religious authorities. The ruling government does not want to trigger any controversy and conflict in federal-state relations on Islam. It is also interesting to see whether the concept of *"Rahmatan Lil 'Alamin"* can be implemented properly and effectively by the PH government. If the PH government fails to champion on Islamic issues, there is a risk that PAS and UMNO are able to gain the support and trust of the Muslims for the next general election scheduled latest by 2023.

However, efforts made by Malaysian Human Rights Commission (SUHAKAM) should be applauded for using religious expression to create awareness about human rights in Malaysia. There are three state religious departments, according to SUHAKAM's Commissioner Nik Salida Suhaila, which have used Friday sermons prepared by SUHAKAM (Bedi 2019). Issues covered in the sermons, among others, are the rights of women, children, and the environment. This is part of its engagement with all the religious departments from the various states. The religious departments of Penang, Kuala Lumpur, and Negeri Sembilan have responded to the sermons submitted by SUHAKAM. Nik Salida said that SUHAKAM is engaging more with religious departments and educating them about human rights such as following a proper standard operating procedure (SOP) in conducting raids during cases of close proximity. SUHAKAM's initiatives can be followed by other government's agencies and non-governmental organizations (NGOs). Through civil engagements and by avoiding conflicts, many issues can be resolved. This will make Malaysia a great nation, full of prosperity for its people.

Future Challenges for Freedom of Expression in Malaysia

Michael Walzer (1983, p. 304) argues that democracy is "the political way of allocating power … What counts is argument among the citizens. Democracy puts a premium on speech, persuasion, (and) rhetorical skill". Democracy, therefore, does not require "simple equality" in the exercise of political power. Though there must be an equal chance to voice out, citizens who make more persuasive arguments in public discussion will have a greater influence. In a democracy, the community should choose which argument is the most persuasive, and the appropriate political authority should decide honestly whether those arguments are practical or good enough to be accepted as policy. Both John Dewey and Benjamin Barber are concerned that citizens in a democracy be able to utilize existing communication systems for democratic means. For Dewey (1927/54, p. 168), democratic communications require that speech rights provide a real opportunity for public participation in democratic processes on a scale that commensurates with the consequences of associated life. For Barber (1984, pp. 273–79), democracies must support local and national institutions and the fora that enable communities to mediate between themselves and to engage in a full range of democratic speech. Both Dewey (1927/54) and Barber (1984) argue that political rights and freedoms are maintained not against, but rather through, society. Both view rights as a mutually agreed-upon social construct that accords to individuals' possibilities and protections they would otherwise lack. Rather than stressing the alienation of individuals from the government,

Dewey and Barber argue that a democratic public and the state should be mutually reinforcing. Democratic states exist not only to protect their citizens from coercion, but also to provide an instrument through which citizens collectively examine, make and enact social decisions to benefit the common good. These arguments from Dewey and Barber are clearly in line with Siebert, Peterson and Schramm's interpretation of social responsibility in relating it to the concept of positive liberty—"freedom for", rather than "freedom from". They wrote:

> Social responsibility holds that the government must not merely allow freedom; it must actively promote it ... When necessary, therefore, the government should act to protect the freedom of its citizens (Siebert, Peterson and Schramm 1956/73, p. 95).

The acts of government mentioned include legislation to forbid "flagrant abuses", and it may also "enter the field of communication to supplement existing media" (McQuail 2000, p. 149). To this end, Emerson (1970, p. 15) and Sunstein (1993, pp. 18–19) have proposed an understanding of speech rights based on whether or not they create an effective system of freedom of expression in a particular social context. In order to maintain a system of free expression, the government must create a workable structure of principles, practices and institutions that respond to real conditions and which advocate realistic goals.

On the other hand, according to David Martin Jones (1995, p. 74), "consensus" as modernized Asian politicians describe the traditional pursuit of balance, does not require a pluralistic consultation of a multiplicity of interests, much less submission to popular taste. Asian political thought overwhelmingly asserts the need for hierarchy and expertise. Ideally, rule is the responsibility of a virtuous elite, or a man of prowess. East and Southeast Asian political understandings place great value on substantive moral consensus that denies or suppresses moral pluralism and social diversity, whether in the traditional Confucian appeal to a past mythical, golden age of virtue and universal harmony to be memorialized and used as a basis to criticize the "chaotic" present, or in the form of contemporary bureaucratic managerial elites mobilizing society via mass organizations, moral exhortation, and the dissemination of national "core values" underpinning social and economic goals. For instance, in January 1989, the Singapore government identified four official core values—communitarianism, familism, decision-making by consensus, and social and religious harmony—which Singaporeans must espouse to ensure national unity (Quah 1990, p. 92). The Islamic faith of the Malays in Malaysia has its communitarian orientation in its idea of the *ummah*, the community of all Muslims, and the religion-dictated practices of charity. Furthermore, the Malay community-spirit is supposedly augmented by the traditional idea of *gotong-royong* (mutual cooperation) in the sharing of labour to assist each other among *kampung* (village) dwellers (Chua 2004, p. 99). There is a view that harmony is achieved not by a proliferation of interests, but by each person precisely fulfilling his ordained relationship or by subtly deferring to the requirements of *muafakat* (consensus). The harmonious, multi-functional Southeast Asian polis still requires that when the wind of the governing elite blows, the popular grass continues to bend (Jones 1995, p. 74).

Much of the restrictions on freedom of expression in Malaysia previously under the BN government have stemmed from the government's desire to weaken political contestation, criticism and dissent. In order to do this and, at the same time, permit legitimate restrictions, I advocate the adoption of social responsibility, which treats free expression as a right, yet carries with it a duty to exercise responsible expression for the common good. Therefore, this gives people the right to religious expression and at the same time protect a multiracial society, like Malaysia, from racial disharmony and hatred. In the context of a "New Malaysia", this advances five important arguments:

1) the creation of a community that balances individual rights with the good of the community;
2) promoting a responsible government that encourages public deliberation;
3) establishing regulations, procedures and practices of truth-seeking, and managing their dissemination;
4) discovering and promoting the common good; and
5) encouraging the creation of a strong civil society for consensus politics in the process of public deliberation.

These can be well adapted to Malaysia, where the tradition of communitarianism and social values can be combined with the principle of freedom of expression. In fact the consociational politics practised by the ruling BN government previously can be revoked in favour of the consensus politics through public deliberation for "New Malaysia" where civil society and the new media, the Internet and mobile phones, can perform significant roles in generating civil deliberation. In implementing this, it is recommended that Malaysia seeks the notion of a deliberative democracy through realizing a two-party system and a strong civil society, paying attention to human rights by balancing the civil and political rights with the economic and social rights, creating a responsible press system, reforming legislations on free expression and expanding the roles of SUHAKAM. The post-2018 general election shows that there are now more openness in practising press freedom and political activism in Malaysia. However, hindering and restrictive structures such as some restrictive laws are still maintained, barring a few proposed suggestions to amend them, making the practice of freedom of expression vulnerable to future restrictions. Therefore, free expression that seeks to contribute to the social good and that is part of the normal democratic process should be protected by the Constitution for the purpose of establishing a fair political contestation and encouraging public deliberation in Malaysia (Azizuddin 2010).

In 2018, the PH government formed a five-member Committee on Institutional Reforms comprising prominent legal minds to look into institutional reforms in the country. Its formation was announced by the government-appointed Council of Eminent Persons and the committee members will report to the council. This committee will identify several key institutions such as the Malaysian Anti-Corruption Commission and Election Commission and study many laws, particularly on political financing and political freedom that are essential to the Constitution and the rule of law. As such, this will bring changes to the country where efficient reforms can take place in the arms of the government, particularly in the legislature and the judiciary, the police and the anti-corruption agencies, and many other government ministries and agencies. The PH government has restructured some government agencies and is considering to abolish and amend several laws. In my view, introducing a new law on hate speech and protecting the race relations and religious harmony in Malaysia is an important step in dealing with religious expression in Malaysia.

I agree with Shad Saleem Faruqi (2018) who suggested several ways to roll back authoritarianism, expand human rights and impose checks on untrammeled powers. He suggested that first, Malaysia needs an independent Law Reform Commission to scrutinize the entire legal arsenal constructed to shackle the media, discourage thought and expression, and suppress information. The commission must report to Parliament. In addition, Parliament must set up a Special Committee on Human Rights to familiarize itself with the work of SUHAKAM. A number of oppressive laws must be repealed. Second, in relation to municipal law and international law, Malaysia adopts the dualistic theory. International law is not law per se unless it is incorporated into domestic law by an Act of Parliament. However, in an age of globalization, it is difficult to build dykes against the incoming tide of international law. Regrettably, Malaysia has not ratified most international treaties and conventions on freedom of expression, media and the right to information. This situation must be changed though, if need be, with reservations in those areas where the allegedly "universal standards" clashed with our deep-seated religious, moral and customary values.

What can be said is that freedom of expression needs to be strengthened in Malaysia. This can be achieved if the government has the political will to implement changes. So far, the PH government has made promises to achieve freedom of expression. The PN government has yet to come out with any commitment in policy or implementation to embrace freedom of expression. Hopefully, this will become a reality and Malaysians, who are consistently seeking for genuine freedom and participation in Malaysian democracy, can get to enjoy the freedom.

George Orwell (1949) pointed out that if large numbers of people believe in freedom of expression, there will be freedom of expression even if the law forbids it. Conversely, if public opinion is sluggish, inconvenient minorities will be persecuted even if laws exist to protect them. Thus, it is clear that in democratic states, like Malaysia, the rights to free expression can effectively be enhanced and protected and unjustified policies curbing legitimate free expression can be minimized. Religious expression that incites racial hatred and political instability or widely regarded as grossly offensive can be controlled, not only by the government, but also by responsible citizens of the country. In this way, freedom of religious expression could bring about a better Malaysia in the future.

To sum up on the future of religious expression in Malaysia, Mahathir, in my interview with him on 11 March 2019, explained about the reality in Malaysia by saying:

> In Malaysia, which has a multiracial, multi-religious population, if you allow a man to insult the religion of another man, there will be riots, the country will not be stable. Like recently they had a picture of a Prophet and all that, and insulted a Prophet. It is a small thing for them, but for the Muslim, it is a big thing, you can't do that. So we have to take serious. Yes you are free, but the limit is that, you don't exercise your freedom at that expense of other people. So that is very important, because the sensitivity of the community must be honoured, must be respected by everyone. So I admit we are not liberal democracy. We are not but we find that it is being eroded because there will always be someone who wants to have full freedom and they will agitate. They will write against those things and all those. But in Malaysia, I think we have a multiracial, multi-religious society and moral values are very important to us. So we cannot follow liberalism that you find in some Western countries.

Therefore, it is a real challenge to practise freedom of religious expression with social responsibility in Malaysia. There is never more pressing issues in the trade-off between freedom of expression on the one hand and the right to be protected from malicious widespread bigotry and hatred on the other. We do not know yet what is the agenda of the PN government for Islam and religious expression in Malaysia. Somehow, Malaysian citizens have no choice but to reject any attempt to undermine freedom and democracy in Malaysia.

BIBLIOGRAPHY

Abas, Mohamed Salleh. 1984. *Selected Articles & Speeches on Constitution, Law & Judiciary*. Kuala Lumpur: Malaysian Law Publishers.
Abbott, Jason P. and Sophie Gregorios-Pippas. 2010. "Islamization in Malaysia: Processes and Dynamics". *Contemporary Politics* 16, no. 2: 135–51.
Abdullah, Nurjaanah. 2007. "Legislating Faith in Malaysia". *Singapore Journal of Legal Studies*: 264–89.
Abdullah, Raihanah. 2001. "Islamic Legal Education: Malaysian Experience". Paper presented at the International Law Conference: ASEAN Legal Systems and Regional Integration, Kuala Lumpur, 3–4 September 2001.
Abidin, Mohd Asri Zainul. 2007. "Apostasy: Between Emotions and Reality". *Drmaza.com*, 22 July 2007. http://drmaza.com/english_section/?p=17 (accessed 22 July 2007).
Adil, Mohamed Azam Mohamed. 2007. "Restrictions in Freedom of Religion in Malaysia: A Conceptual Analysis with Special Reference to the Law of Apostasy". *Muslim World Journal of Human Rights* 4, no. 2: 10–11.
Agence France-Presse. 2017. "Joint Patrols off Mindanao to Counter ISIS Threats—Malaysia", 3 June 2017. http://www.rappler.com/world/regions/asia-pacific/171862-joint-patrols-mindanao-militants-malaysia (accessed 1 July 2017).
Ahmad, Abdul Muati. 2010. "The Genesis of a New Culture: Prime Minister Mahathir's Legacy in Translating and Transforming The New Malays". *Human Communication* 13, no. 3: 137–53.
Ahmad Fauzi, Abdul Hamid. 1998. "Islamic Resurgence in Periphery: A Study of Political Islam in Contemporary Malaysia with Special Reference to the Darul Arqam Movement 1968–1996". Unpublished DPhil thesis, University of Newcastle Upon Tyne, Newcastle Upon Tyne.
———. 2016. "ISIS in Southeast Asia: Internalized Wahhabism is a Major Factor". Middle East Institute, 18 May 2016. https://www.mei.edu/content/map/isis-southeast-asia-internalized-wahhabism-major-factor?print=#_ftn1 (accessed 3 June 2016).

Ahmad, Ismail, Fahmi Abdul Rahim, Jaafar Pyeman, and Asmaddy Haris. 2008. "The Effects of the Introduction Syariah Index to the Bursa Malaysia Stock Index and Bursa Malaysia Stock Index Futures". *The Journal of Muamalat and Islamic Finance Research* 5, no. 1: 113–33.

Ahmad, Mohd Khairie and John Harrison. 2007. "Untapped Potential: Cultural Sensitivity-Islamic Persuasive Communication in Health Promotion Programs". Paper presented at the Global Communication and Development Conference, Shanghai, China, 16–21 October 2007.

Ahmad Sanusi Azmi. 2019. "Kekaburan konsep Rahmatan Lil Alamin". *Malaysiakini*, 26 August 2019. https://www.malaysiakini.com/news/489486 (accessed 9 September 2019).

Ahmad, Zakaria. 1989. "Malaysia: Quasi Democracy in a Divided Society". In *Democracy in Developing Countries: Asia*, edited by Larry Diamond, Juan J. Linz, and Martin Seymour Lipset. Boulder: Lynne Rienner/Adamantine Press.

Ainaa Aiman. 2019. "Don: Our Islamic Education Doesn't Instil Islamic Values". *Free Malaysia Today*, 12 January 2019. https://www.freemalaysiatoday.com/category/nation/2019/01/12/don-our-islamic-education-doesnt-instil-islamic-values/ (accessed 12 January 2019).

Alatas, Syed Farid. 2014. "Salafism and the Threat to Peace". *The Malay Mail Online*, 10 April 2014. http://m.themalaymailonline.com/what-you-think/article/salafism-and-the-threat-to-peace-syed-farid-alatas#sthash.qf4E7iHQ.dpuf (accessed 10 April 2014).

Alexander, Larry. 1993. "Liberalism, Religion, and the Unity of Epistemology". *San Diego Law Review* 30: 775–76.

Ali, M. 2012. "Southeast Asia, Islamic Liberalism in". *Oxford Islamic Studies Online*, 16 April 2012. http://www.oxfordislamicstudies.com/article/opr/t343/e0040 (accessed 3 March 2014).

Ali, Syed Husin. 2008. *The Malays: Their Problems and Future.* Petaling Jaya: The Other Press.

Aliza Shah. 2018. "[Exclusive] Police Will Know If You Watch Porn". *New Straits Times*, 9 July 2018. https://www.nst.com.my/news/exclusive/2018/07/388926/exclusive-police-will-know-if-you-watch-porn (accessed 23 February 2019).

Aljazeera. 2017. "Top Malaysian ISIL Operative Killed in Syria", 9 May 2017. http://www.aljazeera.com/news/2017/05/top-malaysian-isil-operative-killed-syria-170508182519182.html (accessed 1 July 2017).

———. 2018. "Malaysia's Opposition Pulls off Shocking Election Win", 10 May 2018. https://www.aljazeera.com/news/2018/05/malaysia-opposition-pulls-shocking-election-win-180509184811723.html (accessed 20 June 2018).

Anand, Ram. 2015. "409 Cases Investigated Under Sedition Act in Past 7 Years". *The Malaysian Insider*, 18 June 2015. http://www.themalaysianinsider.com/malaysia/article/409-cases-investigated-under-sedition-act-in-past-seven-years (accessed 3 September 2015).

Anbalagan, V. 2014. "Court Reserves Judgment on Church's Leave Application". *The Malaysian Insider*, 5 March 2014. http://www.themalaysianinsider.com/

print/malaysia /course-reserves-judgment-on-churchs-leave-application (accessed 5 March 2014).
Angkatan Belia Islam Malaysia (ABIM). 2010. "Profil ABIM". http://www.abim.org.my/ (accessed 10 March 2010).
Anwar Ibrahim. 1996a. *The Asian Renaissance*. Singapore: Times Book International.
———. 1996b. "Asia's Moral Imperative". *Asian Wall Street Journal*, 13 May 1996b.
Aqilah, Ili. 2019. "Sultan Nazrin: Stop Hate Speech". *The Star Online*, 2 September 2019. https://www.thestar.com.my/news/nation/2019/09/02/sultan-nazrin-stop-hate-speech#Olgy7i0RAoRMgKm6.99 (accessed 4 September 2019).
Aramesh, Kiarash. 2007. "Human Dignity in Islamic Bioethics". *Iran Journal of Allergy Asthma Immunol* 6 (Suppl. 5): 25–28.
Article 19. 2017. "Malaysia: Free Speech is Far from 'Thriving'", 24 April 2017. https://www.article19.org/resources.php/resource/38726/en/malaysia:-free-speech-is-far-from-%E2%80%9Cthriving%E2%80%9D (accessed 29 August 2017).
———. 2018. "Reform Laws Restricting Freedom of Expression". *Malaysiakini*, 22 May 2018. https://www.malaysiakini.com/news/426155 (accessed 5 January 2019).
Asian Pacific Post. 2014. "Foreign Fighter from Asia Joining Islamic Jihad", 15 November 2014. http://www.asianpacificpost.com/article/6448-foreign-fighters-asia-joining-islamic-jihad.html (accessed 5 May 2015).
ASLI (Asian Strategy and Leadership Institute). 2008. *An Analysis of Malaysia's 12th General Election*. Kuala Lumpur: ASLI. http://www.asli.com.my/DOCUMENT/An%20Analysis%20of%20Malaysia.pdf (accessed 3 June 2009).
Associated Press. 2016. "Hacker Who Gave ISIS 'Hitlist' of US Targets Jailed for 20 Years", 24 September 2016. https://www.theguardian.com/world/2016/sep/24/hacker-who-gave-isis-hitlist-of-us-targets-jailed-for-20-years (accessed 24 September 2016).
———. 2017. "Police: Top Malaysian Islamic State Operative Dead in Syria", 9 May 2017. http://newsinfo.inquirer.net/895456/police-top-malaysian-islamic-state-operative-dead-in-syria#ixzz4oT44e8pk (accessed 1 July 2017).
Audi, Robert. 1989. "The Separation of Church and State and the Obligations of Citizenship". *Philosophy and Public Affairs* 18: 259–76.
———. 1997. "Liberal Democracy and the Place of Religion in Politics". In *Religion in The Public Square: The Place of Religious Convictions in Political Debate*, edited by Robert Audi and Nicholas Wolterstorff Lanham. Md: Rowman and Littlefield.
Augustin, Robin. 2018. "Hate Speech is Wrong, Even Against 'Deviant' Shias, says Mujahid". *Free Malaysia Today*, 12 November 2018. https://www.freemalaysiatoday.com/category/nation/2018/11/12/hate-speech-is-wrong-even-against-deviant-shias-says-mujahid/ (accessed 13 September 2019).
Ayton-Shenker, Diana. 1995. "The Challenge of Human Rights and Cultural Diversity". *United Nations Background Note*. New York: United Nations Department of Public Information. http://www.un.org/rights/dpi1627e.htm (accessed 3 June 2009).

Azizuddin, Mohd Sani. 2008. "Mahathir as a Cultural Relativist: Mahathirism on Human Rights". Paper presented at the 17th Biennial Conference of the Asian Studies Association of Australia, Melbourne, 1–3 July 2008.

———. 2009. *The Public Sphere and Media Politics in Malaysia*. Newcastle: Cambridge Scholars Publishing.

———. 2010. *Freedom of Political Speech and Social Responsibility in Malaysia*. Bangi: UKM Press.

———. 2013a. "Politico-Religious Values in Malaysia: Comparing Asian Values and Islam Hadhari". *Cultura. International Journal of Philosophy of Culture and Axiology* 10, no. 1: 141–66.

———. 2013b. "Hate Speech and Free Speech in Malaysia". *New Mandala*, 23 December 2013b. http://asiapacific.anu.edu.au/newmandala/2013/12/23/hate-speech-and-free-speech-in-malaysia/ (accessed 31 December 2013).

———. 2013c. "Report: The Print Media Coverage and Reporting in the 13th General Election in Malaysia (unpublished)". Sintok: School of International Studies, Universiti Utara Malaysia.

———. 2015. *Islamization Policy and Islamic Bureaucracy in Malaysia*. Trends in Southeast Asia, no. 5/2015. Singapore: Institute of Southeast Asian Studies.

———. 2016. "ISIS Recruitment of Malaysian Youth: Challenge and Response". Washington: Middle East Institute, 3 May 2016. http://www.mei.edu/content/map/isis-recruitment-malaysian-youth-challenge-and-response (accessed 4 May 2016).

———. 2018. "Islamic Agenda is the Malaysian Opposition's Achilles Heel". *East Asia Forum*, 3 February 2018. http://www.eastasiaforum.org/2018/02/03/islamic-agenda-is-the-malaysian-oppositions-achilles (accessed 3 June 2019).

Azlee, Zan. 2016. "Here We Go Banning Books Again". *Malaysia Today*, 8 January 2016. http://www.malaysia-today.net/here-we-go-banning-books-again/ (accessed 29 March 2016).

Azmi, Aziz and A.B. Shamsul. 2004. "The Religious, the Plural, the Secular and the Modern: A Brief Critical Survey on Islam in Malaysia". *Inter-Asia Cultural Studies* 5, no. 3: 341–56.

Badawi, Abdullah Ahmad. 2006. *Islam Hadhari: A Model Approach for Development and Progress*. Petaling Jaya: MPH Publishing.

Bakar, Ibrahim Abu and Mohd Nasran Mohamad. 2012. "Human Capital in Islamic Studies at National University of Malaysia". *Advances in Natural and Applied Sciences* 6, no. 6: 852–57.

Bakar, Mohamad Abu. 1991. "External Influences on Contemporary Islamic Resurgence in Malaysia". *Contemporary Southeast Asia* 13, no. 2: 220–28.

Bandura, Albert. 1990. "Mechanisms of Moral Disengagement". In *Origins of Terrorism: Psychologies, Ideologies, Theologies, States of Mind*, edited by Walter Reich. Cambridge: Cambridge University Press, pp. 161–91.

Barber, Benjamin. 1984. *Strong Democracy: Participatory Politics for a New Age*. Berkeley: University of California Press.

Barendt, Eric. 2009. "Incitement to, and Glorification of, Terrorism". In *Extreme Speech and Democracy*, edited by Ivan Hare and James Weinstein. Oxford: Oxford University Press, pp. 445–62.

Barr, Michael D. 2002. *Cultural Politics and Asian Values: The Tepid War*. London: Routledge.

Bedi, Rashvinjeet S. 2019. "Suhakam's Sermons used by Three State Religious Depts". *The Star Online*, 12 September 2019. https://www.thestar.com.my/news/nation/2019/09/12/suhakam039s-sermons-used-by-three-state-religious-depts#AlO2DB1TRrPA5BZz.99 (accessed 12 September 2019).

Bell, Daniel A. 2000. *East Meets West: Human Rights and Democracy in East Asia*. Princeton, New Jersey: Princeton University Press.

Bernama (Berita Nasional). 2007a. "Abdullah Chides Opposition for Spinning out Issues", 27 August 2007. http://www.bernama.com/bernama/v3/news.php?id=281491 (accessed 30 May 2008).

———. 2007b. "Malaysia Not Secular State, says Najib", 17 July 2007. http://www.bernama.com/bernama/v3/news_lite.php?id=273699 (accessed 20 April 2010).

———. 2011. "Most Islamic Studies Graduates Choose Career Path in Education", 1 November 2011. https://my.news.yahoo.com/most-islamic-studies-graduates-choose-career-path-education-110005627.html (accessed 1 November 2011).

———. 2018. "Malays Must Change Their Value System to Succeed—Mahathir", 29 December 2018. http://www.bernama.com/en/news.php?id=1679663 (accessed 9 January 2019).

———. 2019a. "Malaysia Promotes Islamic Values Through *Rahmatan Lilalamin* and the *Maqasid Syariah*", 15 April 2019a. http://www.bernama.com/en/news.php?id=1716777 (accessed 16 April 2019).

———. 2019b. "Kelantan anjur pertandingan bina badan tutup aurat bulan depan", 17 September 2019b. http://www.bernama.com/bm/news.php?id=1768301 (accessed 18 September 2019).

British Broadcasting Corporation (BBC). 2006. "Islam-West Divide 'Grows Deeper'". *BBC News*, 10 February 2006. http://news.bbc.co.uk/2/hi/asia-pacific/4699716.stm (accessed 10 February 2006).

Brown, C.C. 1970. *Sejarah Melayu 'Malay Annals'*. Kuala Lumpur: Oxford University Press.

Buang, Ahamd Hidayat, M. Roslan Mohd. Nor, and Luqman Abdullah. 2008. "The Madrasah System in Malaysia: Its Contribution to the Nation and Challenges". Paper presented at the IAS-AEI International Conference, New Horizons in Islamic Area Studies: Islamic Scholarship Across Cultures and Continents, National Institute of Humanities, Japan and Asia-Europe Institute, University of Malaya, Kuala Lumpur, 22–24 November 2008.

Burhanuddin, J. 2014. "Peranan Kor Agama Angkatan Tentera (KAGAT) Sebagai Organisasi Da'wah Dan Usaha Pengukuhan Daya Juang Anggota Angkatan Tentera Malaysia". In *Prosiding Bicara Da'wah kali ke 15: Pengurusan Da'wah Kontemporari*, edited by Muhamad Faisal Ashaari, Abu Dardaa Mohamad, and

Ahmad Irdha Mokhtar. Bangi: Jabatan Pengajian Da'wah dan Kepimpinan, Fakulti Pengajian Islam, UKM, pp. 20–45.

Bursa Malaysia. 2005. "Syariah Index". http://www.klse.com.my/website/ education/smb_syariahindex.htm (accessed 3 December 2005).

Buyong, Mazni and Rizalawati Ismail. 2011. "Islamic Programs in Malaysian Free-to-Air Television Channels". Paper presented at the International Conference on Islamic Civilization and Malay Identity 2011, Malacca, Malaysia, 14–15 November 2011.

Carmi, Guy E. 2008. "Dignity versus Liberty: The Two Western Cultures of Free Speech". *Boston University International Law Journal* 26: 277–374.

Centre for Independent Journalism. 2012. *Freedom of Expression in Malaysia 2011*. Puchong: Centre for Independent Journalism.

Chalk, Peter. 2015. *Black Flag Rising: ISIL in Southeast Asia and Australia*. Australian Strategic Policy Institute, 8 December 2015. https://www.aspi.org.au/publications/black-flag-rising-isil-in-southeast-asia-and-australia/Blackflagrising_ISIL.pdf (accessed 10 December 2015).

Chan, Joseph. 1995. "The Asian Challenge to Universal Human Rights: A Philosophical Appraisal". In *Human Rights and International Relations in the Asia-Pacific Region*, edited by James T.H. Tang. London: Pinter.

———. 2000. "Thick and Thin Accounts of Human Rights". In *Human Rights and Asian Values: Contesting National Identities and Cultural Representations in Asia*, edited by Michael Jacobsen and Ole Bruun. Surrey: Curzon Press.

Channel News Asia. 2017. "Free Speech Thriving in Malaysia But Fake News a Plague: PM Najib", 19 April 2017. http://www.channelnewsasia.com/news/asiapacific/free-speech-thriving-in-malaysia-but-fake-news-a-plague-pm-najib-8741726 (accessed 29 August 2017).

———. 2019. "PM Mahathir Accuses Chinese Schools Association of Racism over Khat Controversy", 13 August 2019. https://www.channelnewsasia.com/news/asia/malaysia-mahathir-khat-calligraphy-racist-dong-zong-11805520 (accessed 9 September 2019).

Chew, Amy. 2019a. "Outrage in Malaysia as Zakir Naik suggests Chinese Expulsion". *Aljazeera*, 15 August 2019a. https://www.aljazeera.com/news/2019/08/outrage-malaysia-zakir-naik-suggests-chinese-expulsion-190814230715236.html (accessed 9 Septermber 2019).

———. 2019b. "Malaysia's Racial and Religious Divisions Widen as Opposition Seeks Political Gain". *South China Morning Post*, 27 August 2019b. https://www.scmp.com/week-asia/politics/article/3024542/malaysias-racial-and-religious-divisions-widen-opposition-seeks (accessed 11 September 2019).

Chew, Li Hua. 2007. "Legislating Faith in Malaysia". *Singapore Journal of Legal Studies*: 264–89.

Chi, M. 2011. "Perkasa in Minor Protest against MCA". *The Malaysian Insider*, 25 April 2011. http://www.themalaysianinsider.com/malaysia/article/perkasa-in-minor-protest-against-mca#sthash.1q4vZM4B.dpuf (accessed 25 April 2011).

Chin, Emmanuel Santa Maria. 2019. "Zakir Naik gets Police OK for Melaka Prayers". *The Malay Mail*, 2 September 2019. https://www.malaymail.com/news/malaysia/2019/09/02/zakir-naik-gets-police-ok-for-melaka-prayers/1786481 (accessed 9 September 2019).

Chin, James. 2004. "Pak Lah's Islamic Challenge". *Asian Analysis*, September 2004. http://www.aseanfocus.com/asiananalysis/article.cfm?articleID=774 (accessed 25 March 2005).

———. 2019. "Commentary: Almost a Year since Pakatan Harapan swept into Government, has Malaysia Lost its Mojo for Reform?". *Channel News Asia*, 6 May 2019. https://www.channelnewsasia.com/news/commentary/pakatan-harapan-one-year-ge-14-mahathir-anwar-reforms-dap-11505192 (accessed 10 September 2019).

Chong, Debra. 2011. "PM to Meet Church Leaders amid Christian Malaysia row". *The Malaysian Insider*, 11 May 2011. http://www.themalaysianinsider.com/print/malaysia/pm-to-meet-church-leaders-amid-christian-malaysia-row/ (accessed 12 May 2011).

———. 2019. "Convicted of Sedition, Preacher Wan Ji Gets Stay of Jail Sentence". *The Malay Mail*, 12 July 2019. https://www.malaymail.com/news/malaysia/2019/07/12/convicted-of-sedition-preacher-wan-ji-gets-stay-of-jail-sentence/1770740 (accessed 9 September 2019).

Chong, Debra and Emmanuel Santa Maria Chin. 2018. "AG Drops Bid to Appeal Ban on Faisal Tehrani's Books". *The Malay Mail*, 29 October 2018. https://www.malaymail.com/news/malaysia/2018/10/29/ag-drops-bid-to-appeal-ban-on-faisal-tehranis-books/1687686 (accessed 9 January 2019).

Choudhury, Tufyal. 2009. "The Terrorism Act 2006: Discouraging Terrorism". In *Extreme Speech and Democracy*, edited by Ivan Hare and James Weinstein. Oxford: Oxford University Press, pp. 463–88.

Chow, Melissa Darlyne. 2019. "Man Pleads Guilty to Insulting Hindu Religion". *Free Malaysia Today*, 15 March 2019. https://www.freemalaysiatoday.com/category/nation/2019/03/15/man-pleads-guilty-to-insulting-hindu-religion/ (accessed 16 March 2019).

Christmann, Kris. 2012. *Preventing Religious Radicalization and Violent Extremism: A Systematic Review of the Research Evidence*. London: Youth Justice Board for England and Wales.

Chua Beng Huat. 2004. "Asian Values: Is an Anti-Authoritarian Reading Possible?". In *Contemporary Southeast Asia: Regional Dynamics, National Differences*, edited by Mark Beeson. New York: Palgrave Macmillan.

Clifford, Matthew O. and Thomas P. Huff. 2000. "Some Thoughts on the Meaning and Scope of the Montana Constitution's 'Dignity' Clause with Possible Applications". *Montreal Law Review* 61: 301–34.

Comber, Leon. 1983. *13 May 1969: A Historical Survey of Sino-Malay Relations*. Kuala Lumpur: Heinemann Asia.

Commonwealth Legal Information Institute (CommonLII). 2006. Malaysian Federal Court 18. No. 01-3-2005(N). 12 July 2006. http://www.commonlii.org/my/cases/MYFC/2006/18.html (accessed 4 July 2007).

Court of Appeal of Malaysia. 2011. "Judgment of Mohd Hishamudin Yunus, JCA". Civil Appeal No. W-01(IM)-636-2010.

Cram, Ian. 2009. "The Danish Cartoons, Offensive Expression, and Democratic Legitimacy". In *Extreme Speech and Democracy*, edited by Ivan Hare and James Weinstein. Oxford: Oxford University Press.

Daily Express. 2018. "Bernama: Mahathir Warns Free Speech Abusers", 30 November 2018. http://www.dailyexpress.com.my/news.cfm?NewsID=129064 (accessed 9 January 2019).

Daily Mail. 2010. "Mail Online: Malaysian Police Arrest 52 Unmarried Muslim Couples for Being Alone Together in Hotel Rooms", 5 January 2010. http://www.dailymail.co.uk/news/article-1240510/Malaysian-police-arrest-52-unmarried-Muslim-couples-hotel-rooms.html?printingPage=true (accessed 6 January 2010).

Dearden, Lizzie. 2014. "ISIS vs Islamic State vs ISIL vs Daesh: What Do the Different Names Mean—and Why Does It Matter?". *The Independent*, 23 September 2014. http://www.independent.co.uk/news/world/middle-east/isis-vs-islamic-state-vs-isil-vs-daesh-what-do-the-different-names-mean-9750629.html (accessed 5 May 2015).

Dewey, John. 1927/54. *The Public and Its Problems*. Athens, Ohio: Ohio University Press.

Donnelly, J. 2001. "What are Human Rights?". In *Introduction to Human Rights*, edited by G. Clack. Washington: International Information Programs, U.S. Department of State. http://usinfo.state.gov/products/pubs/hrintro/donelly.htm (accessed 7 January 2010).

Dzulkifly, Danial. 2019. "Amanah Seeks to Open Eyes on Malay, Muslim Rights under Pakatan". Microsoft Network (MSN), 6 February 2019. https://www.msn.com/en-my/news/national/amanah-seeks-to-open-eyes-on-malay-muslim-rights-under-pakatan/ar-BBTgKXI (accessed 9 February 2019).

El-Gamal, Mahmoud Amin. 2000. *A Basic Guide to Contemporary Islamic Banking and Finance*. Huston: Rice University.

Emerson, Thomas. 1966. *Toward a General Theory of the First Amendment*. New York: Random House.

———. 1970. *The System of Freedom of Expression*. New York: Random House.

Esposito, John L., ed. 2015. "Dakwah (Malaysia)". In *The Oxford Dictionary of Islam: Oxford Islamic Studies Online*. http://www.oxfordislamicstudies.com/article /opr/t125/e480 (accessed 25 March 2015).

Esscom Times. 2014. "Malaysia Views Seriously ISIS Threat in South Philippines—Hishamuddin", 17 October 2014. http://esscom.gov.my/news-in-english/malaysia-views-seriously-isis-threat-south-philippines-hishammuddin/ (accessed 5 May 2015).

Evans, Carolyn. 2009. "Religious Speech that undermines Gender Equality". In *Extreme Speech and Democracy*, edited by Ivan Hare and James Weinstein. Oxford: Oxford University Press.

Fadli, Mohamad. 2019. "Ask Jais, Mujahid says on Anti-Shia Sermon". *Free Malaysia Today*, 6 September 2019. https://www.freemalaysiatoday.com/category/nation/2019/09/06/ask-jais-mujahid-says-on-anti-shia-sermon/ (accessed 12 September 2019).

Fakhrull Halim, M. 2019. "Liberal atau pelampau sama-sama bahaya". *Malaysiakini*, 1 May 2019. https://www.malaysiakini.com/news/474424 (accessed 1 May 2019).

Farik, Zolkepli. 2015. "Civil Servant and Housewife Detained for IS Links". *The Star Online*, 24 March 2015. http://www.thestar.com.my/News/Nation/2015/03/24/Civil-servant-and-housewife-detained-for-IS-links (accessed 5 May 2015).

Farrah, Naz Karim and Mohd Hariz. 2014. "IS Fighters Taking out Personal Loans". *New Straits Times*, 20 December 2014. http://www.nst.com.my/node/64414 (accessed 5 May 2015).

Faruqi, Shad Saleem. 2001. "Support for Religious Liberty". *Sunday Star*, 25 February 2001.

———. 2002. "Principles that Govern Free Speech". *The Star*, 2 March 2002, p. 22.

———. 2004a. "Human Rights: Now and the Future". *Journal of the Kuala Lumpur Royal Malaysia Police College* 3: 11–28.

———. 2004b. "Constitutional Law, Rule of Law and Systems of Governance in Islam". In *Islam, Democracy and Good Governance: The Malaysia Experience*, edited by Ibrahim Abu Shah. Shah Alam: UPENA.

———. 2006. "Freedom of Religion under the Constitution". *The Sun*, 18 May 2006. http://www.sun2surf.com/article.cfm?id=14147 (accessed 19 May 2006).

———. 2017. "Drift Towards Intellectual Intolerance". *The Star Online*, 12 October 2017. https://www.thestar.com.my/opinion/columnists/reflecting-on-the-law/2017/10/12/drift-towards-intellectual-intolerance-according-to-tauliah-laws-muslims-must-speak-about-islam-only#6o7oJkfJxQYKvkSp.99 (accessed 12 September 2019).

———. 2018. "Reform Needed to Protect Free Speech". *The Star Online*, 27 September 2018. https://www.thestar.com.my/opinion/columnists/reflecting-on-the-law/2018/09/27/reform-needed-to-protect-free-speech-we-need-an-independent-law-reform-commission-to-scrutinise-the/#d73JQvKdebMut6v7.99 (accessed 22 October 2018).

Fazleena Aziz. 2014. "Zahid: Malaysia Working Closely with Interpol". *New Straits Times*, 29 August 2014. http://www.nst.com.my/node/28033 (accessed 5 May 2015).

Fernando, Joseph M. 2006. "The Position of Islam in the Constitution of Malaysia". *Journal of Southeast Asian Studies* 37: 249–53.

Free Malaysia Today. 2015. "Some Youth Think it an Honour to be Part of IS", 13 March 2015. http://www.freemalaysiatoday.com/category/nation/2015/03/13/some-youth-think-it-an-honour-to-be-part-of-is/ (accessed 5 May 2015).

———. 2016. "Retrieved from Zaid lambasts Jamil Khir Baharom", 17 March 2016. http://www.freemalaysiatoday.com/category/videos/2016/03/17/zaid-lambasts-jamil-khir-baharom/ (accessed 30 March 2016).

———. 2018. "Najib Launches New Human Rights Action Plan", 1 March 2018. https://www.freemalaysiatoday.com/category/nation/2018/03/01/najib-launches-new-human-rights-action-plan/ (accessed 9 February 2019).

———. 2019. "More Foreigners Arrested in Fresh Raids on Private Shia Functions in Johor, Selangor", 10 September 2019. https://www.freemalaysiatoday.com/category/nation/2019/09/10/more-foreigners-arrested-in-fresh-raids-on-private-shia-functions-in-johor-selangor/ (accessed 12 September 2019).

Fritz, Nicole and Martin Flaherty. 2003. *Unjust Order: Malaysia's Internal Security Act*. New York: The Joseph R. Crowley Program in International Human Rights, Fordham Law School.

Funston, John. 2006. "Malaysia". In *Voices of Islam in Southeast Asia: A Contemporary Sourcebook*, edited by Greg Fealy and Virginia Hooker. Singapore: Institute of Southeast Asian Studies.

Garza, C. 2012. "Ethnicity, Progress, and Pluralism: The Role and Future of Islam in Malaysia". Working Paper: POLS 4099, 25 April 2012. https://www.academia.edu/6486451/Ethnicity_Progress_and_Pluralism_The_Role_and_Future_of_Islam_in_Malaysia (accessed 3 June 2014).

Gatsiounis, Ioannis. 2006. "In Malaysia, 'Too Sensitive' for Debate". *Asia Times*, 4 August 2006. http://www.atimes.com/atimes/Southeast_Asia/HH04Ae01.html (accessed 8 August 2006).

Ghani, Zulkiple Abdul. 1996. "Diffusion of Da'wah Through Broadcasting Media: The Experience of Radio Television Malaysia (RTM)". Unpublished doctoral thesis, University of Edinburgh, Edinburgh.

Ghazali, Kamila. 2006. "The First Keynote Address of Abdullah Ahmad Badawi at the UMNO General Assembly". *Multilingua—Journal of Cross-Cultural and Interlanguage Communication* 25, no. 1: 129–42.

Global Civil Society Alliance (CIVICUS). 2018. "Malaysia: Acquittal of Individuals Charged for Sedition a Positive Move for Free Speech", 30 July 2018. https://www.civicus.org/index.php/media-resources/news/3341-malaysia-acquittal-of-individuals-charged-for-sedition-a-positive-move-for-free-speech (accessed 21 January 2019).

Goddard, Cliff. 1997. "Cultural Values and 'Cultural Scripts' of Malay (Bahasa Melayu)". *Journal of Pragmatics* 27: 183–201.

Gotbaum, Rachel. 2016. "The News Agency that Breaks Stories for ISIS". *PRI's The World*, 6 April 2016. https://www.pri.org/stories/2016-04-06/news-agency-breaks-stories-isis (accessed 3 June 2016).

Green, Jonathon and Nicholas J. Karolides. 2014. *Encyclopedia of Censorship: Facts on File Library of World History*. New York: Infobase Publishing.

Greene, Abner S. 1993. "The Political Balance of the Religion Clauses". *Yale Law Journal* 102: 1611–33.

Haneef, Mohamed Aslam. 2009. "Contemporary Islamic Economic Thought and Policy: Policies and Institutional Reforms in Malaysia". Paper presented in seminar organized by Bangladesh Institute of Islamic Thought (BIIT), Dhaka, Bangladesh, November 2009. http://www.ierb-bd.org/wp-content/uploads/2010/03/Contemporary-Islamic-Economic-Thought-and-Policy.doc (accessed 26 June 2014).

Harding, Andrew J. 1996. *Law, Government and the Constitution in Malaysia*. Kuala Lumpur: MLJ Sdn. Bhd.

———. 2002. "The Keris, Islam and the Blind Goddess: The State, Islam and the Constitution in Malaysia". *Singapore Journal of International and Comparative Law* 6, no. 1: 154–80.

———. 2010. "Sharia and National Law in Malaysia in Sharia Incorporated: A Comparative Overview of the Legal Systems of Twelve Muslim Countries in Past and Present". In *Sharia and National Law in Malaysia*, edited by Jan Michiel Otto. Leiden: Leiden University Press.

Hargreaves, Robert. 2002. *The First Freedom: A History of Free Speech*. Gloucestershire: Sutton Publishing.

Harisa Hawafi, Siti Aishah Hassan, and Ahmad Fauzi Mohd Ayub. 2017. "The Reliability Analysis for Malaysian Internet and Sexual Activities Inventory and Its Practical Implication". *International Journal of Academic Research in Business and Social Sciences* 7: 719–27.

Hariz Mohd. 2015. "Uni Student Marries IS Fighter on Skype after Facebook Fling". *New Straits Times*, 2 January 2015. http://www.nst.com.my/node/68241 (accessed 5 May 2015).

Haron, H. 2007. *Buletin BAKA*. Siri 1. Bukit Aman: Bahagian Agama dan Kaunseling.

Hasan, Zulkifli. 2008. "Islamic Criminal Offenses in Malaysia and the Extent of its Application", 9 June 2008. http://zulkiflihasan.files.wordpress.com/2008/06/isu-undg-jnyh-msia.pdf (accessed 9 June 2008)

Hashim, Mohamed Suffian. 1987. *Mengenal Perlembagaan Malaysia* [Introduction to Malaysian Constitution]. Kuala Lumpur: Dewan Bahasa dan Pustaka.

Hassan, R. 2009. *Course Material: Islamic Capital Market*. Kuala Lumpur: Islamic Law Department AIKOL IIUM.

Hassan, Saliha. 2003. "Islamic Non-Governmental Organizations". In *Social Movements in Malaysia: From Moral Communities to NGOs*, edited by Meredith Weiss and Saliha Hassan. London: Routledge Curzon.

Henley, Jon. 2009. "Victims of ISIS: Non-Western Journalists Who Don't Make the Headlines". *The Guardian*, 19 October 2009. http://www.theguardian.com/world/shortcuts/2014/oct/19/victims-of-isis-non-western-journalists-dont-make-headlines (accessed 20 October 2009).

Hilley, John. 2001. *Malaysia: Mahathirism, Hegemony and the New Opposition*. London: Zed Books.

Holbrook, Donald. 2014. "Using Quran to Justify Terrorist Violence: Analysing Selective Application of the Qur'an in English-Language Militant Islamist

Discourse". *Perspective on Terrorism*. http://www.terrorismanalysts.com/pt/index.php/pot/article/view/104/html (accessed 5 May 2015).

Hong, Carolyn. 2007. "Furore over Najib's 'Islamic State' Remark". *Straits Times*, 21 July 2007.

Horgan, John. 2005. *The Psychology of Terrorism (Political Violence)*. New York: Routledge.

Horowitz, Donald L. 1994a. *The Qur'an and the Common Law: Islamic Law Reform and the Theory of Legal Change*. Kuala Lumpur: University Malaya Publishers.

———. 1994b. "The Quran and Common Law: Islamic Reform and the Theory of Legal Change". *American Journal of Comparative Law* 42, no. 2: 233–93.

Human Rights Watch. 2015. *Creating a Culture of Fear: The Criminalization of Peaceful Expression in Malaysia*. USA: Human Rights Watch.

Hunt, Luke. 2016. "Malaysia's Growing Crackdown on Dissent". *The Diplomat*, 15 October 2016. http://thediplomat.com/2016/10/malaysias-growing-crackdown-on-dissent/ (accessed 29 August 2017).

Hussain Abdullah. 1990. *Kamus simpulan Bahasa*. 2nd ed. Kuala Lumpur: Dewan Bahasa dan Pustaka.

Inoguchi, Takashi and Edward Newman. 1997. "Introduction: 'Asian Values' and Democracy in Asia". *'Asian Values' and Democracy in Asia*, 27 March 1997. Shizouka: Shizuoka Prefectural Government. http://www.unu.edu/hq/unupress/asian-values.html (accessed 20 September 2000).

INSAP (Institute of Strategic Analysis and Policy Research). 2019. Info Paper: New Policy 'Rahmatan lil Alamin' Prime Minister's Department. https://insap.org.my/wp-content/uploads/2019/06/New-Policy-%E2%80%98Rahmatan-lil-Alamin%E2%80%99.pdf (accessed 9 September 2019).

Institute for Policy Analysis of Conflict (IPAC). 2014. "The Evolution of ISIS in Indonesia". IPAC Report No. 13, 24 September 2014. http://file.understandingconflict.org/file/2014/09/IPAC_13_Evolution_of_ISIS.pdf (accessed 3 June 2015).

International Crisis Group (ICG). 2007. "Islam and Identity in Germany". *Report Europe* 181. Germany: ICG.

Islam, Syed Serajul. 2005. *The Politics of Islamic Identity in Southeast Asia*. Singapore: Thompson Learning.

Jacoby, Mario. 1991. *Shame and the Origins of Self-Esteem: A Jungian Approach*, translated in collaboration with the author by Douglas Whitcher. London and New York: Routledge.

Jakarta Post. 2010. "Malaysia May Charge 200 for Deviating from Islam", 20 December 2010. http://www.thejakartapost.com/news/2010/12/20/malaysia-maycharge-200-deviating-islam.html (accessed 5 January 2011).

JAKIM (Department of Islamic Development Malaysia). 2006. "About Us". http://jakim.intranetportal.my/en (accessed 9 March 2010).

Jamny Rosli. 2018. "There Must Be Limits to Freedom, Dr M says of Human Rights". *The Malay Mail Online*, 1 October 2018. https://www.malaymail.com/news/malaysia/2018/10/01/there-must-be-limits-to-freedom-dr-m-says-of-human-rights/1678304 (accessed 7 January 2019).

Jayamanogaran, Thasha and G. Prakash. 2014. "Cops Launch Probe into Whether Ex-Trainer Influenced Others at National Service Camps". *The Malay Mail Online*, 19 December 2014. http://www.themalaymailonline.com/malaysia/article/cops-launch-probe-into-whether-ex-trainer-influenced-others-at-national-ser#sthash.Z3w2Hyqt.dpuf (accessed 5 May 2015).

Jones, David M. 1995. "Democracy and Identity: The Paradoxical Character of Political Development". In *Towards Illiberal Democracy in Pacific Asia*, edited by Daniel A. Bell, David Brown, Kanishka Jayasuriya, and David M. Jones. New York: Palgrave.

Juriah Abd. Jalil. 2015. "Combating Child Pornography in Digital Era: Is Malaysian Law Adequate to Meet the Digital Challenge?" *Pertanika Journal of Social Sciences and Humanities* 23: 137–52.

Kamali, Mohammad Hashim. 2002. *The Dignity of Man: An Islamic Perspective*. Cambridge: Islamic Texts Society.

Kaplan, Michael. 2015. "Malaysia ISIS Recruits: Counterterrorism Police Detain 10 Suspected Islamic State Group Militants". *International Business Times*, 20 August 2015. http://www.ibtimes.com/malaysia-isis-recruits-counterterrorism-police-detain-10-suspected-islamic-state-2061672 (accessed 20 August 2015).

Kaur, Minderjeet. 2019. "High Court Upholds Ban on 3 Books on Islam". *Free Malaysia Today*, 22 April 2019. https://www.freemalaysiatoday.com/category/nation/2019/04/22/high-court-upholds-ban-on-3-books-on-islam/ (accessed 22 April 2019).

Kayadibi, Saim and Ahmad Hidayat Buang. 2011. "The Role of Islamic Studies in Muslim Civilization in the Globalized World: Malaysian Experience". *Jurnal Hadhari* 3, no. 2: 83–102.

Kefeli, Zurina, Nursilah Ahmad, and Mohammad Haji Alias. 2007. *Employability of Islamic Studies Graduates in Malaysia*. Nilai: Islamic Science University Malaysia.

Khan, Qamar-ud-Din. 1982. *Political Concepts in the Quran*. Lahore: Islamic Book Foundation.

King, Eliza. 2015. "The ISIS Threat in Southeast Asia". *International Policy Digest*, 30 October 2015. http://intpolicydigest.org/2015/10/30/the-isis-threat-in-southeast-asia/ (accessed 3 June 2016).

Kling, Zainal. 2006. "UMNO and BN in the 2004 Election: The Political Culture of Complex Identities". In *Malaysia: Recent Trends and Challenges*, edited by Saw Swee-Hock and K. Kesavapany. Singapore: Institute of Southeast Asian Studies.

Koya, Abdar Rahman. 2019. "Critics Slam Selangor's 'Hate Speech' as Mosques Prepare to Deliver Anti-Shia Sermon". *Free Malaysia Today*, 5 September 2019. https://www.freemalaysiatoday.com/category/nation/2019/09/05/critics-slam-selangors-hate-speech-as-mosques-prepare-to-deliver-anti-shia-sermon/ (accessed 12 September 2019).

Kretzmer, David and Eckart Klein. 2002. "Forward". In *The Concept of Human Dignity in Human Rights Discourse*, edited by David Kretzmer and Eckart Klein. The Netherlands: Martinus Nijhoff Publishers.

Kumar, Pranav. 2012. "Malaysia: Majority Supremacy and Ethnic Tensions". *IPCS Special Report* 134. New Delhi: Institute of Peace and Conflict Studies (IPCS).

Kurzman, Charles. 2002. *Modernist Islam 1840–1940: A Sourcebook*. Oxford: Oxford University Press.

Kwok, Yenni. 2016. "ISIS Has Launched a Newspaper to Recruit Southeast Asian Fighters". *Time*, 11 July 2016. http://time.com/4400505/isis-newspaper-malay-southeast-asia-al-fatihin/ (accessed 29 August 2016).

Lailawati Mohd Salleh. 2005. "High/Low Context Communication: The Malaysian Malay Style". *Proceeding of the 2005 Association for Business Communication Annual Convention*. Kuala Lumpur: Association for Business Communication.

Lee Ban Chen. 2008. *Bagaimana Keris diganti dengan Merpati?* [How to Replace Dagger with Dove?]. Kuala Lumpur: Oriengroup Sdn. Bhd.

Lee, Casey. 2014. "15 Big Movies Banned in Malaysia". *Cinema Online*, 2 April 2014. http://www.cinema.com.my/Articles/features_details.aspx?search=2014.f_bigmoviesbanned_19114 (accessed 30 March 2016).

Lee, Julian C.H. 2010. *Islamization and Activism in Malaysia*. Singapore: Institute of Southeast Asian Studies

Lee Shi Ian. 2014. "Malaysian Women Join Middle East Jihadists as 'Comfort Women', Reveals Intelligence Report". *The Malaysian Insider*, 27 August 2014. http://www.themalaysianinsider.com/malaysia/article/malaysian-women-join-middle-east-jihadists-as-comfort-women-reveals-intelli (accessed 5 May 2015).

Leigh, Michael and Belinda Lip. 2004. "Transitions in Malaysian Society and Politics: Towards Centralizing Power". In *The Asia-Pacific: A Region in Transition*, edited by James Rolfe. Honolulu: Asia-Pacific Center for Security Studies.

Lim Kit Siang. 2003. "Five Questions on the Incompatibility of the PAS Islamic State Blueprint with Democracy, Human Rights, Women Rights and Pluralism". *DAP Malaysia*, 16 November 2003. http://dapmalaysia.org/all-archive/English/2003/nov03/lks/lks2748.htm (accessed 3 January 2012).

Lipi, Emmma. 2019. "Mujahid Rawa meets Zakir Naik, calls his Preaching Work 'Inspiring'". *The Star Online*, 13 March 2019. https://www.thestar.com.my/news/nation/2019/03/13/mujahid-rawa-meets-zakir-naik#JI1B5L0X5Aoji5Re.99 (accessed 9 September 2019).

Loone, S. 2002. *Malaysiakini*, 24 February 2002, pp. 1–2. http://www.malaysiakini.com/news/20020224001284.php (accessed 25 February 2002).

Magarian, Gregory P. 2010. "Religious Argument, Free Speech Theory, and Democratic Dynamism". Washington University in Saint Louis, 16 February 2010. http://www.thedivineconspiracy.org/Z5241W.pdf (accessed 4 April 2011).

Mahathir Mohamad. 1999. *A New Deal for Asia*. Selangor: Pelanduk Publications.

Mahathir Mohamad and Shintaro Ishihara. 1995. *The Voice of Asia: Two Leaders Discuss the Coming Century*. Tokyo: Kodansha International.

Maizatul Nazlina. 2017. "Activist Kassim Ahmad Freed of Insulting Islam". *The Star Online*, 7 August 2017. https://www.thestar.com.my/news/nation/2017/08/07/activist-kassim-ahmad-freed-of-insulting-islam/#EcMOQWhFC4Aw6hj5.99 (accessed 25 February 2019).

Malay Mail Online. 2014. "Bernama: Home Ministry Bans 12 Books Which Threaten Public Order, Morality", 4 February 2014. http://www.themalaymailonline.com/malaysia/article/home-ministrty-bans-12-books-which-threaten-public-order-morality (accessed 31 March 2016).

———. 2016. "PKR Rep Ordered to Pay RM320,000 for Defaming BN Leaders", 29 April 2016. http://www.themalaymailonline.com/malaysia/article/pkr-rep-ordered-to-pay-rm320000-for-defaming-four-bn-leaders (accessed 28 August 2016).

Malaysia. 1971. *Towards National Harmony*. Kuala Lumpur: Government Printer.

Malaysiakini. 2005. "Morality Standards Must Reflect Pluralist Malaysia", 27 April 2005. https://www.malaysiakini.com/letters/35683 (accessed 15 April 2016).

———. 2011. "JAIS Firm on Religious Talk Rule", 28 September 2011. http://www.malaysiakini.com/news/177135 (accessed 29 September 2011).

———. 2013. "M'sia Records Worst-Ever Ranking on Press Freedom", 30 January 2013. http://www.malaysiakini.com/news/220237 (accessed 30 January 2013).

———. 2014. "Varsities Monitor Students to Prevent Militancy", 15 October 2014. http://www.malaysiakini.com/news/277632 (accessed 5 May 2015).

———. 2018. "The Star: Mujahid Sees End to Khalwat Raids—Report", 6 October 2018. https://www.malaysiakini.com/news/446181 (accessed 1 May 2019).

———. 2019. "Home Ministry Lifts Ban on Zaid Ibrahim's Book", 19 September 2019. https://www.malaysiakini.com/news/492515 (accessed 19 September 2019).

Marican, Pawancheek. 2009. "Is Malaysia a Secular State?". *On Malaysian Law*, 23 September 2009. http://www.onmalaysianlaw.com/2009/09/is-malaysia-secular-state.html (accessed 5 November 2009).

Marshall, William. 1993. "The Other Side of Religion". *Hastings Law Journal* 44: 843–58.

Masum, Ahmad. 2009. "Freedom of Religion under the Malaysian Federal Constitution". *Current Law Journal* 2, no. 1: 1–19.

Maududi, Abul A'la. 1995. *Human Rights in Islam*. 2nd ed. Lahore: Islamic Publication.

Maziah Mustapha and Mohd Abbas Abdul Razak. 2019. "A Critical Appraisal of Zakir Naik's Islamic Evangelism". *International Journal of Islamic Thought* 15: 71–83.

Maznah Mohamad. 2002. "Islam and the Politics of Free Speech". *Aliran Monthly* 22, no. 1: 6.

———. 2019. "A Clamour for Islamic Reform in Malaysia: But in Which Direction under a Divine Bureaucracy?". *New Mandala*, 4 June 2019. https://www.newmandala.org/a-clamour-for-islamic-reform-in-malaysia-but-in-which-direction-under-a-divine-bureaucracy/ (accessed 7 September 2019).

McConnell, Michael W. 1999. "Five Reasons to Reject the Claim that Religious Arguments Should be Excluded from Democratic Deliberation". *Utah Law Review*: 639–48.

McIntyre, Alasdair C. 1981. *After Virtue: A Study in Moral Theory*. London: Duckworth.

McIntyre, Ian. 2006. "MB Defends Dress Code". *The Star Online*, 6 December 2006. http://www.thestar.com.my/news/story.asp?file=/2006/12/6/nation/16232962&sec=nation (accessed 4 July 2007).

McQuail, Denis. 2000. *McQuail's Mass Communication Theory*. 4th ed. London: SAGE Publications.

Media Guardian. 2006. "Danish Paper Rejected Jesus Cartoons", 6 February 2006. http://www.guardian.co.uk/media/2006/feb/06/pressandpublishing.politics (accessed 6 February 2006).

Mendes, Errol P. 1994. *Asian Values and Human Rights: Letting The Tigers Free*. Ottawa: Human Rights Research and Education Centre, University of Ottawa. http://www.uottawa.ca/hrrec/publicat/asian_values.html (accessed 11 November 2008).

Merican, Ahmad Murad. 2005. "Religious Ideas: Islam in the Malay Press". In *Covering Islam: Challenges & Opportunities for Media in the Global Village*, edited by Syed Farid Alatas. Singapore: Centre for Research on Islamic and Malay Affairs (RIMA).

Mering, Raynore. 2019. "Cyberspace New Battle Ground Against ISIS, says Mohamad Sabu". *The Malay Mail*, 24 April 2019. https://www.malaymail.com/news/malaysia/2019/04/24/cyberspace-new-battle-ground-against-isis-says-mohamad-sabu/1746610 (accessed 21 September 2019).

Mill, John Stuart. 1991. *On Liberty and Other Essays*. Oxford: Oxford University Press.

Miller, E. 2004. "The Role of Islam in Malaysian Political Practice". *Al-Nakhlah: The Fletcher School Online Journal for Issues Related to Southwest Asia and Islamic Civilization* 4: 1–10.

Ministry of Information. 1986. *Dasar-Dasar Baru kerajaan* [Government's New Policies]. Kuala Lumpur: Ministry of Information.

Mohamad, Marzuki. 2008. "Religion, Human Rights and Constitutional-Contract Politics in Malaysia". *Intellectual Discourse* 16, no. 2: 155–86.

Moses, Balan. 2002. "Ethnic Reporting in the Malaysian Media". *Media Asia* 29, no. 2: 102–7.

Moustafa, Tamir. 2014. "Judging in God's Name: State Power, Secularism, and the Politics of Islamic Law in Malaysia". *Oxford Journal of Law and Religion* 3, no. 1: 152–67.

MSN. 2019. "FMT Reporters: Jais to Probe Book and Forum on Giving up the Hijab", 15 April 2019. https://www.msn.com/en-my/news/national/jais-to-probe-book-and-forum-on-giving-up-the-hijab/ar-BBVXyos (accessed 15 April 2019).

Muhammad Raqib Mohd Sofian, Rizki Briandana, and Azman Azwan Azmawati. 2018. "Minority Group and the Media: Media Coverage on Shia Muslims in Malaysia". *E3S Web of Conferences* 73. https://www.e3s-conferences.org/articles/e3sconf/pdf/2018/48/e3sconf_icenis18_14007.pdf (accessed 1 September 2019).

Muntarbhorn, Vitit. 1994. "Repression and Oppression Still Prevalent in ASEAN". *The Nation*, 15 May 1994, p. 4.

Muslim Scholars Association of Malaysia (MSAM). 2002. *Kontroversi Mengenai Memo Kepada Majlis Raja-Raja Melayu*. Petaling Jaya: MSAM.
Mutalib, Hussin. 1993. *Islam in Malaysia: From Revivalism to Islamic State*. Singapore: Singapore University Press.
Muthiah, W., A. Lai, and A. Raman. 2012. "Singer Fined over Feminine Mannerisms". *The Star Online*, 23 June 2012. http://www.thestar.com.my/news/nation/2012/06/23/singer-fined-over-feminine-mannerisms/ (accessed 2 January 2016).
Muzaffar, Chandra. 1986. *Freedom in Fetters*. Malaysia: Aliran Kesedaran Negara.
———. 1989. *Challenges and Choices in Malaysian Politics and Society*. Penang: Aliran Kesedaran Negara.
———. 1993. *Human Rights and the New World Order*. Penang, Malaysia: Just World Trust.
———. 1996. "Europe, Asia and the Question of Human Rights". *Just Commentary* 23: 4.
———. 2018. "Pakatan Harapan and the Challenge of National Integration". *The Sun Daily*, 25 June 2018. https://www.thesundaily.my/archive/pakatan-harapan-and-challenge-national-integration-KUARCH558809 (accessed 9 January 2019).
Mydans, Seth. 2010. "Churches Attacked Amid Furor in Malaysia". *The New York Times*, 10 January 2010. http://www.nytimes.com/2010/01/11/world/asia/11malaysia.html?pagewanted=print (accessed 11 January 2010).
Nadaraj, Vanitha. 2014. "Asean Must Get Rid of ISIS in Southeast Asia". *The Establishment Post*, 5 September 2014. http://www.establishmentpost.com/asean-must-get-rid-isis-southeast-asia/ (accessed 5 May 2015).
Najib, Tun Razak. 2011. *Driving Transformation*. Kuala Lumpur: Institut Terjemahan Negara Malaysia Berhad.
———. 2017. "Speech by PM Najib Razak at WAN-IFRA 16th Asian Media Awards". *New Straits Times*, 19 April 2017. https://www.nst.com.my/news/nation/2017/04/232093/full-text-speech-pm-najib-razak-wan-ifra-16th-asian-media-awards (accessed 29 August 2017).
Netto, Anil. 2004. "A Black Eye for Human Rights". In *Reflections: The Mahathir Years*, edited by Bridget Welsh. Washington: John Hopkins University.
Neuhaus, Richard J. 1984. *The Naked Public Square: Religion and Democracy in America*. Grand Rapids Mi: Eerdmans.
New Straits Times. 2008. "I.S.A. Blitz", 3 September 2008, pp. 1–9.
———. 2012. "Best Days Are Still Ahead", 1 January 2012, p. 4.
———. 2019. "Malaysian Jailed for 10 Yrs for Insulting Islam on Social Media", 9 March 2019. https://www.nst.com.my/news/nation/2019/03/467536/malaysian-jailed-10-yrs-insulting-islam-social-media (accessed 11 January 2019).
Noor Azimah Abdul Rahim. 2019. "Edunation: PAGE shares Mahathir's view on Education". *The Edge Malaysia*, 16 January 2019. https://www.theedgemarkets.com/article/edunation-page-shares-mahathirs-view-education (accessed 16 January 2019).
North, M. 2007. *World Press Freedom Review 2007: Malaysia*. Vienna: International Press Institute. http://www.freemedia.at/cms/ipi/freedom_detail.html?country=/KW0001/ KW00 05/KW0123/ (accessed 3 June 2009).

Nur Hasliza, Mohd Salleh. 2019. "Putrajaya tak masuk campur urusan tauliah Zakir Naik, kata Mujahid". *Free Malaysia Today*, 23 February 2019. https://www.freemalaysiatoday.com/category/bahasa/2019/02/23/putrajaya-tak-masuk-campur-urusan-tauliah-zakir-naik-kata-mujahid/ (accessed 12 September 2019)

Office of the United Nations High Commissioner for Human Rights. 1993. "General Comment No. 22: The Right to Freedom of Thought, Conscience and Religion (Art. 18)". CCPR/C/21/Rev.1/Add.4, 30 July 1993. http://www.unhchr.ch/tbs/doc.nsf /(Symbol)/9a30112c27d1167cc12563ed004d8f15?Opendocument (accessed 3 June 2010).

Orwell, George. 1949 (1989 ed.). *Nineteen Eighty-Four*. London: Penguin.

Osman, Mohamed Nawab Mohamed, Shahirah Mahmood, and Joseph C. Liow. 2008. *Outlook for Malaysia's 12th General Elections*. Singapore: S. Rajaratnam School of International Studies.

Palatino, M. 2018. "The Jury's Still Out on Freedom of Expression in 'New Malaysia'". *Asian Correspondent*, 9 August 2018. https://asiancorrespondent.com/2018/08/freedom-of-expression-malaysia/ (accessed 26 January 2019).

Parekh, Bhikhu. 2005–6. "Hate Speech: Is There a Case for Banning?". *Public Policy Research* 12: 213–23.

PAS (Parti Islam Semalaysia). N.d. *The Islamic State Document*.

Perez, Evan, Catherine E. Shoichet, and Wes Bruer. 2015. "Hacker Who Allegedly Passed U.S. Military Data to ISIS Arrested in Malaysia". *CNN Politics*, 20 October 2015. http://edition.cnn.com/2015/10/15/politics/malaysian-hacker-isis-military-data/ (accessed 1 November 2015).

Prakash, G. and Ushar Daniele. 2014. "Worrying Trend of Civil Servants Supporting IS Cause". *The Malay Mail Online*, 3 December 2014. http://www.themalaymailonline.com/malaysia/article/worrying-trend-of-civil-servants-supporting-is-cause#sthash.pqkOkYCw.dpuf (accessed 5 May 2015).

Prime Minister's Office. 1986. *Panduan Penerapan Nilai-Nilai Islam* [Inculcation of Islamic Values Guide]. Kuala Lumpur: Prime Minister's Office.

Quah, Jon, ed. 1990. *In Search of Singapore's National Values*. Singapore: Times Academic Press.

Rahimullah, Riyad H., Stephen Larmar, and Mohamad Abdalla. 2013. "Understanding Violent Radicalization amongst Muslims: A Review of the Literature". *Journal of Psychology and Behavioral Science* 1, no. 1: 19–35.

Ramasamy, P. 2019. "Race to the Bottom: Politics of the Umno-PAS Charter". *Malaysiakini*, 11 September 2019. https://www.malaysiakini.com/news/491454 (accessed 11 September 2019).

Ramzy, Austin. 2018. "Hopes for New Era of Malaysian Free Speech are High, but Pending". *New York Times*, 18 June 2018. https://www.nytimes.com/2018/06/18/world/asia/malaysia-mahathir-free-speech.html (accessed 26 January 2019).

Razak, Ahmad. 2013. "Reason Behind Ban on Syiah Teachings". *The Star Online*, 16 December 2013. http://www.thestar.com.my/News/Nation/2013/12/16/Reason-behind-ban-on-Syiah-teachings-Controversial-doctrines-have-led-to-many-seeing-it-as-a-potenti.aspx/ (accessed 16 December 2013).

Refugee Review Tribunal. 2008. "RRT Research Response", 27 March 2008. http://www.ecoi.net/file_upload/1997_1293698291_mys33057.pdf (accessed 28 March 2008).
Regencia, Ted. 2014. "Islamic Support Spread into Asia". *Al Jazeera*, 14 July 2014. http://m.aljazeera.com/story/201471392121686815 (accessed 5 May 2015).
Reichman, Amnon. 2009. "Criminalizing Religiously Offensive Satire: Free Speech, Human Dignity, and Comparative Law". In *Extreme Speech and Democracy*, edited by Ivan Hare and James Weinstein. Oxford: Oxford University Press.
Rineheart, Jason. 2010. "Counterterrorism and Counterinsurgency". *Perspectives of Terrorism* 4, no. 5. http://www.terrorismanalysts.com/pt/index.php/pot/article/view/122/html (accessed 3 June 2012).
Rorty, Richard. 1994. "Religion as Conversation Stopper". *Common Knowledge* 3, no. 1: 1–6.
Rosli, Zakaria. 2019. "Syariah Compliant Sportswear—No Problem for Terengganu". *New Straits Times*, 10 September 2019. https://www.nst.com.my/news/nation/2019/09/520315/syariah-compliant-sportswear-%E2%80%93-no-problem-terengganu (accessed 12 September 2019).
RT. 2016. "ISIS Announces Asia Pivot in Propaganda Video Targeting Malaysia, Philippines", 25 June 2016. https://www.rt.com/news/348302-isis-asia-attacks-propaganda/?utm_source=rss&utm_medium=rss&utm_campaign=RSS (accessed 31 August 2016).
Ryan, Marie. 2010. "Islamizing the Malaysian Economy: The Politics Behind Developing a Malaysian Syariah Economy". Unpublished Master thesis, Lund University Center for East and Southeast Asian Studies, Lund University, Lund.
Sageman, Marc. 2004. *Understanding Terror Networks*. Philadelphia: University of Pennsylvania Press.
Saifulizam Mohamad. 2018. "Islam Terus Utuh Di Era Dr. Mahathir". *Utusan Malaysia Online*, 5 August 2018. http://www.utusan.com.my/rencana/islam-terus-utuh-di-era-dr-mahathir-1.723469 (accessed 26 January 2019).
Salleh Buang. 2015. "Our Defamation Law is Antiquated". *News Straits Times Online*, 19 November 2015. http://www.nst.com.my/news/2015/11/112404/our-defamation-law-antiquated (accessed 27 August 2016).
———. 2019. "Freedom of Speech: Do Not Cross the Line". *New Straits Times*, 2 January 2019. https://www.nst.com.my/opinion/columnists/2019/01/446413/freedom-speech-do-not-cross-line (accessed 3 January 2019).
Salleh, Hasny Md. 2004. *War Against Terrorism: Malaysia's Experience in Defeating Terrorism*. U.S. Army War College, Carlisle Barracks, Pennsylvania 17013.
Sandel, Michael J. 1982. *Liberalism and the Limits of Justice*. Cambridge: Cambridge University Press.
Sani, Asrul Hadi Abdullah. 2011. "Najib Ducks MCA's Islamic State Objection over PAS Invite". *The Malaysian Insider*, 2 May 2011. http://www.themalaysianinsider.com /mobile/malaysia/article/najib-ducks-mcas-islamic-state-objection-over-pas-invite/ (accessed 3 May 2011).

Sarwar, Malik Imtiaz. 2007. "Latifah Mat Zin: Reaffirming the Supremacy of the Constitution", 29 July 2007. http://malikimtiaz.blogspot.com/2007/07/latifah-mat-zin-reaffirming-supremacy.html (accessed 20 April 2010).

Savage, Sara and Jose Liht. 2009. "Radical Religious Speech: The Ingredients of a Binary World View". In *Extreme Speech and Democracy*, edited by Ivan Hare and James Weinstein. Oxford: Oxford University Press, pp. 488–509.

Schwartz, Benjamin E. 2007. "America's Struggle Against the Wahhabi/Neo-Salafi Movement". *Orbis* 51, no. 1: 107–28.

Schwartz, Stephen. 2015. "Zakir Naik, Radical Islamist Video Evangelist". *Huffington Post*, 26 May 2015. https://www.huffingtonpost.com/stephen-schwartz/zakir-naik-radicalislami_b_6945990.html (accessed 7 August 2018).

Shah, Dian Abdul Hamed and Mohd Azizuddin Sani. 2011. "Freedom of Religion in Malaysia: A Tangled Web of Legal, Political, and Social Issues". *North Carolina Journal of International Law and Commercial Regulation* 36, no. 3: 647–87.

Shamsul, A.B. 1997. "Identity Construction, Nation Formation, and Islamic Revivalism in Malaysia". In *Politics and Religious Renewal in Muslim Southeast Asia*, edited by Robert W. Hefner and Patricia Horvatich. Honolulu: University of Hawai'i Press.

Shazwan, Mustafa Kamal. 2014. "Home Ministry Bans 'Noah' Movie for Being 'un-Islamic'". *The Malay Mail Online*, 4 April 2014. http://www.themalaymailonline.com/print/malaysia/home-ministry-bans-noah-movie-for-being-un-islamic (accessed 4 April 2014).

———. 2018. "Despite 'Liberal' Tag, Mujahid Pledges to Push Interfaith Talks as Religious Affairs Minister". *The Malay Mail*, 6 July 2018. https://www.malaymail.com/news/malaysia/2018/07/06/despite-liberal-tag-mujahid-pledges-to-push-interfaith-talks-as-religious-a/1649330 (accessed 1 May 2019).

Sheith Khidhir Abu Bakar. 2018. "Does Pakatan back Mahathir Era's Policy on Islamic Values?". *Free Malaysia Today*, 5 January 2018. https://www.freemalaysiatoday.com/category/nation/2018/01/05/does-pakatan-back-mahathir-eras-policy-on-islamic-values/ (accessed 3 January 2019).

Shelton, Dinah and Alexander Kiss. 2007. "A Draft Model Law on Freedom of Religion (1996)". In *International Human Rights in Context: Law, Politics, Morals*, edited by Henry J. Steiner, Philip Alston, and Ryan Goodman. Oxford: Oxford University Press.

Shepherd, Amy. 2017. "Extremism, Free Speech and the Rule of Law: Evaluating the Compliance of Legislation Restricting Extremist Expressions with Article 19 ICCPR". *Utrecht Journal of International and European Law* 33, no. 85: 62–83.

Sheridan, Lionel A. and Harry E. Groves. 1987. *The Constitution of Malaysia*. Singapore: Malayan Law Journal Ltd.

Shuaib, Farid Sufian. 2012. "The Islamic Legal System in Malaysia". *Pacific Rim Law & Policy Journal* 21, no. 1: 85–113.

Siebert, Fred S., Theodore Peterson, and Wilbur Schramm. 1956/73. *Four Theories of the Press*. Urbana, Illinois: University of Illinois Press.

Silber, Mitchell D. and Arvin Bhatt. 2007. *Radicalisation in the West: The Homegrown Threat*. New York: The New York City Police Department.

Singh, Dya. 2013. "Malaysian Sikhs and the Allah Controversy in Malaysia". *Sikhnet*, 20 November 2013. https://www.sikhnet.com/news/malaysian-sikhs-and-allah-controversy-malaysia-op-ed (accessed 9 September 2019).

Siti A'isyah Sukaimi. 2018. "Clear Explanation on Rahmatan Lil Alamin Concept Needed". *New Straits Times*, 15 December 2018. https://www.nst.com.my/news/nation/2018/11/431623/clear-explanation-rahmatan-lil-alamin-concept-needed (accessed 16 December 2018).

Sivaperegasam, P. Rajanthiran. 2011. "DAP's Opposition of Malaysia as an Islamic State". In *Seminar on National Resilience: Political Management and Policies*, edited by Abdul Rahman Aziz and Mohd Azizuddin Mohd Sani. Sintok: Institute of Tun Dr. Mahathir Mohamad's Thoughts.

Straits Times. 2014. "Second Malaysian ISIS Suicide Bomber Identified as 27-year-old man from Kelantan", 9 December 2014. http://www.straitstimes.com/news/asia/south-east-asia/story/second-malaysian-isis-suicide-bomber-identified-27-year-old-man-kela (accessed 5 May 2015).

──────. 2015. "Malaysia Will Set up Regional Centre to Counter ISIS Propaganda", 10 October 2015. http://www.straitstimes.com/asia/se-asia/malaysia-will-set-up-regional-centre-to-counter-isis-propaganda (accessed 11 October 2015).

──────. 2016. "Young Malaysian ISIS Suicide Bomber 'Killed 14 in Syria'", 18 December 2016. http://www.straitstimes.com/asia/se-asia/young-malaysian-isis-suicide-bomber-killed-14-in-syria (accessed 18 December 2016).

──────. 2018. "PM Mahathir to Overhaul Malaysia's Schools, Saying Too Much Focus on Islamic Studies Now", 22 December 2018. https://www.straitstimes.com/asia/se-asia/pm-mahathir-to-overhaul-malaysias-schools-saying-too-much-focus-on-islam-studies-now (accessed 23 December 2018).

Suara Rakyat Malaysia (SUARAM). 1998. *Malaysian Human Rights Report*. Petaling Jaya: SUARAM Communication.

──────. 2003. *Malaysia: Human Rights Report 2002*. Petaling Jaya: SUARAM Communication.

──────. 2010. *Malaysia Human Rights Report 2009: Civil & Political Rights*. Petaling Jaya: Suaram Komunikasi.

──────. 2013. *Suaram Malaysia Human Rights Report 2010: Civil & Political Rights*. Petaling Jaya: Suara Inisiatif.

Sullivan, Kathleen M. 1992. "Religion and Liberal Democracy". *University of Chicago Law Review* 59: 195–99.

Sunstein, Cass R. 1993. *Democracy and the Problem of Free Speech*. New York: The Free Press.

Suparmaniam, Suganthi. 2015. "Transgender Case: Federal Court Overturns Court of Appeal's Decision". *Astro Awani*, 8 October 2015. http://english.astroawani.com/malaysia-news/transgender-case-federal-court-overturns-court-appeals-decision-75716 (accessed 12 April 2016).

Swift, M.G. 1965. *Malay Peasant Society in Jelebu*. London: Athlone Press.
Syed Umar Arif. 2019. "Dr M Surprised by Outbursts over Khat Issue". *New Straits Times*, 8 August 2019. https://www.nst.com.my/news/nation/2019/08/511232/dr-m-surprised-outbursts-over-khat-issue (accessed 9 September 2019).
Tam, Michelle. 2015. "Malaysian Youth with Islamic State (IS) Militant Updates Followers on Social Media". *The Star Online*, 4 March 2015. http://www.thestar.com.my/News/Nation/2015/03/04/Militant-Facebook-posts/ (accessed 5 May 2015).
Tan, Andrew. 2004. *Security Perspectives of the Malay Archipelago*. Cheltenham, UK: Edward Elgar.
Taylor, Charles. 1985. *Philosophy and the Human Sciences: Philosophical Papers Volume II*. Cambridge: Cambridge University Press.
Teh, Z.A. and E.A. Jamsari. 2013. "Bahagian Agama dan Kaunseling (BAKA), Ibu Pejabat Polis Daerah Kajang: Sejarah dan Pembangunan". In *Prosiding Nadwah Ulama Nusantara (NUN) V: Ulama dan Cabaran Idealisme Semasa*, edited by Azmul Fahimi Kamaruzaman, Ezad Azraai Jamsari, Farid Mat Zain, Hakim Zainal, Maheram Ahmad, Napisah Karimah Ismail, and Rabitah Mohamad Ghazali. Bangi: Jabatan Pengajian Arab dan Tamadun Islam, Fakulti Pengajian Islam, UKM.
Temperman, Jeroen. 2011. "Freedom of Expression and Religious Sensitivities in Pluralist Societies: Facing the Challenge of Extreme Speech". *Brigham Young University Law Review* 3: 729–57.
Thaib, Lukman. 2013. "Muslim Politics in Malaysia and the Democratization Process". *International Journal of Islamic Thought* 3: 45–57.
Tham, Jia Vern. 2018. "Tun M: Pakatan Harapan Will Continue to Govern Malaysia based on Islamic Teachings". *Says*, 5 June 2018. https://says.com/my/news/tun-m-pakatan-harapan-will-continue-to-govern-malaysia-based-on-islamic-teachings (accessed 6 June 2018).
The Borneo Post. 2011. "Bernama: Umno Youth, Perkasa Stage Gathering in Support of Utusan Malaysia", 20 May 2011. http://www.theborneopost.com/2011/05/20/umno-youth-perkasa-stage-gathering-in-support-of-utusan-malaysia-latest/#ixzz38YTGSJsG (accessed 21 May 2011).
The Diplomat. 2015. "Malaysia Debates New Anti-Terror Laws", 31 March 2015. http://thediplomat.com/2015/03/malaysia-debates-new-anti-terror-laws/ (accessed 6 May 2015).
The Edge Markets. 2018. "Bernama: Malay Power, Status of Islam Intact under Pakatan Harapan—Muhyiddin", 29 December 2018. http://www.theedgemarkets.com/article/malay-power-status-islam-intact-under-pakatan-harapan-%E2%80%94-muhyiddin (accessed 3 Janury 2019).
The Malaymail Online. 2014a. "PM: Malaysia to apply Syariah Index from 2015", 28 August 2014a. http://www.themalaymailonline.com/malaysia/article/pm-malaysia-to-apply-Syariah-index-from-2015 (accessed 29 August 2014).

———. 2014b. "Islamic State Militants have Putrajaya in Crosshairs, Bukit Aman says", 11 August 2014b. http://m.themalaymailonline.com/malaysia/article/islamic-state-militants-has-putrajaya-in-crosshairs-bukit-aman-says (accessed 5 May 2015).

———. 2015. "Religious Politics Turning Malaysia More Vulnerable to IS Recruitment, Paper says", 18 January 2015. http://www.themalaymailonline.com/print/malaysia/religious-politics-turning-malaysia-more-vulnerable-to-is-recruitment-paper (accessed 5 May 2015).

———. 2016. "Ex-Army Captain gets Seven Years Jail Term after Pleading to Lesser Terrorism Info Omission Charge", 27 January 2016. http://www.themalaymailonline.com/malaysia/article/ex-army-captain-gets-seven-years-jail-term-after-pleading-to-lesser-terrori#b6jalRqEulkQY2ki.99 (accessed 29 January 2016).

The Malaysian Insider. 2013. "Home Ministry Urged to Ban Books on Syiah Teachings—Bernama", 31 July 2013. http://www.themalaysianinsider.com/malaysia/article/home-ministry-urged-to-ban-books-on-syiah-teachings-bernama (accessed 1 August 2013).

———. 2014a. "Former Political Activist Kassim Ahmad Charged with Insulting Islam—Bernama", 27 March 2014a. http://www.themalaysianinsider.com/malaysia /article/former-political-activist-kassim-ahmad-charged-with-insulting-islam (accessed 28 March 2014).

———. 2014b. "Inspired by ISIS, Solo Terrorists May Strike Here, Police warn", 15 October 2014b. http://www.themalaysianinsider.com/malaysia/article/inspired-by-isis-solo-terrorists-may-strike-here-police-warn# (accessed 5 May 2015).

———. 2014c. "ISIS has Tarnished Islam's Image, says Anwar", 4 October 2014c. https://sg.news.yahoo.com/isis-tarnished-islam-image-says-anwar-062504549.html (accessed 21 September 2019).

———. 2015a. "New Anti-Terror Law a Giant Step Backwards, says Global Human Rights Body", 7 April 2015a. http://www.themalaysianinsider.com/malaysia/article/new-anti-terror-law-a-giant-step-backwards-says-human-rights-body#sthash.XsFpEWHf.dpuf (accessed 5 May 2015).

———. 2015b. "Extremists Stabbing Islam in the Back:- Anwar Ibrahim", 1 February 2015b. http://www.abim.org.my/index.php/press-media-release/item/734-extremists-stabbing-islam-in-the-back-anwar-ibrahim.html (accessed 21 September 2019).

The New Paper. 2015. "Growing Trend? M'sians Taking up to $7.5k Loans to Join Terror Group ISIS", 11 January 2015. http://www.tnp.sg/news/growing-trend-msians-taking-75k-loans-join-terror-group-isis#sthash.bEEOZv0I.dpuf (accessed 5 May 2015).

The Pew Research Center's Religion and Public Life Project. 2014. *The Future of the Global Muslim Population*. http://features.pewforum.org/muslim-population-graphic/#/Malaysia (accessed 20 April 2014).

The Rakyat Post. 2014. "Singer Fined RM1,000 over Revealing Clothing", 18 June 2014. http://www.therakyatpost.com/news/2014/06/18/singer-fined-rm1000-revealing-clothing/ (accessed 18 June 2014).

The Star. 2008. "Repeal, Not Review ISA", 26 May 2008, p. 27.

———. 2010. "Political Management Vital for Race Relations, says Najib", 7 September 2010.

———. 2011. "Artiste Bob Lokman Quizzed over Religious Lecture at Mosque", 12 October 2011.

———. 2013. "Cops Get Tough", 24 May 2013, pp. 1–3.

The Star Online. 2006a. "Mufti: See the Bigger Picture", 17 December 2006. http://thestar.com.my/news/story.asp?file=/2006/12/17/nation/16349115&sec=nation (accessed 18 December 2006).

———. 2006b. "Engineering Firm Sues Utusan for Libel", 18 March 2006. http://www.thestar.com.my/news/nation/2006/03/18/engineering-firm-sues-utusan-for-libel/ (accessed 28 August 2016).

———. 2014a. "Respect and Abide by Ruling over Use of 'Allah'", 25 June 2014a. http://www.thestar.com.my/News/Nation/2014/06/25/Respect-and-abide-by-ruling-over-use-of-Allah-Govt-calls-on-all-parties-to-manage-differences-peacef/ (accessed 26 June 2014).

———. 2014b. "Hisham: Regional Cooperation Essential in Combating Islamic State Threat", 16 October 2014b. http://m.thestar.com.my/story.aspx?hl=Hisham+Regional+corporation+essential+in+combating+Islamic+State+threat&sec=news&id=%7B68B05EF3-FEE1-4A26-A8AF-EC85E08B1502%7D (accessed 5 May 2015).

———. 2015. "Probe into Souvenir Shop with a Militant Theme", 10 January 2015. http://www.thestar.com.my/News/Nation/2015/01/10/Probe-into-souvenir-shop-with-a-militant-theme/?utm_source=dlvr.it&utm_medium=twitter (accessed 5 May 2015).

———. 2017. "Suhakam Stresses on 'Free, Unbought Media' on World Press Freedom Day", 3 May 2017. http://www.thestar.com.my/~/media/online/2017/05/03/05/32/sta_7687.ashx/?w=620&h=413&crop=1&hash=3DE009A95171E1739B07FC47ECA9981DD93A686D (accessed 30 August 2017).

———. 2018a. "Malaysia Tops in South-East Asia for Online Child Pornography", 30 January 2018a. https://www.thestar.com.my/news/nation/2018/01/30/malaysia-tops-in-southeast-for-online-child-pornography/#ZXte5WpgdV3bAPuj.99 (accessed 23 February 2019).

———. 2018b. "Govt Reviewing Existing Acts under Syariah Courts, including RUU355", 4 September 2018b. https://www.thestar.com.my/news/nation/2018/09/04/govt-reviewing-existing-acts-under-syariah-courts-including-ruu355/#mRcOX7FfYxpizFWo.99 (accessed 2 May 2019).

———. 2019a. "High Court Lifts Ban on G25 Book", 9 April 2019a. https://www.thestar.com.my/news/nation/2019/04/09/high-court-lifts-ban-on-g25-book/ (accessed 9 April 2019).

———. 2019b. "Dr M: Zakir Naik is an 'Unwelcome Guest' Malaysia Can't Send Away", 31 July 2019b. https://www.thestar.com.my/news/nation/2019/07/31/dr-m-zakir-naik-is-an-039unwelcome-guest039-malaysia-can039t-send-away#yfTwEP3J7DCSmwr5.99 (accessed 9 September 2019).
The Sun. 2008. "Cabinet: Allah for Muslims only", 4 January 2008. p. 1.
———. 2014. "Battling IS", 27 November 2014, pp. 1–2.
The Sun Daily. 2018. "Public Caning Does Not Reflect True Face of Islam: Mahathir", 6 September 2018. https://www.thesundaily.my/archive/public-caning-does-not-reflect-true-face-islam-mahathir-video-YUARCH576635 (accessed 9 January 2019).
———. 2019. "Don't Fall for Racial and Religious Propaganda at Saturday's Rally: Muhyiddin", 2 May 2019. https://www.thesundaily.my/local/don-t-fall-for-racial-and-religious-propaganda-at-saturday-s-rally-muhyiddin-YK840256 (accessed 2 May 2019).
The Underground. 2011. "Malaysia Scolds Publication for Spreading Rumor, No Apology to Christians", 5 July 2011. http://theundergroundsite.com/index.php/2011/05/malaysia-scolds-publication-for-spreading-rumor-no-apology-to-christians-15960/ (accessed 6 July 2011).
Thomas, Tommy. 2006. "Is Malaysia an Islamic State?". *Malayan Law Journal Article*: 31.
Ting, Helen. 2009. "The Politics of National Identity in West Malaysia: Continued Mutation or Critical Transition?" *Tonan Ajia Kenkyu (Southeast Asian Studies)* 47, no. 1: 31–51.
Today Online. 2014. "Islamic State Recruiter Targeted Local Schoolboy: Malaysia Police", 14 October 2014. http://www.todayonline.com/world/asia/islamic-state-recruiter-targeted-local-schoolboy-malaysia-police?singlepage=true (accessed 5 May 2015).
Travis, Alan. 2008. "MI5 Report Challenges Views on Terrorism in Britain". *Guardian*, 20 August 2008. http://www.guardian.co.uk/uk/2008/aug/20/uksecurity.terrorism1 (accessed 20 June 2010).
TRENDS Research & Advisory. 2017. "Countering the Narrative of Daesh/ISIS in South East Asia", 1 March 2017. http://trendsinstitution.org/countering-the-narrative-of-daeshisis-in-south-east-asia/ (accessed 2 March 2017).
Utusan Malaysia. 2011. "Kristian agama rasmi?", 7 May 2011, p. 1.
Utusan Online. 2014. "Indeks Maqasid Syariah Antarabangsa", 9 April 2014. http://www.utusan.com.my/utusan/Dalam_Negeri/20140409/dn_01/Indeks-Maqasid-Syariah-Antarabangsa (accessed 29 August 2014).
Vanar, Muguntan. 2014. "Claims of French Tourist Kidnapped by Filipino Gunmen in Sabah Refuted". *The Star Online*, 16 November 2014. http://www.thestar.com.my/News/Nation/2014/11/16/Esscom-Sabah-French-hostage/ (accessed 5 May 2015).
Veldhuis, Tinka and Jørgen Staun. 2009. *Islamist Radicalisation: A Root Cause Model*. The Hague: Netherlands Institute of International Relations Clingendael.
Vidino, Lorenzo. 2009. "Europe's New Security Dilemma". *The Washington Quarterly* 32, no. 4: 61–75.

Vreeland, Nena, Glenn B. Dana, Geoffrey B. Hurwitz, Peter Just, Philip W. Moeller, and R.S. Shinn. 1977. *Area Handbook for Malaysia.* 3rd ed. Glen Rock, NJ: Microfilming Corporation of America.

Waldron, Jeremy. 1993. "Religious Contributions in Public Deliberation". *San Diego Law Review* 30: 817–29.

Walzer, Michael. 1983. *Sphere of Justice: A Defence of Pluralism and Equality.* Oxford: Blackwell.

Wan Mansor, W.N., W.K. Mujani, and E.A. Rozali. 2013. "Political Ideologies in Malaysia: Wasatiyyah as a Moderate Solution". This research is funded by the Religion and Social Cohesion grant LRGS/BU/2011/UKM/CMN/04. https://www.conftool.com/skim2013/index.php/Wan_MansorPolitical_Islam_Ideologies_in_Malaysia289.pdf?page=downloadPaper&filename=Wan_Mansor-Political_Islam_Ideologies_in_Malaysia289.pdf&form_id= 289&form_version=final (accessed 3 July 2014).

Wan Mohamad, S.A.A. 2011. "Pengalaman Jabatan Kemajuan Islam Malaysia (JAKIM)". In *Pemahaman dan Penghayatan Nilai Menjana Kepada Prestasi,* edited by Abd Karim Husain and Zainab Ismail. Kuala Lumpur: Penerbit IKIM.

Wilson, Peter J. 1967. *A Malay Village in Malaysia.* New Haven, CT: Hraf Press.

Yatim, Hafiz. 2019. "Selangor Fatwa Declaring Sisters in Islam as a Deviant Group Stands—High Court". *The Edge Markets,* 27 August 2019. https://www.theedgemarkets.com/article/selangor-fatwa-declaring-sisters-islam-deviant-group-stands-%E2%80%94-high-court (accessed 12 September 2019).

Yatim, Rais. 1995. *Freedom Under Executive Power in Malaysia: A Study of Executive Supremacy.* Kuala Lumpur: Endowment.

Yeoh Seng Guan. 2005. "Managing Sensitivities: Religious Pluralism, Civil Society and Inter-faith Relations in Malaysia". *The Round Table* 94, no. 382: 629–30.

Yuan Y. 2003. "Lim Beng Soon: Malay Saying as Politeness Strategies". *Review: Report on SAAL Talk.* Singapore: SAAL (The Singapore Association for Applied Linguistics). http://www.saal.org.sg/sq63.html (accessed 3 June 2010).

Yunus, Arfa. 2016. "Government to Help 'Deviant' Liberal Muslims Return to True Path". *Free Malaysia Today,* 17 March 2016. http://www.freemalaysiatoday.com/category/nation/2016/03/17/govt-to-help-deviant-liberal-muslims-return-to-true-path/ (accessed 30 March 2016).

Zachariah, Elizabeth. 2014. "Malaysia on US Watch List for Limitations on Religious Freedom 2013". *The Malaysian Insider,* 3 May 2014. http://www.themalaysianinsider.com/malaysia/article/malaysia-on-us-watch-list-for-limitations-on-religious-freedom (accessed 3 May 2014).

Zainal Abidin Wahid. 1970. "Glimpses of the Malaccan Empire—I". In *Glimpses of Malaysian History,* edited by Zainal Abidin Wahid. Kuala Lumpur: Dewan Bahasa dan Pustaka.

Zeti Akhtar Aziz. 2006. "Focus on Human Capital Development in Malaysia". *BIS Review* 125.

Zin, Najibah M. 2012. "The Training, Appointment, and Supervision of Islamic Judges in Malaysia". *Pacific Rim Law & Policy Journal* 21, no. 1: 115–31.

Zulhuda, Sonny. 2015. "Cyberlaw on Pornography". Paper presented at the National Law Students Conference 2015 (PEMUDA IV), Universiti Utara Malaysia, Sintok, 2 October 2015.

Zulkiple, A.G. 2014. "Fiqh Broadcasting: A Comparative Study of Television Program Production in Malaysia and Iran". *Advances in Natural and Applied Sciences* 8, no. 4: 286–90.

Zurairi, A.R. 2013a. "US Colonising Malaysia Through 'Liberal Muslims', says Preacher". *The Malay Mail Online*, 18 September 2013a. http://www.themalaymailonline.com/print/malaysia/us-colonising-malaysia-through-liberal-muslims-says-preacher (accessed 18 September 2013).

———. 2013b. "For Some, Liberal Muslims are the Real Extremists". *The Malay Mail Online*, 7 November 2013b. http://www.themalaymailonline.com /malaysia/article/for-some-liberal-muslims-are-the-real-extremists (accessed 8 November 2013).

———. 2014. "Watershed for Muslim Transgenders as Court Rules Anti-Crossdressing Shariah Law Unconstitutional". *The Malay Mail Online*, 7 November 2014. http://www.themalaymailonline.com/malaysia/article/watershed-for-muslim-transgenders-as-court-rules-anti-crossdressing-shariah#sthash.hJcewDWY.dpuf (accessed 12 November 2013).

INDEX

Note: Page number followed by n refers to endnotes.

A
Abdul Ghani Samsudin, 99
Abdul Halim Aman, 145
Abdullah, Abu (Isnilon Hapilon), 122
Abdullah Ahmad Badawi, 9, 64, 70, 76–78, 81, 87, 89
   Islam Hadhari, 44–46, 49, 164
Abdullah Mat Zin, 55
Abu Handzalah (Mahmud Ahmad), 125
Abu Sayyaf, 116, 122, 128
Abu Seman, 98
Academy of Islamic Studies (AIS), 26
Adib Mohd Kassim, Muhammad, death of, 142
Administration of Islamic Law Act (Federal Territories) 1993, 30, 34, 35, 51
   Syariah court in, 34–35
administrative bureaucracy, 28
Afif Bahardin, 109
Ahmad Nizam Amiruddin, 92
Ahmad Tarmimi Maliki, 123

Akhbar Satar, 127
Akyol, Mustafa, 157, 173
"Allah", the word, 52–53, 74–76
   issue, 164
   Malaysian Christians use, 76
   Muslim and Christian communities use, 75
   not used by non-Muslim, 75
Alliance memorandum, 85, 86
Allied Coordinating Committee of Islamic NGOs (ACCIN), 76–77
Amhilni azidka (penalty fee), 33
Aminuddin Yahya, 93
Amirudin Shari, 172
amour propre, 19
Angkatan Belia Islam Malaysia (ABIM), 27, 43
Anti-Discrimination Act, 142
Anti-Fake News Act 2018, 140
anti-Islam, 77, 150, 170
   state of governance, 86
anti-radicalization programmes, 119
anti-religious, 86
anti-terrorism, 10

Anwar Ibrahim, 1, 12, 27, 43, 132, 139, 141
Apandi Ali, Mohamed, 75
Armed Forces Council, 31
Arshad Raji, Mohamad, 142
Ashaari Muhammad, 91
Ashura, 171, 172
Asri Muda, 41
Asri Zainal Abidin, Mohd, 56, 96, 146, 151, 159
Al-Assad, Bassar, 123
Assalamualaikum (May Peace Be Upon You): Observations on the Islamisation of Malaysia (Zaid Ibrahim), 157
authoritative/bureaucratic agency, 49
Ayob Khan Mydin Pitchay, 122, 124
Azmil Tayeb, 153
Azwanddin Hamzah, 143, 144

B
al-Baghdadi, Abu Bakr, 116, 122
Bahagian Agama dan Kaunseling Polis Diraja Malaysia (BAKA PDRM), 32, 63
    Commission on the Improvement of Operation and Management, 32
Bahagian Hal Ehwal Islam (Division of Islamic Affairs), 29
Bahagian Ugama (Division of Religious Affairs), 29
Banking and Financial Institution Act (BAFIA) 1989, 33
Barisan Nasional (BN) government, 1, 89, 139–41, 166
    Islamization policy, 169
batil (invalid), 33
BERSATU Party, 146

blasphemy, 69–70, 84, 99–102, 144
Bob Lokman, 96
Breaking the Silence: Voices of Moderation-Islam in a Constitutional Democracy by G25, 137, 155
British colonial, in Malaysia, 89
British common law system, 165
bureaucracy
    administrative, 28
    broader reforms in, 140
    Islamic. *See* Islamic bureaucracy, institutionalization of

C
caliphate system, 117, 122
censorship, risk of, 23
Centre for Independent Journalism (CIJ), 143
Che Omar bin Che Soh v. Public Prosecutor (1988), 86, 89, 103
civil law system, 89, 94
civil liberties, 12, 135
civil service, 34
civil society movements, 13
coalition, dominant political party in, 1, 139
Coalition of Malaysian NGOs (COMANGO), 93
Communications and Multimedia Act (1998), 50, 72, 96, 140, 143, 144, 164
communitarianism, 81, 177, 178
communitarian orientation, 177
constitutional law, 90
constitutional supremacy, 95
Content Code, 72
Content Code Act 2002, 50
controlled democracy, 68

controversial law, 6
conventional economy, 33
Counter Messaging Centre (CMC), 132
counter-radicalization
    and de-radicalization, 119
    success of, 120
    theory of, 117–20
counterterrorism programmes, 119–20
Crime and Security Act 2001, 10
culturally diverse population, 135
cultural sensitivities, 7, 79
cyber defence, 131
    network, 132
Cyber Defence Operation Centre (CDOC), 132

D
Dangerous Drugs Act 1952, 138
Daulah Islamiah Nusantara, 117
daulat (sovereign), 20
da'wah, 26, 91
    movement of, 40, 42, 49
    Religious Unit and, 47–48
    and youth organizations, 26
Da wa taajjal (financial incentive for early payment), 33
Al-Dawla Al Islamiya fi al-Iraq wa al-Syam (Daesh), 115
death penalty, 69
    for offence, 86
defamation, 3, 108
Defamation Act 1957, 108
deliberative democracy, 178
democracy, 175
    deliberative, 178
    legitimacy, 82
    Malaysian, 7
    as political ideal, 135

Democratic Action Party (DAP), 71, 150
Department of Islamic Development Malaysia (JAKIM), 93
Dewan Undangan Negeri versus Nordin Salleh (1992), 12
Dikir Barat, 107–8
divisive political culture, 47
dominant ethnic groups, 71
dual legal system, 59

E
education
    foreign tertiary institutions, 41
    institutions of higher, 34–36
    in Islamic finance, 39
    Malay-Muslim students, 40
    national, 38
    Nilam Puri Foundation of Higher Learning, 35–36
    non-Islamic studies of, 37
    primary and secondary, 44
    public universities, 37
    religious-based academic qualification, 34
    religious departments, 38
    traditional and modern, 34
education, in Islam, 152–55
    Bahasa Melayu language, 154
    in non-religious public schools, 153
    Pendidikan Islam/Moral (PI/PM), 154
    religious, 38
    syllabus for national schools, 153
Election Commission, 178
Emergency Ordinance (EO), 136
Encyclopedia of Censorship, 105
ethno-religious relationships, 47

extreme religious expression, 113, 166
   glorifying terrorism, 133
   involvement in terrorism, 117–18
   for recruiting and radicalizing, 115
   violence against civilians, 133
extreme speech, 115
extremism, 127
   definition of, 114
   liberal, 149
   radicalization and, 132
   religious, 46, 149

F

face-threatening acts (FTAs), 21
Faculty of Islamic Studies (FIS), UKM, 36, 38
Fadiah Nadwa Fikri, 143
Faisal Tehrani. *See* Mohd Faizal Musa
Farouk Musa, Ahmad, 157–58, 172
Faruqi, Shad Saleem, 58, 86, 150, 173, 178
al-Fatihin (2016), 122
fatwa, 51, 82, 92, 101, 102, 172
Fatwa Committee of the National Council for Islamic Religious Affairs, 92
Federal Constitution of Malaysia (1957), 39, 66, 82, 85, 87, 95
   amendment of, 4
   Article 10 of, 1, 3–5
   fundamental rights in, 6
   "reasonable regulation" in, 13
   Universal Declaration of Human Rights and, 76
Federal Constitution on Citizenship, 4

Federal Territories. *See* Administration of Islamic Law Act (Federal Territories) 1993
Federal Territories Religious Council (MAIWP), 150
Federal Territory Syariah Offences Act 1997, 98
Ferizi, Ardit, 129–30
fighting against ideology, 128
Film Censorship Act 2002, 50, 71, 107
Film Censorship Board of Malaysia (FCBM), 107
forbidden speech, 84, 94
14th General Election in 2018 (GE14), 139, 145, 167, 169
freedom of expression, in Malaysia, 2–11, 65, 78, 138, 163
   and constitutes sedition, 8
   in Constitution under Article 149, 5
   and critiques, 11–16
   future challenges for, 175–80
   human dignity. *See* human dignity
   implementation of political freedom, 7
   limitation on, 23
   in national security, 2–3
   Parliament, 12
   political freedom, 7
   press freedom, 9
   "reasonable regulations" on, 12
   restrictions on, 7, 13, 177
   struggle for, 157
   suspension, during war, 14
freedom of political speech, 105, 136, 137, 140
freedom of religion, 59, 60, 75
   and intra-religious expression, 90–94

freedom of speech, 54, 60, 67, 101
free speech, 67, 68, 140
    First Amendment of, 14
    issue of, 101
    in Malaysia, 136
    Muslim community to use, 78
    principle of, 133
    in propagating violent
        radicalization, 113–14
    in radicalization, 113
Fuziah Salleh, 146–48

G
Gagasan Sejahtera (GS), 139
gender identity disorder (GID), 103
gender neutral language, 83
gharar (risk), 33

H
Hadi Awang, Abdul, 147
Hadith, 99–100
Hajjah Halimatussaadiah binti Haji Kamaruddin v. Public Services Commission Malaysia & Anor (1994), 102
halus (soft), 18
Hamid, Abdul, 6, 86, 99
haram in Malaysia, 33, 94
harga diri (self esteem), 19
hate speech, 1, 7–8, 70–72, 141–45
    ban on, 22
    Hate Speech Act (2016), 143
    in Malaysia, 70–72, 114
    negative impacts in Malaysia, 9
Hate Speech Act (2016), 143
Herald, The, 74–76
Hiebert, Murray, 3
hijab, 159
Hilmi Hasim, Muhammad, 131

Hindu Rights Action Force (HINDRAF), 71
homegrown terrorists, 127
Homeland Security Presidential Directive No. 6 (HSPD-6), 130
hudud (punishment) law, 88
    implementation of, 127
human capital development, 34–47
    da'wah and, 36
    education and. *See* education
    financial investment for, 34
    in Islamic studies, 35
    public universities, 37
    training in Islamic finance, 39
human dignity, 16–22
    characteristics of, 22
    concept of, 17, 21
    in Holy Qur'an, 17
    human rights/liberties with, 16
    Islam and, 60
    Malay customs (*adat*), 18
    maruah, 19–21
    morality and, 69
    regulation of speech, 22
human liberties, 16
human rights
    campaign, 11
    concepts of, 16
    struggle in Malaysia, 10
    theories of, 16
Human Rights in Islam (Maududi), 87
Human Rights Watch, 15, 137

I
Ibrahim Ali, 71
Ikatan Muslimin Malaysia (ISMA), 93
IKIM.fm, radio, 48
illiberal democracy, 79

imam (leader), 83
Institut Da'wah dan Latihan Islam (INDAH), 39
institutional transformation, 28
Institut Kajian Strategik Islam Malaysia (IKSIM), 150
intelligence sharing, 129
inter-ethnic relationship in Malaysia, 37
inter-faith commission, 76–78
Internal Security Act (ISA), 6, 10, 12, 78, 92, 136, 138
internal security problems, 68
International Centre for Education in Islamic Finance (INCEIF), 39
international community, 166
International Convention on the Elimination of All Forms of Racial Discrimination (ICERD), 142–43
International Covenant on Civil and Political Rights (ICCPR), 113, 138, 143
International Crisis Group (ICG), 119
International Islamic University Malaysia (IIUM), 34, 126
Internet Crime Against Children-Child Online Protective Services (ICACCOPS), 74
inter-racial relations, 141
inter-religious expression, 164
    blasphemy, 69–70
    hate speech, 70–72
    interfaith commission, 76–78
    in Malaysia, 67–69
    obscenity, 72–74
    in press, 74–76
intra-religious expression, 164–66
    blasphemy, 99–102
    communitarian approach, 81

dress code, 102–4
    freedom of religion and, 90–94
    multireligious society, 81
    offensive and racist expressions, 82
    perspective of, 82–83
    private speech, 104–10
    publication and broadcasting, 97–99
    public speech, 94–97
    religious expression model, 83–85
    religious-themed books banned, 106
    secular/Islamic state in Malaysia, 85–89
Iranian Revolution (1979–82), 26, 41
Iraq
    defeat of ISIL in, 131
    ISIL-held territory in, 126
    Syria and. *See* Syria
Islam, 7
    and education. *See* education, in Islam
    in government policy, 41
    jurisdiction of, 163
    and justice, 158
    in Malaysian political life, 168
    model and social system, 27
    in national schools, 152
    portrayed, 48
    radical, 127
    "*Rahmatan Lil 'Alamin*" brand of, 146
    teachings of, 52
    TV al-Hijrah programmes in, 50–51
    values and laws, 27
Islamic Banking Act (1983), 33

Islamic banking business, 33
Islamic bureaucracy,
  institutionalization of, 24, 28
   administration of Islamic law,
     29, 30
   economy, 32–34
   Jabatan Kehakiman Syariah
     Malaysia, 29–30
   Jabatan Kemajuan Agama Islam
     Malaysia, 29
   judiciary, 30–31
   Malaysian National Council for
     Islamic Affairs, 39
   public service sector, 29–30
   security services, 31–32
Islamic civilization, 37, 44
Islamic Consultative Body (ICB), 42
Islamic Development Foundation, 29
Islamic finance, education and
  training in, 39
Islamic financial business, 33
Islamic identity, 27, 28, 48
Islamic law, 43, 86, 163
   administration of, 29, 30
   aspects of, 44
   enforcement of, 164
   implementation of, 57
   jurisdiction based on, 49
   in Malaysia, 36
   public and private aspects, 89
   by religious authorities, 52
   system, 89
Islamic Missionary Foundation
  Malaysia, 58
Islamic movements, 128
Islamic Religious Council, 51
Islamic religious education system,
  38
Islamic religious institutions, 96

Islamic Renaissance Front (IRF),
  157
Islamic State and the Levant (ISIL),
  115, 134, 149, 166
   ability of, 115
   Amaq, 120
   Dabiq, 120–21
   extreme ideology, 166
   fighting against ideology, 128
   funding, 126–28
   Katibah Nusantara, 116, 121
   Malaysians' involvement in,
     123–28
   media propaganda, 120–23
   political parties and aggressive,
     127
   recruiters, 123–24
   social media campaign, 120
   strategy of recruiting, 123–26
   terror group, 125
   threats in Malaysia, 128–32
   using online media, 128
   violent methods used by, 166
Islamic State Document, The
  (Maududi), 87
Islamic State for Iraq and Syria
  (ISIS), 115
Islamization policy, 25, 164
   human capital development,
     34–47
   implementation of, 43
   Mahathir Mohamad, 164
   Malaysia's Constitutional
     Framework and, 58–63
   media, 47–54
   moral policing, 54–57
   multiple facets. *See* multiple
     facets of Islamization process
   political Islamist movement, 26

revivalism of conservative
  Islamism, 26–27
social and economic policy, 27
state-driven, 28
strengthening, 34
substantive programmes, 43
Syariah index, 57–58
universal Islamic values, 42
Islam Tanpa Keekstreman: Berhujah Untuk Kebebasan (Akyol), 157

J

Jabatan Agama Islam Wilayah Persekutuan (JAWI), 54
Jabatan Kehakiman Syariah Malaysia (JKSM), 29–30
Jabatan Kemajuan Agama Islam Malaysia (JAKIM), 29, 38, 46, 49, 50, 58, 94, 99, 149, 158, 164
  new motto, "1Malaysia 1Ummah", 46
  roles and functions of, 150
  and State Islamic Religious Councils, 150
Ja'fari jurisprudence, 92
JAIPk. *See* Perak Islamic Religious Department (JAIPk)
Jamaah Islah Malaysia (JIM), 27
Jamaah Islamiah, 127
Jamil Khir Baharom, 96–97, 150
Jaringan Melayu Malaysia (JMM), 143
jihad, 45, 115, 117, 123
jihadism, 118–22
jihadist movement, 45, 116
Johor Islamic Affairs Department (JAINJ), 171
JPA. *See* Public Service Department (JPA)
judiciary system, of Islam, 30–31

Federal Territories, 30
  functions, 30
  power of, 30
  structure of, 30
  Syariah, 30–31
jurisdiction
  based on Islamic law, 49
  civil and *Syariah*, 62
  Islamic, 62
  under state law, 61
jurisprudence, of Islam, 40

K

"*Kafa*" programme, 153
"Kajol" or Mohd Hafiz Jeffri, 108
kasar (rough), 18
Kassim Ahmad, 99, 101, 102
Kelang Islamic College, 35
Khairy Jamaluddin, 13
khalwat (close proximity), 56–57, 60, 148, 149
Khat, 154–55
Khilafa (the caliphate), 87
Koh Tsu Koon, 13
Kok, Teresa, 144
Kor Agama Angkatan Tentera (KAGAT), 31–32
Kuala Lumpur Convention Centre (KLCC), 147
Kuala Lumpur International Airport (KLIA), 125
Kumpulan Mujahidin (Militan) Malaysia (KMM), 45, 127

L

legal moralism, principle of, 73
legal system, in Malaysia, 165
legislation
  of Islam, 29, 40
  Malaysia, 14

lesbian, gay, bisexual and transgender (LGBT), 93, 151
   activists, 151
   community, 151
   rights, 141
liberal democracy, 65, 66
   socialism and, 87
liberal extremisms, 149
liberal Muslims/Islam, 93, 165
Lim Beng Soon, 21
Loh Kooi Choon v. Government of Malaysia (1977), 85

M
Madhavan Nair versus Public Prosecutor (1975), 12
madrasah, 152
   religious school system, 34
Mahathir Mohamad, 26, 28, 29, 37, 41–43, 49, 67, 73, 87, 89, 101, 139–40, 146, 150, 152, 155, 158, 164, 167–70
   hate speech, 141–45
   Inculcation of Islamic Values, 146, 147
   interview with Naik, 160
   Islamization policy. *See* Islamization policy
   LGBT rights and same-sex marriages, 141
   Pakatan Harapan, 145
   religious expression in Malaysia, 180
Mahmud Ahmad (also Abu Handzalah), 125
MAIWP. *See* Federal Territories Religious Council (MAIWP)
Majlis Agama Islam dan Adat Istiadat Melayu, 29–30
Majlis Kebangsaan Bagi Hal Ehwal Ugama Islam Malaysia, 39
Majlis Raja-Raja (Council of Rulers), 39
Makkal Osai, 70
Malay Dilemma, The (Mahathir Mohamad), 67
Malay language, 70
   syllabus, 155
Malay-Muslim
   communities, 97
   culture, 67
   students, 40
Malaysia Internet Crime Against Children Investigation Unit (MICAC), 74
Malaysia/Malaya, 140
   communitarian orientation, 177
   community and traditions, 18
   compromising and obliging styles, 21–22
   Constitutional Framework, 58–63
   constitutional supremacy, 95
   constitution and pluralism, 94
   counter subversive activities in, 10
   culture, 18–19, 21
   democracy, 7
   dominant ethnic groups in, 71
   education system in, 152
   Federal Constitution, 1, 3, 12
   fragile social balance, 78
   freedom of expression in. *See* freedom of expression, in Malaysia
   Guang Ming newspaper, 9
   hate speech, 9
   human rights struggle in, 10
   identity, 49

independence, 87
inter-religious expression in, 67–69
in ISIL. *See* Islamic State and the Levant (ISIL)
Islamic-based institutions in, 38
Islamic law in, 36
Islamic practices in, 146
Jyllands-Posten newspaper, 9
legal system, 165
legislation, 14
liberal Islam, 93
moderation solution in, 46
multi-ethnic society, 164
national security in, 2–3
political system, 20
press freedom in, 9
proper conduct of speech, 18, 19
psyche and interaction, 19
race and religious issues in, 1
rights groups, 53
Sarawak Tribune newspaper, 9
secular/Islamic state in, 85–89
terrorist attacks in Indonesia and, 122
TV al-Hijrah television station in, 50–51
unmarried Muslim couples in, 56
Utusan Melayu and *Utusan Malaysia*, 9
Malaysian Anti-Corruption Commission, 178
Malaysian Armed Forces, 31, 32
Malaysian Chinese Association (MCA), 9
Malaysian Communications and Multimedia Commission (MCMC), 141
Malaysian Constitution, 77

Malaysian Consultative Council of Buddhism, Christianity, Hinduism and Sikhism (MCCBCHS), 77
Malaysian Defamation Act 1957, 108
Malaysian government
  amendment of Federal Constitution (1971), 4
  in restricting free expression, 11
Malaysian Human Rights Commission (SUHAKAM), 13, 138, 174–75, 178
Malaysian Indian Congress (MIC), 70
Malaysian Islamic Party (PAS), 15, 26, 87, 88, 96, 97, 139
  United Malays National Organisation and, 145–46, 167, 169, 170
Malaysian law, 72
Malaysian National Council for Islamic Affairs, 39
Malaysian revivalism, 41
Malaysians Against Moral Policing, 54
malu, 19–20
  social emotion of, 19
  unpleasant sense of, 20
Manji, Irshad, 98
Maqasid Syariah, 57, 148
  concept of, 148
Martinez, Patricia, 99
maruah, 19–20
Maunsell Sharma & Zakaria, 109
media
  community, 68
  as "double-edged weapon", 68
  of Islamization, 47–54
Meor Atiqulrahman bin Ishak & Ors v. Fatimah bte. Sihi & Ors (2000), 103

militant Islamic movements, 45
Mingguan Malaysia, 156
misusing communication networks, 144
Mohd Faizal Musa, 155–57
    Home Affairs Ministry's ban on books, 155
moral disengagement, 118
    theory of, 117
moralism, Malaysia, 73
moral policing, 54–57
muafakat (consensus), 177
Muhammad (Prophet), 9, 69, 84, 92, 144
Muhammad Juzaili bin Mohd Khamis & Ors v State Government of Negeri Sembilan & Ors (2015), 103
Muhyiddin Yassin, 94, 146, 147, 159, 167
Mujahid Yusof Rawa, 142, 144, 146, 148–51, 160, 172, 174
multi-ethnic society, 164
multiple facets of Islamization process
    education. *See* education
    human capital development. *See* human capital development
    institutionalization. *See* Islamic bureaucracy, institutionalization of
    media, 47–54
multiracial society, religious freedom and expression in, 74
Muslim(s)
    "Allah" used by, 164
    and Christians, 76
    communities, 90
    Holy script of, 160
    model, 56
    and non-Muslims relationship, 61, 150. *See also* non-Muslims
    population, 27
    terror organizations, 160
    women, 159
Muslim law, 39
Muslim Scholars Association of Malaysia (MSAM), 99
Muslim Welfare Organisation of Malaysia, 26

N

Naik, Zakir, 159–61, 169, 174
Najib Tun Razak, 1, 13–16, 46–47, 57, 58, 64, 88, 89, 130, 135–39, 164
    Anwar Ibrahim, opposition leader, 141
    Barisan Nasional, 139
    blame "foreign activists", 136
    "free speech is thriving in Malaysia", 136
    Malaysia's culturally diverse population, 135
    Pakatan Harapan, 139
    political conspiracy, claims of, 141
    13th General Election in 2013, 137
    UN international standards, 138
    use of Sedition Act, 137
nama baik (one's good name), 19
National Cultural Congress (NCC), 39
National Dakwah Council (MDN), 150
national education system, 38
National Fatwa Council (NFC), 92, 107, 131

National Harmony and Reconciliation
    Commission Act, 142
National Human Rights Action Plan
    (NHRAP), 138–39, 162n1
national Islamization policy, 44, 168
national legal system, 62
national security, 23, 135
    and individual freedom, 14
    in Malaysia, 2–3
National Transformation 2050
    (TN50), 138
National Transformation Policy
    (NTP) (2011–20), 14
National University of Malaysia
    (UKM), 37, 38
New Economic Policy (NEP), 42
Nik Abduh Nik Abdul Aziz, 96
non-governmental organizations
    (NGOs), 136, 175
    coalition of, 77
    Hindu community, 71
    Islamic, 70
    Muslim, 76
    and public, 23
    right-wing, 143
    secular-liberal, 101
    smaller parties and, 139
non-Muslims
    activities, 151
    "Allah" not used by, 75, 164
    communities, 88, 90
    to convert Muslims, 110
    Muslims and, 150
    propagations by, 165
    protection of rights, 151
    publications, 75
    related law, 36–37
non-political speech, 104
Noor, Farish A., 99

O
obscenity, 72–74
    Content Code, 72
    test of, 72
Official Secret Act (OSA), 6, 12
1Malaysia Development Berhad
    (1MDB) issue, 139, 141

P
Pakatan Harapan (PH) government,
    139–40, 148–49, 166
    Barisan Nasional and, 139–41,
        155
    candidates, by-elections, 145
    concept of *Maqasid Syariah*, 148
    hate speech, 141–45
    Inculcation of Islamic Values,
        145–52
    Islamization policy, 169
    Mahathir Mohamad claimed, 145
    main challenge for, 171
    Malay-Muslims to support, 170
    policy of Islamization, 154
    recent developments under,
        158–61
    religious publications, 155–58
    "unsafe" under, 159
Pakatan Rakyat (PR), 15, 139
Parliament's legislative power, 6
PAS. *See* Malaysian Islamic Party
    (PAS)
PATRIOT Act, 10
Peaceful Assembly Act 2012, 138
Penal Code, 1, 11, 71
Pendidikan Islam/Moral (PI/PM), 154
Penerapan Nilai-nilai Islam, 49
People's Justice Party (PKR), 15
Perak Islamic Religious Department
    (JAIPk), 92

Perikatan Nasional (PN) government, 167
Persatuan Kebajikan Islam Malaysia (PERKIM), 26
Persatuan Kebangsaan Pelajar Islam Malaysia (PKPIM), 27
person's dignity, social concept of, 19
Pertubuhan Peribumi Perkasa (PERKASA), 53–54, 71
Philippines, attacks against civilians in, 116
Police Act (1967), 11, 14
political authority, 69
political decision-making, 68
political defamation, 109
political freedom in Malaysia, 7
political instability, 68
political Islam
    future challenges for, 167–71
    in Malaysia, 165
    "*Rahmatan Lil 'Alamin*" policy, 169
    and religious expression, 167–68
political Islamist movement, 26
political speech, freedom of, 136, 137
pornography, 72
    banning, 73
    and sexual exploitation, 74
    women's involvement in, 73
post-independence Malaya, 26
pre-independence memorandum, 85
press freedom, in Malaysia, 9
press, religious expression in, 74–76
Prevention of Crime (Amendments and Extensions) Act 2013 (POCA), 130, 131
Prevention of Terrorism Act 2015 (POTA), 15, 130–31, 137
Primary School Evaluation Test, 154

Printing Presses and Publications Act 1984 (PPPA), 6, 12, 14, 98, 105, 136, 157–58
private/non-political expression, 109
private speech, 104–10
publication and broadcasting, 97–99
public/political expression, 109
Public Prosecutor versus Ooi Kee Saik & Ors (1971), 8
Public Service Department (JPA), 31
public service sector, 28–29
public speech, 94–97
public universities, 37
Pusat Penyelidikan Islam (PPI), 39

Q
Al-Qaeda, 115, 116, 124
Quran, 96, 99–100, 103

R
racial conflicts, 2, 4
racial discrimination, 143
racist expressions, 82
radicalization, 113
    and counter-radicalization, theory of, 117–20
    definitions of, 117
    free speech in, 113
    ISIL media propaganda, 120–23
    modern age, 118
    process of, 117
    recruitment process, 118
    and terrorism, involvement in, 117–18
Radio and Television Malaysia (RTM), 47, 48
radio, establishment of, 48
"*Rahmatan Lil 'Alamin*", 146, 148, 150, 151, 162, 166, 169, 174

"*Rahmatan Lil Kafirin*", 151
regional cooperation, 129
regulation of speech, 22
religions, 67
    arguments, 65–66
    authorities, 51
    diversity of, 67
    of Federation, 58, 59
    and liberal extremisms, 149
    of Malays, 48
    and political authority, 69
Religious and Racial Hatred Act, 142
religious conflicts, 2
religious expression model, 82–85
    forbidden speech, 84
    future challenges for, 171–75
    implementation of, 167
    issues of, 159
    sacred expression, 83
    speech as religious duty/obligation, 84
religious freedom, 52, 53, 61
religious groups, 90
religious knowledge, 32
religious publications, 155–58
religious revivalism, 40
religious sensitivities, 66
revivalism of Islam, 26
    of conservative Islamism, 26
    of *da'wah* movement, 40
    primary cause of, 41
    religious, 27, 40
riba (usury), 33
right to privacy, 17
Risala (the prophethood of Muhammad), 87
Royal Malaysian Air Force (RMAF), 109

Royal Malaysia Police Rehabilitation Programme, 127
Rushdie, Salman, 69–70, 84

S
Salafi movement, 119
Salafism, 120
same-sex marriage, 141
Sarawak Tribune newspaper, 9
Satanic Verses (Rushdie), 69, 84
secular/Islamic state in Malaysia, 85–89
secularization process, 67
secular-liberal NGOs, 101
Securities Commission Act 1993, 33
Security Offences (Special Measures) Act 2012 (SOSMA), 80n5, 125, 126, 137, 140
Sedition Act (SA), 1, 6, 8, 12, 15, 71, 137, 140, 143, 144
    Najib's use of, 137
Selangor Islamic Religious Administration Enactment (2003), 96
Selangor Islamic Religious Department (JAIS), 96, 98, 159
73rd United Nations General Assembly (2018), 141
sexual exploitation, 74
Sexual Offences against Children Act 2017, 138
shame
    and dignity, 20
    malu, 21
    psychology of, 20
shame-anxiety, 20
Shia doctrine, 92, 94, 97
Shia Muslims, 97, 171–72

Shi'ism/Shia Islam, 52, 53, 82, 84, 92, 94, 165
Sikh community, 165
Sinar Harian newspaper, 48, 97
Sisters in Islam (SIS), 172
social contract, 20
    derhaka (disloyal), 20
    sovereign (*daulat*), 20
socialism, 87
social media, 115, 124
    campaign, 120
    and free expression, 128
    by ISIL, 132
    monitoring of, 128
    Muhammad (Prophet) on, 144
social value system, 21
Societies Act (1966), 92
Special Branch's Counter-Terrorism Division (SB-CTD), 126
speech as religious duty/obligation, 84
state and federal statutory laws, 40
state-driven Islamization policy, 25, 28
state laws, 90, 91
Sufaat, Yazid, 131
SUHAKAM. *See* Malaysian Human Rights Commission (SUHAKAM)
Sultan Nazrin Muizzuddin Shah, 114–15
Sunni doctrine, 165
Sunni Islam, 90, 94, 165
Syariah Advisory Council, 33
Syariah Approved Securities, 57
Syariah court, 29–30
    banking, 33
    capital market, 33
    compliance, 33
    department of law and, 36
    economy and conventional economy, 33
    fatwa committees, 92
    in Federal Territories, 34–35
    financial markets, 33
    judges, appointment of, 34, 35
    law, 56, 59
    lawyer (*peguam syarie*), 35
Syariah Court of Appeal, 30
Syariah Courts (Criminal Jurisdiction) Act 1965, 147, 148
Syariah Criminal Offences (Federal Territories) Act 1997 (Act 559), 51, 90, 102, 173
Syariah index, 57–58, 64, 164
    concept of, 57
    implementation of, 165
    by JAKIM, 58
    jurisdictions, 62
    objective of, 57
    progress and traits of, 63
Syariah laws, 82, 86, 89, 165
    and civil laws, 148
    critical stand against, 93
    implementation of, 88
    infrastructure of, 148
    issues of Islamic administration and, 158
    and Malay unity, 139
Syria
    defeat of ISIL in, 131
    Indonesian and Malaysian jihadists in, 122
    and Iraq, 121
    ISIL-held territory in, 126
    militants in, 124

T

tahfiz, 152
Takaful Act 1984, 33
tauliah (qualified approval), 95, 96, 173–74
Tawhid (the Unity of God), 87
Terengganu through Sukan Terengganu (SUTERA), 173
terrorism
    activities, 166
    and extremist movements, 129
    groups, 118
    homegrown, 127
    involvement in, 117–18
    in Malaysia, 121
    in United States, 130
terrorist attack
    in Indonesia and Malaysia, 122
    in New York, 6
    in Sri Lanka, 131
terror organizations, 116
13th General Election in 2013, 1, 13, 15, 16, 137
TV al-Hijrah, 50–51
    broadcasting programmes of, 50
    mission of, 50
    vision of, 50
12th General Election in 2008, 15, 16

U

ummah, 41, 45, 81, 119, 177
undesirable publications, 106
United Malays National Organisation (UMNO), 1, 26, 41, 43, 53, 85, 101
    and Malaysian Islamic Party, 101, 145–46, 167, 169, 170
    members, 101
    nationalist party, 101
Universal Declaration of Human Rights, 76
universal Islamic values, 42
universal religion, 103
Universities and University Colleges Act (UUCA), 13, 14, 140
Universiti Sains Islam Malaysia (USIM), 151
University Kebangsaan Malaysia 4 (UKM 4), 13
unmarried Muslim couples, 56
Unveiling Choice (Maryam Lee), 159
US Commission on International Religious Freedom (USCIRF), 53
US-led war on terror, 10
Utusan Malaysia, 9, 48, 53–54, 71, 97, 100, 156
Utusan Melayu, 9

V

violence against civilians, 133

W

Wahhabi movement, 119
Wan Ji Wan Hussin, 144, 145
Wasatiyyah, 46–47, 164
    concept of, 46–47, 57
women's involvement, in pornography, 73

Z

Zaidi jurisprudence, 92
Zainah Anwar, 99, 100
Zunar (Zulkiflee Anwar Ul Haque), 140–41

ABOUT THE AUTHOR

Professor Dr Mohd Azizuddin Mohd Sani is Professor of Politics and International Relations at the School of International Studies (SoIS), Universiti Utara Malaysia (UUM). He has taught in UUM for twenty years. He was a Visiting Fellow at the ISEAS – Yusof Ishak Institute, Singapore in 2014.

www.ingramcontent.com/pod-product-compliance
Lightning Source LLC
Chambersburg PA
CBHW050327020526
44117CB00031B/1819